1996 CUMULATIVE SUPPLEMENT

Purchasing Manager's
DESK BOOK
of
PURCHASING
LAW

Second Edition

DONALD B. KING
JAMES J. RITTERSKAMP, JR.

PRENTICE HALL
Englewood Cliffs, New Jersey 07632

Prentice-Hall International (UK), Limited, *London*
Prentice-Hall of Australia Pty. Limited, *Sydney*
Prentice-Hall Canada, Inc., *Toronto*
Prentice-Hall Hispanoamericana, S.A., *Mexico*
Prentice-Hall of India Private Limited, *New Delhi*
Prentice-Hall of Japan, Inc., *Tokyo*
Simon & Schuster Asia Pte. Ltd., *Singapore*
Editora Prentice-Hall do Brasil, Ltda., *Rio de Janeiro*

10   9   8   7   6   5   4   3   2   1

Library of Congress Cataloging-in-Publication Data

King, Donald Barnett.
  Purchasing manager's desk book of purchasing law.—2nd ed./
Donald B. King, James J. Ritterskamp, Jr.
    p.   cm.
  Rev. ed. of: Purchasing manager's desk book of purchasing law /
James J. Ritterskamp, Jr.
Kept up to date by supplements
  Includes index.
  ISBN 0–13–443615–6
    1. Sales—United States.   2. Contracts—United States.
3. Purchasing agents—Legal status, laws, etc.—United States.
I. Ritterskamp, James J.   II. Ritterskamp, James J. Purchasing
manager's desk book of purchasing law.   III. Title.
KF915.R58   1993
346.73′072—dc20   93-25715
[347.30672]   CIP

ISBN 0-13-443615-6

PRENTICE HALL
Career & Personal Development
Englewood Cliffs, NJ 07632

A Simon & Schuster Company

Printed in the United States of America

This supplement is dedicated to
our mothers:

Mrs. James (Linn) Ritterskamp

Douglas D. Ritterskamp
James J. Ritterskamp III

Mrs. George (Marian) Brooks King

Donald B. King
Clay B. King

Acknowledgments

Gracious acknowledgment is made to all those who have made this Supplement possible—to the editors and others at Prentice Hall and to James J. Ritterskamp, Jr., a lawyer and purchasing manager, for laying a basis with his initial work. Acknowledgment is made to Mr. Mark McColl, my very capable faculty research assistant, a third year law student and newspaper writer, for his assistance in making the manuscript more "user friendly." In addition, other acknowledgments are due to persons I have worked with closely throughout their research and writing, which has been tailored specially for this publication: Juris Doctors of law and alumni of Saint Louis University School of Law; Ziaoxue Zhao for his writings on practical cultural-legal considerations in negotiating business contracts with the Chinese; James Wang for exploring electronic technologies effects on the law; Elsia Robinson for her analysis of NAFTA point of origin rules affecting the purchases of goods; and Brian Sandler for viewing provisions of the International Sales convention, advantages to purchasers, and use of contract provisions in such sales. Working with them in the development of these writings has been intellectually stimulating. In addition, Karen Grossman Tabak has contributed important material that deals with the purchasing manager and possible problems he or she may face when retiring older staff in the department. Faculty secretary Pam Boyer is credited for her word processing and other skills.

About the Authors

Donald B. King has taught commercial law for thirty-seven years. During this time he has written or edited twelve books, and over forty articles and essays. The *Commercial Transactions* casebook he first coedited in 1968 is now in its fifth edition. He has coauthored a book on Sales Law and has written books on "Consumer Protection Experiment in Sweden" and "Consumer Protection in Chinese." Professor King also was the editor of books on "Commercial and Consumer Law from an International Perspective" and "Essays on Comparative Commercial and Consumer Law." His teaching has been concentrated in the fields of commercial law, consumer law, secured transactions, products liability, and comparative law. He has taught at the University of Washington, Dickinson Law School, Wayne State University, and Saint Louis University. He also was a Visiting Professor at the University of Cincinnati, Stetson Law School, and Sichuan University in China.

He is founder and Honorary President of the International Academy of Commercial and Consumer Law, a select group of sixty international authorities. He has done comparative research and given lectures on commercial and consumer law in a number of countries throughout the world.

He received his Bachelor of Science degree in psychology from Washington State University and his Juris Doctor from Harvard Law School. Professor King has also earned a Masters from New York University and a Masters in psychiatric social work from Saint Louis University. He is a member of the Missouri, Washington State, and Supreme Court bars, is an elected member of the American Law Institute and was recently given the honor of "Life Member," an honor held by less than 600 lawyers out of the 847,000 lawyers in the United States. Professor King also has been elected a President of the Central States Law School Association for 1995, which consists of over forty law schools from thirteen states. The Saint Louis University Du Bourg Society has named him an Honorary Dean and Honorary Vice President.

James J. Ritterskamp, Jr. coauthored and contributed to several books on purchasing, and wrote a monthly column, *Ritterskamp Views the Law,* which was carried in numerous purchasing magazines, including *Purchasing Management, Midwest Purchasing,* the *St. Louis Purchaser, Purchasing Professional,* and the *New South Purchaser.* He was best known for his legal seminars conducted for the National Association of Purchasing Management, for Regional Purchasing Management Associations, and for private organizations throughout the country.

He served as president of numerous professional associations, including the Purchasing Management Association of St. Louis, the National Association of Educational Buyers, the National Association of College Stores, and the National Association of College and University Business Officers. He taught accounting, law purchasing, and economics at Washington University and Vassar College.

He received his Juris Doctor degree from the School for Law of Washington University in St. Louis, and held various academic posts at the Illinois Institute of Technology in Chicago, The University of Chicago, and Vassar College in New York. In 1986, he came out of retirement to become President of Rocky Mountain College in Billings, Montana for one year.

Preface

The law moves quickly ahead. Since the second edition of the *Purchasing Manager's Desk Book of Purchasing Law,* several trends have continued and some other developments have taken place:

- The reform of Sales law, as found in Article 2 of the UCC, is moving forward and a draft of all of Article 2 has now been completed.
- The new American free trade zone becomes crucial with the passage of NAFTA.
- The law relating to computers may now develop legislatively as "hub-spoke" provisions are advocated for the new Sales law.
- Some purchasing managers, faced with having to reduce staff, must confront the legal boundaries placed on their actions. Also, new law is developing with regard to various types of discrimination that may be alleged and which must be awarded.
- As both the international purchases and those within NAFTA countries increase, it becomes crucial for the purchasing managers to be aware of the main facets of the law and the cultural differences which may affect his or her negotiations and contracting.
- The International Sales of Goods law becomes more important since it is automatically a part of U.S. law for sales between U.S. businesses.

While there is some discussion of these matters in the second edition, it is believed that the materials in the supplement will be of further assistance and keep the purchasing manager on the "cutting edges" of the law and new international trade developments. As in the second edition, not only is attention paid to making the Purchasing Manager more technically proficient, but to also add to his general reservoir of knowledge. This is necessary in an increasingly complex business world of yearly changes, which both includes and transposes national boundaries.

Contents

Complexities of Society and Law

CONTINUING COMMERCIAL LAW DEVELOPMENTS, FOLLOWS PAGE 22 OF ORIGINAL TEXT

In the mid-1990s, as in all legal history, there are new developments occurring every month. In our modern times of complexity and accelerated change, major developments take place more often than before.

Last year, it was pointed out that the Uniform Commercial Code, with its drafting beginning in the 1940s, is in need of some changes. There are new businesses, as well as technological and legal developments. Even theory changes over the course of time as mentioned in Chapter XXVII. The Sales Article of the Uniform Commercial Code is now being revised as discussed in Chapter XXX and in this Supplement. The Sales Article is further being changed to cover computer software and licensing, and some special principles are being added.

Commercial law history also has been made with the adoption of the Convention on the International Sale of Goods by this country and many others. This development is discussed in Chapter XXVIII.

With the development of the North American Free Trade Association, there is now a growing body of regional country law throughout the world and despite some crisis, it will undoubtedly continue to grow. The already well-established European Community is effectuating many of its goals and expanding.

1

Recently, an international set of commercial law principles has been developed. Formulated by a group of leading legal experts from around the world, this may have an impact with regard to purchases from sellers abroad.

Finally, the changing political scene in the United States has brought with it major proposals for change in the legal and court procedural systems.

The Role of Your Legal Counsel

REELING IN LEGAL BILLS

Legal reform has become a catchy political phrase. The Republicans included legal reform as part of their "Contract With America" and passed a version of tort reform within the first 100 days of Congress in 1995. President Clinton has expressed doubts about the legislation and has indicated he will veto the bill.

Is legal reform necessary? Maybe, but with some planning, it's possible to cut down on legal bills without the help of Congress. Purchasing managers sometimes become involved in disputes that concern the company. Some helpful hints for the company to keep legal expenses down include the following:

- *Outline what you plan to spend in the litigation.* Many law firms are much more receptive these days to alternative billing resolutions. When you make initial contact, attempt to get an outline of what the attorney plans to do, and how much the various stages of processing the suit will cost. Some firms willing to take a flat fee for services.

- *Meet with your attorney.* Don't be afraid to ask for progress reports. Although it's true that a daily—or even weekly—assessment is unrealistic, a meeting every few months is a good way to judge where you're at and if the budget is still holding.

- *Get involved.* Some consultants believe it is often helpful in civil cases if principals meet face-to-face sans lawyers. Also, attempt to find out more

3

about the law, and its terms. You might be able to offer some insight into your attorney's strategy.

- *If you are in need of a foreign lawyer, communication is a key.* Make sure you provide your attorney with clear instructions on how to proceed, and be careful to choose an attorney that is skilled in the area in which you need assistance. Both Martindale-Hubbell and the ABA provide directories, or guides, of international firms. Still, it is most advisable to consult with others who have had occasion to utilize these forms.

USE OF A FOREIGN LAWYER, FOLLOWS PAGE 28 OF ORIGINAL TEXT

If the purchasing manager or his company needs to consult a foreign attorney, several things must be taken into account. For one thing, the fluctuation of exchange rates makes it important to specify in what currency the fee shall be paid.

In instances where the purchasing manager, some officer in his company, or the company attorney consults a foreign lawyer, it should not simply be assumed that the foreign attorney will charge a "reasonable rate" in American terms. One should always inquire as to the rate and reach an agreement as to the rate or amount to be paid. Despite what the foreign attorney says as to rate schedules governing the matter, it almost always is subject to agreement between the parties just as it is in hiring an outside attorney in the United States. No commitment or work should be given until there is such an agreement with the foreign attorney.

In a number of countries, there are fee schedules which the foreign attorney follows if there is no other specific agreement. While these are generally set by what might be fair in ordinary circumstances, there are some situations where they may work out unfairly. One example is where a foreign lawyer was contacted and asked to incorporate a subsidiary company in his home country. Although he did only a few hours work before the company informed him that they had changed their minds, he sent a huge bill based on a fee schedule which set the fees by the amount involved—in this case sixty million dollars was the amount of capital the subsidiary would have had. The fee schedule allowed that amount regardless of the few hours put in or the fact that the company later decided against it. Large contract amounts can also create large lawyer fees, regardless of the simplicity of the transaction.

Sometimes a foreign attorney may charge by the hour. While

American companies may be used to American attorneys charging from one hundred to five hundred dollars an hour, some foreign attorneys charge from five hundred to a thousand dollars per hour. If one doesn't inquire first, that fee may have to be paid. While unfavorable exchange rates may make the fee higher, in many instances it is simply a matter of very high fees being charged. This is all subject to negotiation and agreement with the attorney in advance of any work.

Nota Bene to Purchasing Officer: Never make a commitment with a foreign lawyer for legal work or even ask him to perform any without a written agreement as to the fee. If the work is in stages or if contingencies are involved, the fee for each should be agreed upon. The currency that is to be used in setting and paying the fee also should be specified.

Liabilities of a Purchasing Manager Regarding the Staff

DISCRIMINATION GENERALLY

Think of the word "discrimination," and the image that is likely to come to mind for many Americans is a picture of the great civil rights movements of the 1960s and the struggle of African Americans to gain equality in a society that viewed the world through tinted glasses. The great focus of that time was on racial discrimination, but the legislation spawned by the work of Dr. Martin Luther King and others is broad based. Federal law protects not only race, color, and national origin from employment discrimination, but also religion and "sex," or gender.

Under Title VII of the 1964 Civil Rights Act, it is illegal for employers to discriminate based on race, color, religion, sex, or national origin. Title VII—which covers private employers, local and state governments, and educational institutions with 15 or more employees—makes it illegal to discriminate in the hiring and firing of employees, and in other terms and conditions of employment (e.g., employment compensation, job assignment and the use of company facilities).

For example, as noted above, it is illegal to discriminate against an employee based on his or her religion. An employer is therefore prohibited from such activities as refusing to allow the observance of a Sabbath or religious holiday, or scheduling an examination that conflicts with an employee's religion, *unless* the employer can prove that abiding by the employee's wishes would cause an undue hardship. An employer is allowed to claim that it is an undue hardship if the accommodation of an employee's religious needs requires costs that exceed the ordinary administrative expenses.

The 1964 Act is probably the most well known, but there have been several other Federal acts passed since that time that all deal with various forms of discrimination. The Age Discrimination in Employment Act, Title I of the Americans with Disabilities Act, and the Civil Rights Act of 1991 have all been passed since Lyndon Johnson signed off on the original Civil Rights Act. The following paragraphs offer a brief look at some of the legislation governing this area.

The Age Discrimination in Employment Act (ADEA)

Under this 1967 law, persons 40 years or older are protected from discrimination in hiring, termination, compensation, and promotions because of their age. The Older Workers Benefit Protection Act (OWBPA), which became effective in 1991, emphasizes that employee benefits and plans are subject to the ADEA. The ADEA applies to private employers with 20 or more employees.

The Equal Pay Act (EPA)

This legislation was actually passed before the Civil Rights Act of 1964. Enacted in 1963, the EPA, as amended, prohibits an employer from discriminating in compensation between men and women who perform essentially the same job. In addition, an employer may not lower the salary of either sex to come in compliance with this law. Violations in this area may also be violations of Title VII.

The Americans With Disabilities Act (ADA)

Title I of the ADA prohibits private employers with 15 or more employees from discriminating against qualified individuals that have a mental or physical impairment. An individual is qualified if they have the skill and knowledge to perform the job with or without reasonable accommodations. An employer is required to make a reasonable accommodation, which can include such things as making existing facilities accessible to employees with disabilities or restructuring and modifying jobs, if it is not going to pose an undue hardship. An undue hardship would mean that accommodation is significantly difficult and expensive in light of a business' size and financial wherewithal. An employer does not have to make an accommodation if it means lower quality or production standards.

The Civil Rights Act of 1991

In the wake of some controversial decisions by the Supreme Court, Congress passed additional legislation to protect against unlawful employment discrimination. This amendment to the Civil Rights Act of 1964 is aimed at intentional discrimination and disparate impact actions.

All of these acts are enforced by the United States Equal Employment Opportunity Commission (EEOC). The EEOC investigates complaints of employment discrimination against private employers. It is the EEOC's mission to seek full relief for every victim of discrimination. Remedies against an employer that has been found to have discriminated against an employee may include compensatory damages, back pay, and the payment of attorney's fees; placement in the position the victim would rightfully have occupied were it not for the discrimination; and preventive actions to ensure that this doesn't happen again. It is illegal to retaliate against a person who files a discrimination charge or participates in an investigation.

For further information on these Federal laws, purchasing managers may contact the EEOC at the following address: U.S. Equal Employment Opportunity Commission, 1801 L Street, N., Washington, D.C. 20507; or call 1-800-669-4000.

AGE DISCRIMINATION AND THE PURCHASING MANAGER*

Age Discrimination and the Law

Legal issues involving discrimination related to race, sex, age or disability as well as sexual harassment are complex. Many questions have yet to be clarified as the laws evolve. The question of age discrimination in particular is governed by a number of statutes. Title VII of the Civil Rights Act of 1964 and the Age Discrimination in Employment Act of 1967 (ADEA) make it unlawful for an employer to refuse to hire an individual or to discharge an individual or to discriminate in any manner based upon age, with several exceptions. Additionally, the law prohibits the retaliatory dis-

*By Karen Grossman Tabak, CPA and consultant.

charge of individuals who testify on behalf of those alleging discrimination or harassment. The ADEA was amended by the Older Workers Benefit Protection Act enacted in 1990 (OWBPA) which involves benefit costs. Furthermore, workplace issues may be covered by the Employee Retirement Income Security Act (ERISA) relating to pension plans as well as the Americans with Disabilities Act (ADA). This latter law addresses issues that may be particularly important to older workers who become ill or disabled. The ADA requires that employers allow workers to return to work after an injury once they are able to perform substantially all of their duties, although they may not have completely recovered. In the many thousands of cases resolved by the courts over the past two-and-one-half decades, the burden of proof has shifted back and forth between the employee and the employer in proving or disproving age discrimination. Age discrimination may be found by the courts if it can be shown that:

a) the employee was age forty or over,

b) the employee was performing his or her duties,

c) the employee was fired, demoted, reduced in salary, or otherwise negatively treated

d) younger employees (those younger than age 40) were treated more positively.

In proving such allegations, statistics may be utilized to support claims that a significantly greater number of older employees were fired, transferred, or demoted than younger employees. However, the courts have yet to provide clear and concise guidelines for managers and supervisors in terms of statistical analysis and in terms of evidence.

What Can Managers Do?

While there is no way to guarantee a successful defense against charges of age discrimination, there are steps purchasing managers can take to limit the extent of potential liability to the organization from accusations of discriminations.

1) Ensure that your firm has a clear, written policy defining and prohibiting both discrimination and sexual harassment.

2) In conjunction with the human resources department, familiarize yourself and your subordinates with the policies. This should be an ongoing process.

3) Clarify the internal procedures to be taken when employees believe they or their colleagues are the subject of discrimination. Consider posting complaint procedures.

4) Inform the human resources department or top management when complaints of discrimination arise.

5) Document performance-related problems and maintain accurate records! Often supervisors are reluctant to include negative comments in employee evaluations. Thus, when termination occurs with an older employee due to poor performance, there is little evidence to support the company's position of poor performance.

6) Avoid age-bias in training programs. Be sure that employees of all ages are selected to attend training programs.

7) Create an environment that discourages discrimination. Avoid stereo-typing older employees and reinforce the commitment to a discrimination-free workplace.

Cost of Age Discrimination Law Suits

Age discrimination cases are costly. There will be legal fees in defending the company as well as the cost of experts. Should a company be found guilty of age discrimination, they may be liable for actual, compensatory, and liquidated damages. An often overlooked cost is the time required of company personnel in preparing the defense and gathering documents, as well as testifying in court. While some of these costs may be covered by the company's insurance policy, the distractions of employees and the emotional toll may cost the employer more than the damages awarded by the court.

Computation of Damages

When damages are awarded by the court, they fall into several types.

a) *Actual damages* or economic damages may include compensation lost to the trial date, interest on these funds and the present value of lost compensation in the future.

b) Damages may also be awarded to the plaintiff for emotional distress. These are called *compensatory damages.*

c) *Liquidated damages* will be awarded if the jury determines that the discrimination was willful. To obtain the liquidated damages, the actual or economic damages are doubled.

The computation of the actual damages in age discrimination cases is usually handled by an economist. Economists are trained in the analysis of wage increases and interest rates. Accordingly, they are able to determine an appropriate settlement that leaves the plaintiff in the same situation as if he or she had not been discharged or demoted.

Lost Income to Trial Date

The first computation the economist makes is the determination of lost income from the date of discharge/demotion to the trial date. To make this calculation, the economist determines:

> the period of time from the date of discharge to the trial date;
>
> the annual compensation received by the employee prior to discharge including fringe benefits such as medical insurance, life insurance, pension benefits, and other retirement programs;
>
> and any compensation received by the plaintiff including fringe benefits from replacement employment.

The economist then makes an assumption as to the growth of wages had the plaintiff remained in the original position. If the economist assumes the wages would have grown during the period, the calculation of the lost income to the trial date is then the computation of the future value of an annuity using the formula:

> $\Sigma[(pmt(1+r) + pmt(1+r)^2 \ldots + pmt(1+r)^n]$ – compensation from replacement employment
> where pmt = the annual compensation received from employment before discharge
> r = the annual growth rate in wages
> n = the period of time from discharge to the trial date

If the economist determines the compensation would not have grown during this period or chooses to take a more conservative approach, the calculation is simply to multiply the annual compensation the employee would have received had the action not taken place by the period of time from the date of discharge to the trial date and then deduct any compensations received from replacement employment. Additionally, there may be interest computed on this money as the plaintiff has theoretically been denied the benefit of this money.

Present Value of Future Income Lost

To determine the value of the compensation lost into the future, additional assumptions must be made. First, there must be an assumption about the ability of the plaintiff to find employment with a new employer (or to remain employed at a lower-paying position within the company) and the level of compensation the plaintiff will receive. Furthermore, there must be a determination as to the salary and benefits the employee would be receiving had he or she not been discharged or demoted. The difference between these two amounts—the compensation from the new position minus the compensation from the old position—will be the annual rate of loss. Next, the economist will make an assumption as to the number of years the employee would have remained in the work force. This determination can be made by asking the plaintiff his or her estimated retirement date, or by assuming that the plaintiff would have retired upon becoming eligible for full social security benefits based upon year of birth and the social security laws. The retirement age is 65 for those born in 1937 and before; however for those born after 1937, the age at which one qualifies for full social security benefits (called full retirement age) rises gradually from age 65 to age 67. Individuals born in 1960 will not qualify for full social security benefits until age 67. As an alternative assumption, the economist may assume the plaintiff would have delayed retirement and taken advantage of increased social security benefits by working to age 70 or beyond. Perhaps the most difficult decision is that of the appropriate discount rate. Remember that in a settlement, the plaintiff will receive the money at the settlement date and then be able to invest this money. The settlement must be large enough to hypothetically set up an account that will allow the plaintiff to annually withdraw an amount equal to the difference between their salary, based upon not being terminated, and their new compensation. We assume they continue to withdraw an amount that grows as their salary would have grown and by the time they reach the assumed retirement age, the balance of this hypothetical account will be zero. We know that this account will earn interest, and we also know that wages will grow over time. Accordingly, we must determine the difference between the rate of interest the plaintiff will earn on the money in a secure investment and the rate of future wage increases. The difference will become the net real discount rate. To maintain consistency in taxability of both the settlement and the earned income, we use an investment vehicle that is also taxable such as United States Government bonds. Hence, the discount rate will be the difference between the interest rate on United States government bonds and the growth rate in wages. Historically, this is below 2.5%. However, the Internal Revenue Service is currently reconsidering the taxability of such settlements and the related interest. Should the IRS determine that these amounts are not taxable, then consistent treatment requires that we reduce the annuity payment amount to take into account the effects of taxes. Additionally, we use an investment vehicle that is not taxable, such as municipal bonds. This will lower the net real discount rate. To compute the amount of money needed to compensate the plaintiff, we use the formula for computing the present value of an annuity:

$$\Sigma[\text{pmt}/(1+r)+\text{pmt}/(1+r)^2 \ldots + \text{pmt}/(1+r)^n]$$

where pmt = the difference between the compensation the plaintiff would be earning had he or she not been discharged and the compensation the plaintiff is assumed to be earning
n = the number of years to retirement
r = the discount rate, in the case, the difference between United States government bonds and the growth rate in wages or 2.5%

The combination of the loss to the trial date and the present value of future lost income will be the amount of the actual damages.

Clearly, age discrimination can be costly. Careful attention to managing employees and the demographics of the workforce is now an important requirement of all supervisory personnel.

THE FAMILY AND MEDICAL LEAVE ACT

In 1993, Congress passed the Family and Medical Leave Act (FMLA). This law requires companies with 50 or more employees to provide up to 12 weeks of unpaid leave for a "serious health condition" of an employee or a member of his or her immediate family. Likewise, an employee who celebrates the birth or adoption of a child is eligible for leave under this law. (29 U.S.C. 2601-2654.)

The FMLA applies to all public employers, as well as private employers with more than 50 workers on the payroll during each of the 20 or more work weeks in the current or the preceding calendar year.

Employees must work at sites with more than 50 employees, or companies with 50 or more employees within 75 miles of this site, and have at least 12 months experience, and at least 1,250 hours at their jobs in the past 12 months preceding commencement of their leave to be covered by the FMLA. (29 U.S.C. 2611 (2), (4).)

A "serious health condition" is an "illness, injury, impairment, or physical or mental condition that involves inpatient care in a hospital, hospice, or residential medical care facility; or continuing treatment by a health care provider." (29 U.S.C. 2611 (11).)

It should be noted that the employee only needs to give his or her employer verbal notice that the employee needs leave, and the employer must let the employee know that the leave counts against his or her FMLA entitlement. When the leave is finished, the employee must be returned to his or her old position or a similar one with the same pay and conditions. Employers are in violation of the law if they do not allow leave, or try to discourage it, or if they discipline an employee who takes leave.

This law is likely unfamiliar territory for most firms, and many problems can be avoided if both sides cooperate. Employees should let their employers know that they need leave as soon as they can. It also behooves them to find out exactly what their benefits are before an emergency takes place, so they'll know exactly where they stand.

Caveat Bene: When employees don't ask enough questions, misunderstandings later occur. The purchasing manager should, in consultation with the company attorney, provide employees with information concerning this Act and these benefits.

Purchasing Ethics and the Law

PRESIDENT'S NEW CODE OF ETHICS FOR BUSINESS*

Those who plan to conduct business in a foreign country may in the near future be asked to adhere to a corporate code.

President Clinton's administration has been in contact with businesses and Congress about putting in place a voluntary code of conduct that would be used to guide the efforts of American companies doing business outside the borders. A sample draft code asks companies, among other things, to avoid using child labor and to have respect for collective bargaining.

Clinton broached the idea of drafting a code for doing business overseas in May 1994 when he decided to renew most-favored-nation trading status for China. The five basic principles that were included in a draft code called for having a safe workplace; practicing fair employment procedures (including not having children as part of the labor force); protecting the environment; encouraging freedom of expression; and complying with U.S. laws in the prohibition of illicit payments.

It should be noted that the document as it stands would not be mandatory, but is intended to be voluntary.

*Information obtained from the Daily Labor Report, *White House Initiates Consultations on Voluntary Code for Firms Abroad,* March 31, 1995.

FOREIGN CORRUPT PRACTICES ACT, FOLLOWS PAGE 180 OF ORIGINAL TEXT

The Foreign Corrupt Practices Act was passed in 1977 to prohibit certain payments to foreign officials, made directly or through third parties, which are more commonly referred to as bribes or corrupt payments. During the Watergate investigations of payments to U.S. political candidates, it was discovered that numerous corporate political slush funds to foreign officials evaded normal accounting controls. Congress responded quickly by passing the Act. The U.S. is the only nation in the world that prohibits its domestic corporations from bribing another country's public servants.

The original 1977 Act included only three substantive sections. One established accounting standards which would disclose foreign payments. The other two governed payments to foreign officials and to "other" persons, who "knew or had reason to know" the payments would be passed on to a foreign official. The law contained no definitions and only a brief exclusion for payments that were "ministerial" in nature. The so-called "grease" payments often needed to pass goods through customs were allowed. The law was ambiguous, and U.S. business requested that guidelines be issued. None were forthcoming.

Continued pressure from U.S. business finally brought about the 1988 trade law which substitutes the "reason to know" language for a requirement that any payment to a third person be made "knowing that" it would be passed on to a foreign official. But new definition provisions state that "knowing" may well include reason to know. Having "a firm belief" or being "aware" is sufficient to constitute "knowing."

Another important addition is the further clarification of permissible "grease" payments. Payments are allowed for a "routine government action," which includes obtaining permits to do business, processing papers, providing certain routine services such as police protection or telephone or power, and "actions of a similar nature." But it does not include any decision by a foreign official regarding new business or retaining old business, decisions which are more than merely routine government actions.

The law further includes an affirmative defense for several payments not prohibited. They include payments permissible under the written laws of the other nation, and reasonable and bona fide expenditures such as travel and lodging if related to the promotion or performance of the contract. The FCPA in 1988 also included some clarification of the accounting provisions.

In addition, what was known as the Eckhardt provision was removed in 1988, which prohibited bringing a suit directly against an employee without first having received a judgment finding the employer in violation of the Act.[1] Corporate officers may now find themselves scapegoats, and required to defend charges while the company remains free of any litigation.

There have been attempts to govern payments to foreign officials on the international level, particularly by the Organization for Economic Cooperation and Development and the United Nations. The OECD established guidelines but the U.N. has done nothing. A few individual nations attempt to prohibit payments by their entities, but some nations encourage such payments by allowing them to constitute deductions against taxes as ordinary business expenses.

[1]See *United States v. McLean*, 738 F.2d 655 (5th Cir. 1984).

Quality and Warranties

STRICT LIABILITY IN TORT FOR DEFECTIVE PRODUCTS, FOLLOWS PAGE 364 OF ORIGINAL TEXT

Breach of warranty remains in the mid-nineteen nineties as the main remedy for the purchasing manager who finds the goods purchased to be defective. But there also is strict liability in tort if the defect in the goods causes property damage or personal injury. It also covers property damage to the goods themselves if it is the result of a violent occurrence, rather than slow deterioration. While this seems like a strange distinction courts generally have drawn it. They find such damage to the goods to be covered by strict liability in tort because the damage is caused by the unreasonable dangerousness of the defect, whereas they find gradual deterioration caused by the defect to be more the subject of warranty law.

In terms of economic loss brought about by the defectiveness of the goods, such as lost profits, the issue may be whether strict liability in tort or warranty law is applicable. The general trend seems to be to hold that warranty, which allows disclaimers of liability by contract, is the applicable law. Strict liability, as mentioned shortly, does not allow for such contractual disclaimers.

Strict Liability for products is best exemplified by the Restatement of Tort Section 402A:

"SPECIAL LIABILITY OF SELLER OF PRODUCT FOR PHYSICAL HARM TO USER OR CONSUMER

(1) One who sells any product in a defective condition unreasonably dangerous to the user or consumer or to his property is subject to liability for physical harm thereby caused to the ultimate user or consumer, or to his property if

   (a) the seller is engaged in the business of selling such a product, and

   (b) it is expected to and does reach the user or consumer without substantial change in the condition in which it is sold.

(2) The rule stated in Subsection (1) applies although

   (a) the seller has exercised all possible care in the preparation and sale of his product, and

   (b) the user or consumer has not bought the product from or entered into any contractual relation with the seller."

There are several "caveats" which cover special situations where the American Law Institute takes no position as to the applicability of §402A; these remain a matter of caselaw:

"The Institute expresses no opinion as to whether the rules stated in this Section may not apply

(1) to harm to persons other than users or consumers;

(2) to the seller of a product expected to be processed or otherwise substantially changed before it reaches the user or consumer, or

(3) to the seller or a component part of a product to be assembled."

In part, it is a development of warranty law, with the elimination of privity, and to a slight extent takes on characteristics formerly found in warranty law. Nevertheless, it is based primarily on a separate theory in tort and is explicitly separated from warranty liability. Since the Restatement section represents one of the most important modern formulations of strict liability, it is important to look at its underlying bases.

One basis given as underlying Section 402A, is that the seller "by marketing his product for use in consumption, has undertaken and assumed a special responsibility toward any member of the consuming public who may be injured by it." This portion of the statement of the underlying theory seems to reflect the undertaking by the seller of the business enterprise or risk involved activity. It is merely the marketing of the product which will later be used and consumed, which is the undertaking itself and carries with it a certain responsibility.

A second basis for the Restatement strict liability for products is that "the public has the right to expect and does expect, in the case of products which it needs and for which it is forced to rely upon the seller, that reputable sellers will stand behind their goods." This theory places greater emphasis upon the general expectancy of the public that products on the market will be ones which are sound or which the seller will stand behind or be liable for damage caused by their defects. While there is some emphasis upon the factor that the products are needed by the public and that the public is forced to rely upon the seller for the product, there are, however, no limitations specially found as to products which are considered necessities of life or any particular reliance upon the seller.

A third reason given as underlying Section 402A is that "public policy demands the burden of accidental injuries caused by products and intended for consumption be placed upon those who market them, can be treated as a cost to production against which liability insurance can be obtained." While there may be several reasons in this more general statement, the brunt of the statement is directed toward making the loss a part of the cost of production. In so doing, it is pointed out that liability insurance protection can be undertaken or losses be treated as a cost of production.

Another basis for Section 402A, is that the "consumer of such products is entitled to the maximum of protection at the hands of someone, and the proper persons to afford it are those who market the product." This particular policy lays heavy emphasis upon the need for protection in a modern society permeated by the use of goods and the great possibility of accidents occurring.

The drafters of Section 402A are clear that it is a strict liability in tort. They do not set forth precisely, however, what must be its basis. They have said that "on whatever theory" there are the justifications for strict liability just discussed. It is clear that the drafters intend not to choose any particular basis so much as to enunciate the fact that strict liability does exist on any of the theories mentioned.

Currently there is a new proposed §402A on Strict Liability for Defective Products. This draft is the product of extensive work over a number of years by the Reporter and consultants. It is important because it redefines defect into certain main categories and will undoubtedly serve as the basis of the law for years to come.

RESTATEMENT PROPOSAL: REVISION
OF §402A STRICT LIABILITY

As mentioned earlier, if goods purchased are defective, there is a basis for recovery of damages on three possible major bases: negligence, warranty, and strict liability. §402A of the Restatement of Torts 2d in the formulation of strict liability of the manufacturer and seller is often followed by the courts. This allows the purchaser to recover if the product is defective in quality, design, packaging, labeling, or carrying any need warnings. It is likely that the courts will continue to follow this formulation until a new one has been considered and passed by the American Law Institute (ALI).

The new formulation of §402A was debated on the floor of ALI and is scheduled for further discussion. For the purchasing manager, it is valuable to have an understanding of this new development. Some of the goods or products purchased by his or her company may be defective and damage may be caused to the goods themselves, or to other goods, or to persons. The first section of the Proposed §402A is similar to the former §402A set forth on page 13 of the 1995 supplement. It states:

§1 Commercial Seller's Liability for Harm Caused by Defective Products:

(a) One engaged in the business of selling products who sells a defective product is subject to liability for harm to persons or property caused by the product defect.

(b) A product is defective if, at the time of sale, it contains a manufacturing defect, is defective in design, or is defective because of inadequate instructions or warnings.

However, several differences are readily apparent. For one, the liability is limited to commercial sellers. Although most of the sellers to purchasing agents will be commercial ones, there may be a few instances where the seller is an individual not engaged in commercial sales. If the latter is so, the new §402A appears inapplicable. The drafters also indicate that an "occasional" or "casual sale" of surplus property outside the seller's regular business is not covered.

The rule stated in this section applies not only to sales transactions but also to other forms of product distribution that are the functional equivalent of product sales. Commercial lessors of products for consumer use are thus liable for injuries caused by defective products that they lease to consumers.

Interestingly, the drafters also state that the rule of this new section also applies to housing, although sales of real property historically have not been within the ambit of product sales. But providers of services unaccompanied by products are not covered.

Another difference is that the new §402 has been phrased in terms of major categories of defects:

1) Manufacturing Defects

2) Design Defects

3) Inadequate Instructions or Warnings

It is these major categories of defects that will have some different standards applied in later sections.

The first category of manufacturing defects has a long history and as drafters point out:

> By the early 1960s, American courts recognized that a seller of any product having a manufacturing defect should be liable in tort for harm caused by the defect regardless of the plaintiff's ability to maintain a traditional negligence or warranty action. Liability would attach even if the manufacturer's quality control in producing the defective product was reasonable.

The defenses of contractual privity or direct connection remain ineffective against strict liability.

In regard to the other two major categories or defect, the drafters state:

> Questions of design defect and defects based on inadequate instructions or warnings arise when the specific product unit conforms to the intended design but the intended design itself, or its sale without adequate instructions or warnings, renders the product not reasonably safe. If these forms of defect are found to exist, then every unit in the same product line is potentially defective.

Although the drafters still recognize these as defects in the product for which the purchaser can recover, they also see these defects as deserving slightly different treatment. The rule developed for manufacturing defects is inappropriate for these defects, they believe. Instead these cases require determinations that the product could have reasonably been made safer by a better design, instruction or warning. Sections 2(b) and (c) and 4(b) (2), (3), and (4) rely on a reasonableness test traditionally used in determining whether an actor (manufacturer or seller) has been negligent.

These standards for design of products and accompanying warnings would appear to be a negligence standard, however, the drafters point out that there are some differences between it and what some dealing with design defects, if the product causes injury while being put to a reasonably foreseeable use, the seller is held to have known of the risks that attend such use. (See § 2, Comment i.)

Second, some courts have sought to limit the defense of comparative fault in certain products liability contexts. In furtherance of this objective, they have avoided characterizing the liability test as based in negligence, thereby affording freedom to fashion comparative or contributory fault doctrine in a more restrictive fashion. (See § 7, Commend d.) Third, some courts are concerned that a negligence standard might be too forgiving of a small manufacturer who might be excused for its ignorance of risk or for failing to take adequate precautions to avoid risk.

Some courts might focus negligence considerations on the conduct of the defendant and say it was not liable because its meager resources made it too burdensome to discover design risks or give warnings. But under the new 402A concept of strict liability reasonableness, a defendant is held to the standard of knowledge available to the relevant manufacturing community at the time the product was manufactured. Also, the liability of nonmanufacturing sellers in the distributive chain is strict in the sense that it is no defense that they acted reasonably and were not aware of a defect in the product, be it manufacturing, design, or failure to warn.

The drafters likewise acknowledge the overlap of legal theories of liability:

> As long as the functional criteria are met, courts may utilize the doctrines of negligence, strict liability, or the implied warranty of merchantability, or simply define liability in the functional terms set forth in the black letter.

The drafters continue that part of the law that limits this strict liability to personal injury or property damage. They exclude from this rule damage to the product itself, economic losses, or emotional upset.

Section 2 of the Restatement sets forth in more detail these three basic categories:

> For purposes of determining liability under § 1:
>
> (a) A product contains a manufacturing defect when the product departs from its intended design even though all possible care was exercised in the preparation and marketing of the product;
>
> (b) A product is defective in design when the foreseeable risks of harm posed by the product could have been reduced by the adoption of a reasonable alternative design by the seller or a predecessor in the commercial chain of distribution and the omission of the alternative design renders the product not reasonably safe;
>
> (c) A product is defective because of inadequate instructions or warnings when the foreseeable risks of harm posed by the product could have been reduced by the provision of reasonable instructions or warnings by the seller or a predecessor in the commercial chain of distribution and the omission of the instructions or warnings renders the product not reasonably safe.

In regard to the last category (a), it is reemphasized that liability for the defective product exists regardless of the manufacturer's high standard of quality control and reasonableness.

It also is pointed out that the rationale for holding wholesalers and retailers strictly liable for harm caused by manufacturing defects is that, as between them and innocent victims who suffer harm because of defective products, the product sellers as business entities are in a better position than are individual users and consumers to insure against such losses. In most instances, wholesalers and retailers will be able to pass liability costs up the chain of product distribution to the manufacturer.

In regard to defect categories—defective design and defectiveness of warnings or instructions—the drafters set forth the different standards of reasonableness. They state that subsections (b) and (c), which impose liability for products that are defectively designed or sold without adequate warnings or instructions and are thus not reasonably safe, achieve the same general objectives as does liability predicted on negligence. Their goal can be seen in the following statement: The major emphasis is on creating incentives for manufacturers to achieve optimal levels of safety in designing and marketing products. Most would agree that society does not benefit from products that are excessively safe—automobiles designed with maximum speeds of 20 miles per hour—any more than it benefits from products that are too risky. Society benefits more when just the right, or optimal, amount of built-in product safety is achieved. They note that a reasonably designed product still carries with it some elements of risk that must be protected against by the user or consumer. If something risky cannot be designed out of the product at an acceptable cost then the user population bears the risk. However, what is an "acceptable" or an "unacceptable" cost is not indicated! But evidence of state of the art technology is relevant to show that a safer design for the product could have been used. Furthermore, even if the design is similar to others being used, it can still be shown by the purchaser that a safer design was feasible.

Where risks and benefits of less safe products are generally known, liability may be precluded. For example, John is seriously injured driving his small car, which is less crashworthy than some larger ones. The drafters note: product sellers must provide reasonable instructions and warnings about risks of injury associated with their products. *If* a design change is not a reasonable alternative for the particular style of product that is being sold, such a change is not necessary. For example, sellers down the chain of distribution must warn when doing so is feasible and reasonably necessary. In any event, sellers down the chain are liable if the instructions and warnings provided by predecessors in the chain are inadequate.

Consumer expectations are a highly relevant factor in this reasonableness standard of risk-utility balancing in design issues. But consumer expectations alone are not the determinative factor in regard to design.

In terms of warnings, the drafters have made it clear that "product sellers must provide reasonable instructions and warnings about risks of injury associated with their products." Warnings of obvious risks or obvious risk avoidance is not required. But what is obvious? If the product is so misused, modified, or altered that this creates risks that are sufficiently unreasonable and unusual, liability for design or warnings may be precluded.

Section 3 of the new §402A deals with inferences of manufacturing defectiveness without proof of specific defect. Section 4 deals specifically with drugs and medical devices. Section 5 deals with causation or causal connections problems. Did the defect cause the harm? Section 6 deals with defects that increase harm beyond what otherwise might have occurred. Was the careless driver more seriously injured because the car was defective? Because it is foreseeable that there will be some accidents, did the car manufacturer reasonably produce and design the car to give reasonable protection to those involved in accidents?

Section 7 deals with apportionment of liability where both parties have been at fault. This recognizes comparative fault where each must bear some of the responsibility and loss. This determination is up to the jury; or if there is no jury, it is up to the judge. It likewise will depend on the circumstances when the plaintiff's conduct is failure to discover a defect, or inattention to a danger that should have been eliminated by a safety feature. In such cases, a trier of fact may decide to allocate little or no responsibility to the plaintiff. Conversely, when the plaintiff voluntarily and unreasonably encounters a risk, the trier of fact may decide to attribute all or a substantial percentage of responsibility to the plaintiff.

Section 8 deals with disclaimers, waivers, and contractual defenses. It states disclaimers and limitations of remedies by product sellers, waivers by product purchasers, and other similar contractual exculpations, oral or written, do not bar or reduce otherwise valid products liability claims for harm to persons. This reaffirms the traditional §402A strict liability that overrides any contractual defenses, as the drafters point out. A commercial seller of a product is not permitted to escape liability for harm to persons through limiting terms in a contract governing the sale of a product. It is presumed that the plaintiff lacked sufficient information, bargaining power, or bargaining position necessary to execute a fair contractual limitation of rights to recover. There is an exception for used "as is" products. Also, the section may be inapplicable where the risk or waiver has been fully understood and negotiated by parties with equal bargaining power.

Delivery Terms and Risk of Loss

SHIPMENT AND DELIVERY TERMS, FOLLOWS PAGE 395 OF ORIGINAL TEXT

Recently, a major development has taken place in regard to abbreviated shipment terms. The use of these terms has been discussed in Chapter XX. With just a few letters e.g. F.O.B, New York or C.I.F. St. Louis, major legal obligations and consequences ensue. Matters of price, delivery, risk of loss, insurance and other obligations are set forth in the law for these letters or abbreviated terms. The use of the definition in the Uniform Commercial Code remains the same and the discussion in the main text remains relevant as long as the purchasing manager makes sure it is specified in the contract that the UCC applies.

A new development is the issuance of new trade terms and definitions by the International Chamber of Commerce. These may be used in both domestic and foreign trade, and the purchasing manager will surely be encountering their proposed use by some suppliers. They are called "Incoterms 1990" and will undoubtedly be used during the last half of this century and into the next.

Nota Bene: The purchasing manager may prefer to use shipment terms which he or she is more familiar with and want to specify that the Uniform Commercial Code shipment terms apply as well as specifically contracting to precise duties and risks. Sometimes even the UCC shipment terms do not make it clear whose employees have the duty to load the goods into the truck or unload them, or who undertakes the risk while the goods are at the carrier's storage facility or dock. While custom or usage or past practice may be looked to under UCC §1–205, sometimes this is not clear and an express contract term on the matter is preferable.

However, the use of the shipment may be in the control of the other party and that party may insist on using a shipment term of the Incoterms. Or the purchasing manager who is engaged in numerous international purchases may find it to his or her advantage to use them.

Nota Bene: If the purchasing manager decides to use Incoterms, he or she should obtain a copy of them with the precise legal definitions contained therein. It is obtainable only from the International Chamber of Commerce, 38, Cours Albert 1er, 75008 Paris, FRANCE (Phone (1) 49.53.28.28. or FAX (1) 42.25.86.63.) which controls its publication rights. The purchasing manager also should consult with the company lawyers to be sure of its understanding and consequences.

The type of terms which the purchasing manager may encounter are in four major groupings:

Group E Departure	EXW	Ex Works
Group F Main carriage unpaid	FCA	Free Carrier
	FAS	Free Alongside Ship
	FOB	Free On Board
Group C Main carriage paid	CFR	Cost and Freight
	CIF	Cost, Insurance and Freight
	CPT	Carriage Paid To
	CIP	Carriage and Insurance Paid To
Group D Arrival	DAF	Delivered At Frontier
	DES	Delivered EX Ship
	DEQ	Delivered EX Quay
	DDU	Delivered Duty Unpaid
	DDP	Delivered Duty Paid

Also, the ship with the port of destination named may be used, or DEQ (Delivered Ex Quay) with the named port of destination.

There are some Incoterms which are applicable and may be used for any type of transportation or combinations thereof:

FCA   Free Carrier (. . . named place)

CPT   Carriage Paid To (. . . named place of destination)

CIP   Carriage and Insurance Paid To (. . . named place of destination)

DAF   Delivered At Frontier (. . . named place)

DDU   Delivered Duty Unpaid (. . . named place of destination)

DDP   Delivered Duty Paid (. . . named place of destination)

If the goods are to be picked up at the supplier's factory, warehouse, or place of business then the EXW or Ex Works term is appropriate with the place named immediately after those letters.

While the purchasing manager should consult the Incoterm publisher and the company attorney for precise meaning, a summary of the four major categories and their consequences is made here for general orientation. It is envisioned by the drafters of the Incoterms that these terms will be used most frequently with certain types of transportation. For example, if shipment is by air, then FCA (Free Carrier) may be used with the name of the city or place where shipment is made. If the shipment is by railroad, FCA likewise may be used. If the goods are shipped by sea or by inland waterway, there are some other specialized terms which may be used. There are the more common ones such as FAS (Free Alongside Ship) with the port of shipment named (e.g., St. Louis if goods are shipped from St. Louis to New Orleans), or FOB (Free on Board) with the port of shipment named. The CFR term is Cost and Freight with named city or port of destination following these letters. Or there is CIF (Cost, Insurance, and Freight) with the named port, the term DES (Delivered Ex Ship).

Article 2A of the Uniform Commercial Code—Leases

This revised list should replace the list currently found on page 441. The following states had adopted Article 2A as of March 10, 1995:

Alabama	Kentucky
Alaska	Maine
Arizona	Maryland
Arkansas	Michigan
California	Minnesota
Colorado	Mississippi
Connecticut	Missouri
Delaware	Montana
District of Columbia	Nebraska
Florida (original 1987 Act)	Nevada
Georgia	New Hampshire
Hawaii	New Jersey
Idaho	New Mexico
Illinois	New York
Indiana	North Carolina
Iowa	North Dakota
Kansas	Ohio

Oklahoma	Utah
Oregon	Vermont
Pennsylvania	Virginia
Rhode Island	Washington
South Carolina	West Virginia
Tennessee	Wisconsin
Texas	Wyoming

Computer Purchases and Controversies

LEGISLATIVE REFORM OF COMPUTER LAW

The current Article 2 of the Uniform Commercial Code (UCC) is not sufficient to handle transactions involving the sale and licensing of computer software. Under current law, several courts have even held that such transactions involving computer software do not fall within Article 2 of the UCC. These courts hold that such sales are not transactions in goods, but rather are transactions for services. This holding is common when the software contract entails substantial services (i.e., when the contract is for custom designed software).

Software contracts differ from contracts involving ordinary goods in two important features: 1) software contracts transfer intangible goods; and 2) software contracts often entail a license of rights to use rather than a sale. There needs to be a shift from case law to the legislative front to tackle these differences and resolve the problem of the scope of Article 2.

The Article 2 Drafting Committee had been given just this task. In November 1992, the Article 2 Drafting Committee decided to complete a section-by-section review of Article 2. The Drafting Committee asked the ABA Business Law Section Task Force on Software Contracting to prepare this analysis of Article 2 and make proposals regarding necessary changes and accommodations. These proposals will be summarized shortly.

The Drafting Committee has three alternatives which it could use to structure the additions and adjustments to Article 2 to handle computer software transactions.[1] The alternatives are:

(1) Defining Article 2 to include software licensing contracts; adjusting Article 2 sections to deal with the intangible character of the transactions; and adopting new sections to deal with licensing issues.

(2) Adopting a "hub and spoke" structure for Article 2, in which Article 2 would contain the fundamental principles applicable to all commercial contracts; and creating sub-articles which would deal with specific types of transactions, such as Article 2A (leases), Article 2B (sales), and Article 2C (licenses).

(3) Removing software contracts from Article 2 entirely and developing a new article specifically for licensing of intangibles, including software contracts (Article 2B Licensing of Intangibles).

Because the Drafting Committee has proposed fewer changes in the area of contract formation and other basic issues, the "hub and spoke" approach seems feasible.

CATEGORIZING OF PROPOSED LEGISLATION

The Report of the ABA Task Force on Software Contracts is an important one. Instead of reviewing the proposal for changes, additions, and adjustments to Article 2 in a sequential fashion up the code section numbers, the proposal can best be understood by summarizing it in the following categories:

(1) General principles are different.

(2) General principles are same, but major changes are necessary.

(3) General principles are same, but minor technical changes are necessary.

(4) General principles of Article 2 are applicable without any changes.

(5) New sections need to be added.

---

[1]These three possible approaches are set forth in: Raymond T. Nimmer, Donald A. Cohn, & Ellen Kirsch, *License Contracts Under Article 2 of the Uniform Commercial Code: A Proposal,* 19 Rutgers Comp. & Tech. L. J. 281, 283 (1993).

This summary will not reflect every change, adjustment or difference. It is intended only to highlight important proposed changes in Article 2.[2]

General Principles Are Different

§2–201—In proposed revisions to Article 2 this section concerning the Statute of Frauds requirement is eliminated. However, this would be in conflict with the federal patent and copyright laws which require a writing to transfer ownership in intellectual property. Therefore, the ABA Task Force suggests that while the writing requirement be eliminated for other contracts, a writing could be mandated for some contracts to the extent mandated by federal patent and copyright laws.

§2–307—This "gap-filler" concerning delivery in lots is in direct contrast with the presumption of the custom developed software industry practice. Even with mass-marketed software, the industry practice is generally to contract, as part of the initial transaction, for upgrades, corrections, and enhancements. Therefore, this "gap-filler" is inappropriate for software transactions.

§2–309—Since licensing generally involves long-term or perpetual ongoing relationships as opposed to short-term purchases of goods, this gap-filler, providing for termination at any time by either party, will require significant redrafting to handle termination and cancellation of licensing relationships.

§2–401—This section concerns issues of transfer of title. Because title transfer is not applicable to many software transactions, as access to or use of the software is important, rather than physical transfer, the ABA Task Force suggests that rather than dealing with title transfer, the revisions should contain provisions determining when a license becomes binding, and determining when a licensee has access to an intangible would be necessary.

§2–403—Again, concepts of title transfer are not applicable to licensing. Also, there can be no good faith purchaser with regard to software licenses. The ABA Task Force suggests that mass-marketed software which resembles a good, may warrant separate treatment here than the custom software developed for a licensee.

---

[2]To see the complete sectional analysis, see ABA Business Law Section Task Force on Software Contracting, UCC Article 2 Sectional Analysis, *Issues Relating to the Inclusion of Software Contracting*, Feb. 10, 1993.

General Principles Are Same, But Major Changes Necessary

§2–101 & §2–102—The short title and the scope of Article 2 shall have to be broadened to reach software contracts, including software licensing, and software assignments of intangible intellectual property, and the sections should be broadened to cover contracts, including licensing and assignments, of other types of intellectual property.

§2–103—The definition section for Article 2 will have to provide definitions for the new terms involving software contracts and licensing, such as licensor, licensee, license, intangible, intellectual property, etc. Terms already defined in this section may have to be modified. For example, "receipt" will have to be redefined to deal with different ways that intangible property is delivered (i.e., electronic transmission or "downloading").

§2–105—This section defining merchant will need to be broadened to cover software and other intangible property in light of the enlarged scope of Article 2. The drafters will need to decide which persons will be included in the merchant definition—the inventor, the designer or the author—and will need to decide whether a dealer who may have no specialized knowledge of the software and its application shall be considered a merchant.

§2–207—This section dealing with additional terms in acceptance should be revised to deal with the enforceability of "shrink wrap" licenses. A "shrink wrap" license is a preprinted set of vendor-oriented terms and conditions printed on the exterior of the mass-marketed software package or on the envelope containing the mass-marketed software. The license contains a warning which states that if the consumer breaks the package or envelope, she has agreed to the terms of the license.

§2–312—In this section on warranty of title, changes will be needed to address the right to use and access software and other intangible intellectual property without reference to "title." Changes will be needed to make clear that licensing of software does not involve any transfer of title. The section also has a provision providing a warranty against infringement and obliging buyer to hold a merchant seller harmless against claims arising out of compliance with buyer's specifications. This will need substantial revision, as it is in contrast with the actual practice of the software industry. The buyer's or licensee's specifications are only functional specifications as to what the program should do; it is the programmer who puts together the technical lines of computer code which can infringe upon the patent or copyright of other third parties. The drafters could consider adding a provision that would require licensor to warrant that licensee's use of the software will not infringe upon any patent or ownership rights of third parties.

§2–313, §2–314, §2–315, & §2–316—In these sections dealing with warranties, the ABA Task Force recommends that a "substantial conformity tender rule" be adopted for Article 2 as it relates to software contracting instead of the "perfect tender rule," with modifications to protect licensee, in event of less than perfect tender of intangibles. Because software generally does not operate without deficiencies or "bugs," the "perfect tender rule" is inappropriate to software transactions. This problem is particularly expected in the context of custom-developed software contracts in which there is an expected lengthy period of adjustment and refinement on a developed software program after the first operational testing. The drafters may wish to consider a substantial performance or a material impairment standard in light of the assumption that software is inherently "imperfect."

In the area of express warranties, there are questions as to whether the vendor should be held to the promises of a demonstration "shell" program (a non-working program which shows layout and proposed features of future software) of the non-working demonstration product. In the section on implied warranties, the drafters may provide protection for the consumer and licensee from the hidden presence of computer viruses and the resulting injury to the user's computer system. Because latent defects in software will be virtually impossible to discover by examination, drafters may wish to provide additional safeguards in the section on exclusion and modification of warranties to protect licensees and consumers.

§2–508—This section provides seller to cure improper delivery or tender. Again, the concept of delivery is not appropriate to contracts involving software licensing, and needs to be adjusted to reflect methods of transfer applicable to software transactions. Also, perfect tender should not be required by seller (see §2–313 supra), and a modified provision allowing for "substantial tender" should be drafted for software contracting.

§2–510—Because this section deals with the effect of breach, it will need to be modified to allow for use of a "substantial tender" rule for determining breach in software contracting. See §2–313 supra.

§2–512—Where buyer is to pay before inspection of software, the drafters will again wish to modify the perfect tender rule to a substantial conformity tender rule, to provide protection to the software seller. See §2–313 supra.

§2–513—The provision regarding buyer's inspection rights will have to be modified to adjust concept of delivery to include methods of transfer used in software transactions and to provide for a substantial tender rule (see 2–313 supra). Also, drafters will want to consider what inspection rights buyers and licensees should have considering that most defects in software and other intangible technology are latent defects and are not generally discoverable from a simple inspection.

§2–601–§2–617—These provisions which address breach, repudiation and excuse will all need to be adjusted to reflect the use of a "substantial performance" or "substantial conformity" test instead of the use of a perfect tender rule. See §2–313 supra. Also, in several of the sections, the concept of delivery needs to be adjusted to include transfers in software contracts. In §2–602 buyer's rightful rejection, the section needs revision to reflect the fact that in many software transactions there is no transfer of ownership. Section 2–603, dealing with the merchant buyer's obligations to rightfully rejected goods, will need substantial revisions for application to licensing contracts. Licensees have no rights to sell the software as they do not have title to goods, nor do licensees generally have greater rights than right of licensee alone to use or access the software. The section providing buyer's salvage rights in rightfully rejected goods (§2–604) will need much additional revision, in great part because the physical media of the software license is not the truest measure of the software's value. The drafters may wish to consider granting the licensee a right to continued use of the rightfully rejected software absent instructions from licensor; continued use of an intangible will likely not deteriorate the intangible property to the licensor's disadvantage. For the section defining acceptance (§2–606), the ABA Task Force suggests that different rules should apply to mass-marketed software, as there is no practical opportunity to inspect it before purchase without substantial opportunity to operate software. The Task Force suggests consideration of a partial acceptance notion. The ABA Task Force also questions the appropriateness of §2–607 in creating the obligations of buyer or licensee of mass-marketed software after acceptance where the buyer's inspection of the physical media and packaging will not discover latent defects or where transfer is done without opportunity to inspect.

§2–703—This section providing seller's remedies needs revision to adjust the definition of delivery to address the granting of use and access in software transactions. The concept of resale by the seller of wrongfully rejected goods, while it may apply to mass-marketed software, does not apply to the custom-developed software context. The drafters also need to consider what remedies they wish to provide for licensors. Licensors may generally be able to cancel licensee's access or use of software by means other than retaking physical possession. Also, with software and other intangible intellectual property licenses, a licensee's breach may involve more than just the user fee or royalty. For example, licensee could have wrongfully disclosed trade secrets of licensor. The drafters may wish to provide remedies for licensors in these and similar situations.

§2–711—Substantial revision will be necessary on this section which provides buyer's remedies when seller fails to deliver or buyer rightfully rejects goods. As is, this section provides the buyer with the right to hold goods after rightful rejection and to resell them. A licensee may not have the right to transfer his rights to a third party (see §2–603 supra). Besides, the transfer of the right to access the software may be valueless without the licensor's obligation to provide support and maintenance. The drafters need to provide the licensee with remedies when licensor defaults or when licensee rightfully rejects software. The drafters have many options for remedies, including granting the licensee: the right to refund payments; the right to continued use of software after licensor's default; or the right to contract with a third party to maintain the software program.

General Principles Are the Same, But Technical Changes Are Necessary

§2–204, §2–205, §2–206 & §2–208—These sections dealing with formation of contract, offer, acceptance, and course of performance need to be redefined so that the scope of the sections include the transfer of, or granting rights to, software and other intangible intellectual property.

§2–301—This Section needs to be adjusted to include forms of transfer which are not done by physical delivery. For instance, the licensee of a software licensing contract expects only the right to access the intangible property, and the licensor's obligation is only to provide that access; there is no physical delivery.

§2–305—"Delivery" is an inappropriate measure to determine time of payment. Rather, transfer of right to use or access software or other intangibles should be the measure. Also, "price" should be redefined to reflect the software industry practice of making a continuing stream of payments, as royalties or user fees.

§2–308—This "gap-filler" provides for place of delivery in the absence of specification in the contract. Since the concept of physical delivery is not applicable to software transactions, drafters will need to take into account the means of tender of software and other intangibles, keeping in mind that right to access and right to use are generally the rights to be transferred.

§2–310—Again, this section will need to redefine delivery and receipt to include methods of transfer involved in software contracts and licensing. This section will also have to provide for relationships where the transfer is ongoing.

§2–503 & §2–504—These sections, which deal with the manner of seller's tender of delivery and shipment by seller, require adjustment so that the delivery concept will include transfers of rights to use or to access intangible intellectual property. The drafters may want to consider providing for the method of transfer for electronic or remote access contracts.

§2–511—No revisions are necessary to this section concerning tender of buyer's payment, other than adjusting the definition of delivery to include methods of software and other intellectual intangible property transfers.

General Principles Applicable Without Significant Changes

§2–202—The parol evidence section will not require revision to accommodate software contracts.

§2–302—The unconscionability section will not require revision to accommodate software contracts.

§2–303—The section allocating risk will not require revision to accommodate software contracts.

§2–304—The section providing how the purchase price may be payable will not require revision to accommodate software contracts.

§2–319–§2–323—These sections deal with shipment and delivery issues and are therefore either not relevant to most software contracts (e.g., licensing contracts where remote access rights are used), or are not unique in their impact upon software transfers where software is treated like any other commodity (e.g., mass-marketed software).

§2–326—Note that when dealing with intangibles, such as software, creditors may not have the right to a security interest.

§2–328—Provisions for sale by auction require no revision to accommodate software contracts.

§2–402—In this provision dealing with the rights of seller's creditors, there is some question as to whether a security interest can be created in intellectual property.

§2–509—Risk of loss during shipment is not important to many software transfers. Risk of loss might be important in the mass-marketed software transactions, and could probably be governed by the sections provisions as is.

New Sections Need to Be Added

Presumption of Confidentiality—The ABA Task Force proposes that the drafters may wish to consider a gap-filler which will provide a presumption of confidentiality in software or other intangible intellectual property contracts.

Default in Licensing of Intangibles—The default concept in the context of licensing intangibles is not currently defined in Article 2. The Task Force suggests looking to Article 2A for guidance with respect to rights to notice and cure and other similar provisions. Should the test of default be material breach or impairment of a license?

Mass-Marketed Software—Mass-marketed software could be treated separately from the licensing of intangibles. Sales of mass-marketed software could be treated as sales of goods.

Gap-Fillers—The revisions of Article 2 could provide provisions to fill in when the parties' contract is silent as to: location restrictions; revocability of license; term of license; number of users and copies; rights to future maintenance, support and enhancements; and licensee transfer rights.

Caveat Bene: It must be remembered that most license and computer contracts are printed ones. As such they are subject to the infirmities of standard form contracts, e.g., reality of consent; unconscionability; matters discussed in Chapters IX and XXVII of this book.

Computer Purchases and Contracts

PRAGMATIC AND LEGAL EFFECTS OF THE INFORMATION SUPERHIGHWAY*

The Information Age

A remarkable aspect of the information age is the speed at which it is impacting our lives. Less than five years ago the average American would have ventured to guess that the Internet was a network marketing scheme somehow connected to Amway Products. Now E-mail, World Wide Web, Gopher, and Mosaic are a regular part of the lives of millions. It is a means of communicating that has taken the world by storm.

It is estimated that by the year 2000, computers of various forms will outnumber people in the U.S. An estimated 35 million people in the world are already connected by the infobahn. Another estimate gives the median income of the Internet user as $55,000. The business world has been quick to take advantage of the superhighway or infobahn for efficiency and operational reasons. But now the prospect of reaching millions of well-to-do potential customers is another reason businesses are taking the infobahn seriously.

Internet dilettantes Speaker of the House Newt Gingrich and Vice President Al Gore are but two of a growing number of politicians getting online. Now it is possible to send E-mail to President Clinton, read the

*A. James Wang, Juris Doctor, MBA, MS.

latest legislation, or discuss deficit fighting with former Senators Rudman and Tsongas.

Electronic commerce is no longer just a catchy phrase. In the modern business world of international competition, satellite links, and laptop computers, high technology gives the business player the competitive edge and wider markets. And as expected, Commercial Sales law is being tested in ways that were not imagined when current laws were written.

Legal Role

Traditionally, law has usually played a more or less reactive catch-up role to technology. For instance, the invention of the telegraph in the 19th century had an enormous impact on business practices. Yet no clarification on the rules of business law were forthcoming for almost 30 years. In their 1868 treatise on the law of telegraphs, Scott and Jarnagen wrote, "It is becoming more and more important that the rules governing negotiations made by telegraph would be clearly defined and settled, as contracts thus made are constantly increasing in number and magnitude." History is repeating itself again as we watch legal rules struggle to maintain pace with advances in technology.

It is understandable why cyber-commerce has blossomed and grown. Modern businesses are adopting new technologies much faster than in the past. The old adage of "time is money" is ringing truer than ever. Just as the telegraph and telephone bridged buyer and seller located hundreds of miles apart, new communications technologies are making the world a much smaller place. Businesses are using the Internet to search throughout the globe for better bargains, employees, consultants, and to conduct market surveys. Most of all, businesses are looking to the Internet as a window to a broader market.

Purchasing managers may require their suppliers to meet the requirements of their computerization and electronics systems. For example, one of the requirements suppliers must meet to be qualified as potential vendors to General Motors is that they must be "electronically connected." Information must be up-to-date and instantly available for management schemes like just-in-time manufacturing to work properly. Information technology has become the competitive edge.

Going electronic is also more economical in many instances. The Internet is the giant computer network created by the Defense Department during the 1960s and 1970s. With proper access to the

Internet, it is possible to send messages to every corner of the world at zero incremental cost. Although access to the Internet may cost the user a monthly fee, there are generally no further costs. The savings really add up for firms doing business globally. In some parts of the world (e.g., Eastern Europe), the Internet is often more reliable than the phone systems. Current estimates have the number of Internet users as over 25 million in the U.S. alone and growing. Practically every Fortune 500 company uses E-mail. A one-page E-mail sent from California to New York costs about 16 cents, compared with $1.86 by fax, $4.56 by Telex, and $13.00 by overnight express in 1992. The cost of access to the Internet has steadily been slashed as the three major providers—Prodigy, CompuServe, and American Online—compete aggressively. Computer software giant Microsoft is poised to enter the field in a few months and further depress access fees.

Even in the home, electronic commercial transactions will soon become as common as cable TV. Indeed, some of the home shopping channels have linked up with the cable companies to allow home viewers to purchase items being advertised on TV by entering codes into a controller box. Businesses are seeing green at the prospects of millions of consumers on the information superhighway. The astute consumer can search far and wide for the desired product as well as the best price. Shopping on the electronic malls is already existent. Electronic transactions will be the high-speed vehicle a considerable portion of commerce will ride in.

The boom in business done electronically means that an equivalently growing number of transactions are taking place without the traditional meeting of parties or even phone conversations. Electronic contracting becomes important as more people than ever before are making purchases over international boundaries. There is a broadening of horizons in search of the best products at the best prices.

What could possibly go wrong with commercial transactions done electronically? A guide to Internet purchasing appearing every five days on the "biz.marketplace" news groups gives some advice on how to buy via the net. Of paramount importance in any Internet transaction is to save all E-mail and written correspondence relating to the transaction. The guide suggests the use of COD (Cash On Delivery), credit cards, or third-party escrow services. It also reports an average of one complaint per month concerning transaction fraud; a very low number considering the thousands of buy-sell matches negotiated through the net.

The legal difficulty with an electronic commercial transaction is that it is neither written nor signed as would be required by a strict reading of the Statute of Frauds. In addition, the Best Evidence Rule would require production of the original document. The question then is which document is the original document when it exists only in cyberspace and not in any file drawer? The authentication requirement places the burden on the proponent to prove that the document is what he or she claims it is.

U.C.C. 2-201(26) provides that a notice is deemed received when it is delivered at the place of business where the contract was made or at any other place held out by the recipient as the place for receipt of such communications, and U.C.C. 2-201(25) provides that the recipient has knowledge of a fact when the recipient has received notice of it. Considered together, this could prejudice the computer illiterate who fails to or is unable to read the electronic mail he or she has already received on his or her computer.

Statute of Frauds

The Statute of Frauds has its roots in 17th century England. Its purpose was to protect the unwary and unwitting from contractual obligations. The prevailing law of commercial transactions still upholds the statute: the Uniform Sales Act demands a memorandum in writing and the Uniform Commercial Code requires only a "writing."

The terms "memorandum in writing" and "writing," when applied to media other than ink and paper raises some uncertainty. Telegraphs were eventually accepted as a valid means of memorializing a contract. The reasoning was that the mechanics of ink flowing through a pen was analogous to electricity flowing through a wire. When teletype came about, the courts readily held that the teletyped message satisfied the writing requirement. In addition, courts have shown a willingness to accept a bewildering variety of substitutes including scratchings on furniture and tractor fenders and writings on eggshells in rulings related to wills.

Telegraphs, facsimiles, and contracts on paper napkins all have a common denominator in that there is a physical object that is visually legible. The writing requirement reflected the central importance paper represented in commercial transactions. This was primarily so because it was easier to detect alterations made to the actual paper document. Electronic transactions are steadily becoming difficult to alter as the use of electronic safeguards have increased. Various computer security measures can be taken to keep tab of the primary document and to signal whether changes to the document have been made or whether the document has been displayed on a computer screen or printed on a printer.

The signature requirement of the Statute of Frauds requires the defendant's party's signature on the contract. Ordinarily this implies a handwritten signature on paper in ink. Courts have accepted as substitutes letterheads, typewritten or printed names, stamp marks, and embossed marks. The basis is the parties' intent to use them as endorsements of the contract and therefore satisfies the signature requirement.

As a practical matter, signatures cannot be telegraphed but the courts are quick to accept typed signatures as signatures within the context of the Statute of Frauds. A natural progression in this line of thinking would place equal acceptance to the typed signature on an electronic document.

Because the U.C.C. defines "signed" to include any symbol executed or adopted by a party with present intention to authenticate a writing, a party may use an electronic identification code to signal that the transaction pertains to a particular party.

Best Evidence Rule

Modern commentators give a more narrow reading to the Best Evidence Rule, restricting it to a requirement that parties produce available original documents rather than copies. Electronic mail consists of electronic pulses instead of writings on paper. The determination of which—if any—of the transmissions should be considered an original document is difficult.

Federal evidence rules 1001 advisory committee's note reads:

> Present day techniques have expanded methods of storing data, yet the essential form which the information ultimately assumes for useable purposes is words and figures. Hence the considerations underlying the rule dictate its expansion to include computers, photographic systems, and other modern developments.

This advisory note, which would be looked to by courts utilizing the federal rules, recognizes that words and figures can be stored in media other than ink on paper. The federal rules also provide that if data is stored on a computer or similar device, any printout or output otherwise readable by sight, shown to reflect the data accurately, is an original. Therefore, E-mail and other forms of electronic communications should satisfy the Best Evidence requirements readily. The fact that electronic documents can be faithfully copied electronically without any degradation in quality should make the Best Evidence Rule an insignificant requirement.

Technology has a penchant of filling voids, especially where some financial reward exists. It seems only a matter of time before a more or less foolproof system of authenticating an electronic transaction will be developed. Recognition by the laws of Commerce will make electronic commerce safe and dependable.

Requirements that documents or communications be "written" or "in writing" are out of place in the context of modern commercial practices. The American Bar Association is currently working to revise the Uniform Commercial Code—especially Section 2-201—to accommodate electronic transactions. The working group on Electronic Writings and Notices of the subcommittee on Electronic Commercial Practices recently proposed an Article 2 redraft for comments by members. A revised definition of the term "record" was proposed. Many of the panel members felt that a "blanket" allowance of electronic transmission of notices may be inappropriate at the present time. A definition of "record," a new term, has been proposed:

> Record means a durable representation of information which is in, or is capable of being retrieved or reproduced in perceivable form. A record may be in writing or in any electronic or other media.

All references to "writing," "writings," and "confirmatory memoranda" are to be replaced by "record" or "records" from Section 2-201 through Section 2-207.

Likewise, the National Conference of Commissioners on Uniform State Laws (NCCUSL) in its draft for Revised Article 2 of the Uniform Commercial Code has offered the following new definition for "record";

> Record means information that is inscribed on a tangible medium or that is stored in an electronic or other medium and is retrievable in perceivable form.

These new definitions are designed to embrace all means of communicating or storing information including but not limited to E-mail, tapes, and disks.

The term "record" encompasses "writings"; that is, any writing is a record. The corollary is not true; that is, any record is not necessarily a writing. A record need not be permanent or indestructible, but does not include any oral or other communication that is not stored or preserved by any means. The information must be stored on paper or some other medium. Information that has not been retained other than through human memory does not qualify as a record.

The proposed revisions are a palpable improvement over the current definition and paves the way for electronic commerce to reach new levels in scope and effectiveness.

Authentication Requirement

The laws of evidence require the proponent of an article to provide proof that the submitted article is what the offering party claims it is and therefore, authentic. Proof of the parties' signature using expert testimony is one way of authentication. Witnesses to the signing may testify as another means of authentication.

The authentication requirement raises the issues of fraud and deceit and reliability of transmission. The wide use of telegraph has resulted in ample contracts disputes involving fraudulent use of telegraphs and operator mistakes by the telegraph company. An alternate means of authentication are the telegraph forms that are filled out by the telegram senders. Faxes are still susceptible to transmission errors and the quality of the faxed document is still of inadequate quality to detect fraud.

The authentication requirement as applied to Internet transmissions is potentially tricky. There is almost no way to stop a determined criminal talented enough to commit fraud via the Internet. From a disgruntled coworker using the computer of someone who has just stepped away from their workstation to high-tech electronic eavesdropping to gain account passwords, the possibilities are too many to enumerate. Technological advances in preventing and fighting online fraud is indirectly providing means to meet the authentication requirement.

Notice

U.C.C. 1-201 (25) and U.C.C. 1-201 (26) taken together deems that a notice is received when delivered at the place of business where the contract was made or at any other place held out by the recipient as the place for the receipt of communications and that such receipt is knowl-edge of a fact. If the contract was transacted online, this presumes that the Internet address is a place held out as the place for the receipt of communications. This means that one is assumed to have read his or her E-mail. This substantially prejudices the computer illiterate who fails to or is unable to read the mail he or she has already received on his or her computer.

Conceivably, a person could enter into a commercial transaction over the Internet to buy a thousand widgets, and then fail to check his or her electronic mail thinking that all was well. Unbeknownst to the buyer, there is an E-mail message in his or her computer from the supplier in-forming the buyer that the price on the widgets has doubled. U.C.C. 1-201 (25) and U.C.C. 1-201 (26) applied here would imply that he or she had knowledge of the price increase.

U.C.C. 1-201 (25) and U.C.C. 1-201 (26) were designed to require that a person should read the mail he or she receives. It loses its practi-cality if it requires that just because a person uses an Internet address, he or she is required to use it faithfully. A feature that signals that a sent document was opened by the recipient would solve this dilemma. Or per-haps a return receipt note akin to certified mail.

Technology Aspects: Authentication and Security

Addressing the authentication requirement as one of the paramount problems with electronic commerce crosses several lines. The battle against crime may bring some benefits to safeguarding commercial transactions by meeting the authentication requirement. Computer secu-rity is a relatively new field that is growing rapidly. Fueled largely by in-dustry and market demands, hundreds of hardware and software have been marketed and sold in the name of computer security. If judicial no-tice is granted to reliable forms of computer security, it would serve the dual purpose of satisfying the authentication requirements.

The federal government in its battle against computer crimes, eco-nomic crimes, and pornography has provided considerable funding to a variety of research efforts sometimes even resorting to hiring hackers themselves. It has funded the creation of the Computer Emergency Response Team (CERT), a group formed to safeguard the Internet.

The boom in demand for the services of computer security experts is an indication of how seriously industry is taking the problems of computer security with regard to ex-employees, hackers and viruses. Concerns about unauthorized access—by hackers, competitors, and disgruntled employees—has been the main stumbling block for conducting business on the Internet.

The 1986 Electronic Communications Privacy Act (ECPA) makes it illegal for anyone other than the sender and the receiver of the message to read messages exchanged over public electronic mail systems. There is, however, the practical difficulty in its enforcement. Instead, the push has been to protect the information itself by various means.

Every innovation seems to have inspired the diabolical minds. For example, faxes have been used by forgers to defraud banks. Spurious individuals can easily cut and paste executive's signatures from company mailings onto payment orders and fax the orders to a bank. The quality of faxed documents are generally not good enough to discern whether the document and signature is authentic or not. For this reason, banks are unwilling to accept payments orders by fax.

Technical advances likewise have made it more efficient for criminals to ply their trade. Police in New York recently reeled in the head of one of the biggest illegal gambling operations known as "Spanish Raymond." His operation made good use of the indispensable fax machine, but police were able to bug his fax lines to gather the incriminating evidence against him.

In the battle against various types of crime, government and industry—often together—have persevered to come up with interesting solutions. For instance, not long after the first telephone system was in place, Bell's invention was probably used in some sort of crime. It invariably became desirable to ascertain whether a defendant placed a phone call from a particular place to another at a particular time. Today it is possible to obtain the Caller-ID service from the telephone company. All phone signals carry an electronic coded signal containing the phone number, listing name and time of call. By subscribing to the Caller-ID service, this data is displayed on an electronic device. E-mail users are assigned unique Internet addresses. The sender's address is electronically linked to whatever message is sent. Although this would probably meet the evidentiary requirement, there is always the possibility that a fraudulent user has obtained someone else's account and password. In addition, there are methods to disguise an Internet address to prevent traceability. This has created the need for cybersleuths like Tsutomu Shimomura who ensnared Kevin Mitnick, the wanted superhacker on the run since 1992.

Retinal scanners, voiceprint recorders, and cryptographic authentication are presently available. One ongoing study funded by the federal government looks into the feasibility of a grant plan requiring every computer, telephone, fax machine, and so on to incorporate an electronic chip that would provide a unique identification key. Two keys would be required to decrypt the coded information that will be appended to every transmission or record from the device. One of the keys is resident with the device and the other is a common key held by federal authorities. This plan would give every device a unique signature that only law enforcement authorities can decipher. This is comparable to a Caller-ID function usable only by law enforcement, a valuable crime-fighting tool against money laundering and computer crimes.

Another computer security measure under development is what is widely referred to as Public Key. This system was developed by the National Security Agency and licensed to a consortium called Public Key Partners consisting of companies such as the Silicon Valley firm Cylink. This is a signature system designed to ensure that transactions are made in good faith. The Department of Defense hopes to use this technique for its contracting and the Internet Revenue Service wants to incorporate this signature system to its electronically filed tax returns.

The electronic signature is created when the document is encrypted using a secret code. The difference is that unlike conventional encryption/de-encryption routines, a different, public key is used to read the document. If the document has been altered in any way by someone without the secret code it will no longer produce exactly the same signature sequence when combined with the public key.

Signature authentication as a desired part of sealing a contract has spawned a multitude of hardware and software devices. United Parcel Service delivery persons carry specially designed handheld computers that can digitally store the customer's signature. On receipt of the parcel, the customer signs on the special electronic writing pad and the signature is digitally transmitted back to the central office. Although this again is not altogether foolproof, the risk of fraud is slight and exists whether or not the customer signs on an electronic signature pad or a sheet of paper. The benefits of this technology far outweigh the drawbacks of fraud.

A race is on to develop the standard for Internet transaction security protocols. Two different security standards are emerging—the Secure HTTP (Hypertext Transfer Protocol) and SSL (Secure Sockets Layer). SSL basically encrypts the customer's order and credit card number at the beginning of the transaction. Secure HTTP is a more sophisticated system. It includes authentication of the customer's identity by the server through digital signature verification and other features. A battle is brewing over which standard will emerge as the de facto standard for commercial net transactions. Although these security standards are primarily meant for retailing on the Internet, its applicability to other facets of commercial transactions in terms of the authentication and signature requirements are evident.

The growth of other computer technologies opens up more challenges to the Commercial Law. Artificial intelligence and neural networks could have far-reaching effects into commerce. A neural network can be made to learn the job functions of a purchasing agent by monitoring his or her activities over a period of time, and in due course, even perform them. This is a further test to existing commerce law because now the computer is not just the means of communicating a transaction but also involved in the direct formulation of contract.

Purchasing Decisions by Computer

Computers making buying decisions? Hardly absurd considering the fateful Black Monday in October 1987 when computer programs of such pedigree caused the biggest one-day drop in the Dow Jones Industrial Average. Computers running artificial intelligent software make thousands of transactions on the stock market all around the world everyday without any human input. So much so that computer trading is suspended if a stock market crash is in progress. But the simple irony is that even the decision to suspend computer trading is computer triggered.

In the slim-profit grocery industry, managers monitor sales from data gleaned directly from the check-out registers and warehouses. More sophisticated systems have the added ability to automatically raise a flag if a particular item is selling very briskly or is sold out. It is not inconceivable that the computer can search the cybermall for the best prices, determine when and what quantity needs to be ordered, and send an electronic purchase order to the appropriate supplier.

Farfetched or not, it is possible for a personal computer to make purchasing decisions for man. Although the Statute of Frauds and the Best Evidence Rule requirements can be stretched to cover even these types of electronic transactions, it is evident that such technology advances can leave commercial law struggling to keep pace.

Conclusion

Commercial transactions will experience more changes as technology continues to leapfrog itself. Perhaps a cue can be taken from copyright law, itself a victim of innumerable technological surprises. Surprises in the form of T.V., radio, compact discs, and video recorders when considered in the light of the original 1909 Copyright Act. The 1976 Copyright Act as well as the 1988 Berne Convention makes ample room for advances in technology. Flexible language such as "..., now known or later developed, ..." is found in multiple parts of the 1976 Copyright Act. Copyright law as it now stands is seemingly ready for the next barrage of gadgets and electronic toys Sony, Nintendo, and Disney come up with in the 21st century.

The Statute of Frauds requirement seems particularly out of place in the context of cyber-commerce. There is some talk about abolishing the requirement altogether. Even England, the birthplace of the Statute of Frauds, has dropped the requirement completely.

The Best Evidence Rule is at its maximum utility when applied to force a party to produce the murder weapon and not some replica of it. As applied to computer documents, the rule seems inappropriate. Of more value would be rules to require stating the original disposition of the electronic document; type of file whether test, graphic, etc., and location of document, where stored on a hard drive, removable disk, or the full Internet address if stored in cyberspace.

The scope of U.C.C. 2-201 (25) and U.C.C. 2-201 (26) should be limited to account for the fact that no one should be expected to religiously read his or her computer mail on a daily basis. A proper remedy instead would be to consider that computer mail sent to a person is considered unread unless the person acknowledges receipt by means of some response.

The spread at which electronic messages are transmitted and the possibility that all E-mail may not be read by the recipient also means that other rules (e.g., the Mailbox rule and the rules pertaining to revocation or withdrawal of offer) need to be reexamined.

Existing commercial law must be reexamined in the light of the growing numbers jumping on the information bandwagon. Otherwise, commercial law as it now stands will be a speedbump in the information superhighway.

The following sources were used in writing this section, and may be referenced for additional information:

1. Daniel King, "How to Conduct Transactions on the Usenet Marketplace," *biz.marketplace,* April 7, 1995.

2. "I Was a Hacker for the FBI," *Information Week,* March 13, 1995.

Purchasing From Foreign Vendors

This revised list should replace the list currently found on page 543.

The following countries had adopted the Convention on the International Sale of Goods (CISG) as of May 25, 1994:

Argentina	Hungary
Australia	Iraq
Austria	Italy
Belanis	Lesotho
Bulgaria	Mexico
Canada	Netherlands
Chile	Norway
Czechoslovakia	Poland
Denmark	Rumania
Ecuador	Russian Federation
Egypt	Singapore
Finland	Spain
France	Sweden
Germany	Switzerland
Ghana	Syrian Arab Republic
Guinea	Uganda

Ukraine

United States of America

Venezuela

Yogoslavia

Zambia

SELLER AND PURCHASER ADVANTAGES IN THE CISG AND SAMPLE CONTRACT CLAUSES*

The United Nations Convention on Contracts for the International Sale of Goods (CISG) covers many subjects similar to the Uniform Commercial Code (UCC). However, these two laws are not identical in nature or terms. The CISG is a treaty passed by the Senate in 1979, and took effect on January 1, 1980. Since the CISG passed as a treaty, its effect is felt across all fifty states, including Louisiana. Many other countries have passed the CISG and have become contracting states (a contracting state is one that has approved the application of the CISG and has adopted it into its laws). Therefore, the CISG is a fairly new law that has yet to be interpreted to clarify its meanings, while the UCC has been in effect for many years, and has been subject to many years of revision, fine tuning, and interpretation.

The CISG's effect can be felt when a business in a contracting state negotiates with another business in a contracting state. The application of the CISG is automatic, unless the parties otherwise agree. On the other hand, the UCC does not become effective unless the parties agree to its application, and they have stated so in their contracts. This section will discuss a number of aspects regarding the CISG that a seller and purchaser must be aware of, as well as the advantages or disadvantages for each when comparing it with the UCC. Also, the UCC is used as a gap filler for many CISG contracts between U.S. parties and other foreign countries. Its purpose is to identify those circumstances not covered in their contract by the CISG and apply the UCC to those circumstances. There will be various sample clauses that can be inserted into the parties' standard contracting terms. Critical contract terms will be discussed; however, only those that are historically the most dickered over between the parties will be included.

The issues under discussion will take the point of view of both purchaser and seller. Each point of view will be between a domestic and a

---

*Bryan N. Sandler, Juris Doctor, Attorney-at-Law, St.Louis, Missouri.

foreign party negotiating a contract. Sometimes, the parties will both be from contracting states, while at other times they will not. Again, the exemplary clauses will be from the point of view being presently expressed, unless otherwise noted.

The topics that will be discussed are: 1) when there is a valid offer, 2) when there has been acceptance or rejection of the offer, 3) what terms control the contract, i.e. the Battle of the Forms, 4) the ability to disclaim warranties, 5) the ability to exclude the recovery of consequential and/or incidental damages, 6) limitation of liability clauses, 7) the ability to "opt in" the CISG when one or both of the contracting parties are not Contracting States, 8) the applicability of the UCC as the gap-filling law when no other law has been chosen, and 9) the ability to use the CISG over the UCC or other domestic laws of either party.

The effects of the CISG upon U.S. purchases or sellers have yet to be felt. One reason is the slow utilization of the CISG, thus the lack of caselaw interpreting its Articles. One of the main goals of the CISG is to have a uniform international law applied throughout the world. However, this is difficult, because there is no national reporting service publishing the opinions for national interpretation.

U.S. parties are leery to use the CISG, because of the widespread acceptance and applicability of the UCC within the U.S. The UCC is known, familiar, and predictable for U.S. parties. However, foreign countries, especially third-world countries, or those with less bargaining power than the U.S., feel that it is time for a change. Therefore, they openly adopt the application of the CISG. This eager adoption by less powerful countries of the CISG is due to the national representation present when the CISG was in its initial stage of formation, and at its conclusion.

Applicability of the CISG When Both Businesses Are From Contracting States

When both parties are members of a contracting state to the CISG, the CISG will automatically apply to their contracts, unless otherwise agreed to, under Article 1. Thus, there is no need for two contracting parties to have a clause in their contract, applying the CISG, if they choose to have the Convention applied.

When two contracting parties wish to have the CISG excluded, they must specifically state that the CISG is not applicable, in clear language. The following is an example of a clause that the parties may wish to use:

> The parties to this contract agree specifically that the laws of the State of (Missouri), except for the Convention for the International Sale of Goods, shall be applicable to the formation, application and interpretation of this contract.

This clause makes the laws of the State (e.g. Missouri or whatever named state) applicable to the formation, application, and interpretation of the contract. However, the parties may choose any law, other than that state, to be applied, as long as it has some relation to the parties or place of contracting.

There is no advantage to either party wishing to have the CISG apply or not. However, there is a perceived benefit that each party may wish to have a certain law apply rather than the CISG. For example, a U.S. party may wish to have the UCC apply because of its familiarity and long tradition of precedents. On the other hand, the foreign party may wish not to have their disputes settled under "American Law," or the perceived "American Law" advantage. Many foreign parties may wish to have their law, or some neutral third country's law, applied to the dispute.

Caveat Bene: An American party must be aware, when they are negotiating with another party who is a member of a contracting state, that any oral agreement between them, with few exceptions, will create a binding contract with the other party. The CISG does away with the statute of frauds, unless specifically called for by the parties in the contract.

The growing familiarity and perceived neutrality of the CISG may make it a law that all countries will want to apply when dealing with foreign parties. However, today there seems to be some hesitance regarding its widespread application; this is due to its lack of interpretation through caselaw of the various Articles within.

Another selection that the parties may choose is to apply the CISG to some of the contractual terms, and supplement it with another law to fill the gaps. This may make the parties more willing to have the CISG apply to some clauses of the contract, while the other clauses are governed by a different agreed upon law. Article 94(1) allows the parties to derogate from the Convention by joint or reciprocal unilateral declarations renouncing the Convention. The end result is a hybrid of negotiations between the parties using both the CISG and another law to either supplement or fill in the gaps the CISG creates. The following is a sample clause that could be utilized by the parties:

The parties to this contract agree specifically that the laws of the UCC shall govern all aspects of this contract that are not specifically governed by the United Nations Convention on Contracts for the International Sale of Goods, as well as the interpretation and application of the clauses within.

A Business in a Contracting State and a Business in a Non-Contracting State

The CISG is applicable to contracts between a business in a contracting state and a business in a non-contracting state. This is due to Article 1 (1)(b). This Article makes the CISG applicable to contracts where one of the parties is a contracting state, merely by the application of private international law leading to the application of the law of the contracting state—the CISG. Article 1(1)(b) allows the CISG to sometimes be applied under conflicts of law rules where one of the laws will lead to the application of the CISG, no matter whether both businesses are in contracting states.

There is another exception to the applicability of the CISG, where the business in the contracting state, like the U.S., has adopted the CISG with the exclusion of Article (1)(b).

Any business in a contracting state, by excluding Article 1 (1)(b), has effectively limited the scope of the CISG to those situations where they are contracting with another signatory to the Convention, or where the two parties have chosen to apply the CISG to their contract; as previously stated, the parties may do so by using the sample clause. The CISG allows the parties freedom of contract with very few restrictions, thus allowing its applicability to even two businesses in non-contracting states.

Contracts Between Two Businesses in Non-Contracting States

The Convention allows for freedom of contract by the parties. Article 6 of the CISG states:

> The parties may exclude the application of this Convention or, subject to Article 12, derogate from or vary the effect of any of its provisions.

A party may opt into the applicability of the CISG by simply inserting a clause in their contracts. The only restrictions to the applicability of the

CISG to these contracts is the prohibition or non-acceptance of the choice of law provision in the contracts by the domestic law. Restatement (Second) Conflicts of Law §187, states that the law chosen must be "reasonable" or have a substantial relationship to the transaction. Therefore, the law chosen by the parties must not be totally unrelated to the transaction, nor may it be too obscure for the court.

Article 12, which states that those countries that require a contract to be concluded by a writing may not derogate or vary the effect of this Article (Article 12). Article 12 states that where one party's Contracting State has adopted the CISG with the provision of Article 11 and Article 96, they may not derogate from the CISG except by a formal writing (i.e., no termination or modification by agreement or any offer, acceptance, or other indication of intention to be made in any form but in writing). But the U.S. has not adopted these exceptions and oral contracts are binding.

Still, the private international law of the U.S.—conflict of law—may lead to the application of a law not provided for in the contract.

A second example includes a foreign country determining, correctly or not, that the choice of law provision is a result of unequal bargaining positions, rather than mutual agreement between the parties. Thus, it will choose to ignore the choice of law provision, choosing the UCC, and apply its own domestic law to the controversy—*lex fori*. Some courts will go so far as to state that they will apply the local law to govern all transactions regardless of the choice of law provision in the contract.

The following is an example of a clause that would effectively choose the CISG as the applicable law to the contract:

> This contract shall be governed by the United Nations Convention on Contracts for the International Sale of Goods supplemented by the law of the state of—(any state the parties desire) _____ U.S.A.

The other item that may be substituted is that the CISG may be supplemented by the law of the foreign country; however, as an American seller or purchaser you want the UCC applicable.

OFFER

Before we move on to the next material, it will be beneficial to define a few terms and concepts that will be discussed. In the following material, the terms purchaser and seller will not be used, in its place will be offeror and offeree. This is due to the fact that a purchaser and seller may be either offeror or offeree, depending on the situation. It can be very important, both legally and practically, who is the offeror and who is the offeree (i.e., dealing with the problem of the battle of the forms, or deciding when and if there is a valid contract).

> EXAMPLE 1: A purchaser may send out to many sellers a letter desiring their response to his or her needs for a particular part. In response, the Seller will return a quote that will be considered the offer. Here the purchaser is the offeree, because he or she has received an offer, and the Seller is an offeror, because he or she has sent the offer. The purchaser, by sending out these letters, is not the offeror because his or her initial contact with the sellers will be considered an invitation to make an offer and not an offer in itself.

> EXAMPLE 2: Same facts as EXAMPLE 1, however, the purchaser sends out the letters with a set price it will pay for the parts that it needs. The seller then responds with a letter back to purchaser approving the transaction. The purchaser will be deemed the offeror because he has set a definite price along with the other requirements of Article 14, and the seller will be the offeree, in that he is responding to the offer.

> EXAMPLE 3: A purchaser may be responding to a catalog for the parts that it needs. He or she then sends in an order with his company's contract terms on the back. The seller will then send the parts to him or her at the specified price. Here the seller is the offeree because his or her catalog will be considered an invitation to others to make offers thus, when he or she receives the offer from the purchaser he or she will be the offeree. The purchaser will be the offeror, since he or she has sent the offer to the seller.

What Constitutes an Offer?

The CISG defines an offer as:

> A proposal for concluding a contract addressed to one or more specific persons constitutes an offer if it is sufficiently definite and indicates the intention of the offeror to be bound in case of acceptance. A proposal is sufficiently definite if it indicates the goods and expressly or implicitly fixes or makes provision for determining the quantity and the price.

This definition is very similar to the UCC definition of an offer, with one exception; the CISG makes the price an essential term in an offer. However, they are different also. The CISG allows for the acceptance of proposals or catalog orders; if a price is stated in them, these proposals will constitute offers. The common law that supplements the UCC, on the other hand, will treat such widespread advertisements as invitations to make an offer and not offers themselves. But the UCC will also find a valid offer without a price stated in the offer, while the CISG requires price to be included in all valid offers. The UCC provides a way to determine price when there is a binding contract.

Caveat Bene: Without any special contractual clauses, the purchaser who finds it of paramount importance to have a binding contract and valid offer right away will prefer to UCC. This is due to the absence of the requirement for price within the offer. However, if the exact price as contrasted to a reasonable price is more important, the CISG will be advantageous because the offeree can then send the first form, in response to the invitation to make an offer, stating a price and thus become the offeror.

Under the CISG, it is wise for a domestic offeror to include a price in their offer to the foreign offeree. It is also important for a domestic offeree to have the offeror include a price, thus reducing the possibility that the offeror may not perform on the agreement, because there is no valid offer: without a valid offer there can be no acceptance.

The CISG also follows the UCC, which emphasizes agreement by any means and supplemental Restatement law. But in determining when an offer becomes effective under the CISG: this occurs when it reaches the offeree. Therefore, if the purchaser or seller are governed by the CISG and wish to modify this to make the offer effective upon dispatch, they must do so by a specific clause. The following is a sample clause:

> This offer becomes effective at the time of dispatch by the offeror. The offeror has the right to revoke this offer by sending a revocation before the offeree dispatches an acceptance.

When Can an Offer be Revoked?

Article 15(2) reaches the conclusion that an "irrevocable" offer can be withdrawn by the offeror as long as it reaches the offeree before the offer.

For example, a major difference between the CISG and the UCC is the assumption that once there is acceptance there is a valid contract. The UCC assumes that there is a valid contract upon a valid acceptance; the CISG does not. The CISG only determines that there has been a valid acceptance, but says nothing about a valid contract; hence withdrawal of the offer is possible for this set of terms. The only aspect of an acceptance, under the CISG, is that it makes an offer irrevocable. Article 18(2) tells us when an acceptance becomes effective, thus creating a binding contract.

For example, if the offeree has dispatched his or her acceptance and the offeror has not received the acceptance, the offeror may send a notification, to the offeree, that the offer is revoked, thus canceling the acceptance. The acceptance is only valid once the "indication of assent has reached the offeror," and not at the time it is dispatched by the offeree.

There is a period of time where there is no valid contract between the two parties, but the offer is irrevocable, therefore, giving an unscrupulous offeree a chance to back out of the deal. Article 22 allows the offeree to withdraw its acceptance before it becomes effective. This is in theory correct; however, in today's increasing technological advances, such as the facsimile and the telephone, most parties will not have this time period where there is no valid contract.

For example, when the offeree has sent its acceptance in response to an "irrevocable" offer, the offeree decides that he or she can get a better deal from someone else. Before the "indication of assent" reaches the offeror the offeree may send a rejection via fax or in person, thus rejecting the offer and nullifying acceptance.

Another difference between the CISG and the UCC, is the mail box rule. It is used in the common law, as reflected by the Restatement and courts, to determine when there is a valid acceptance, thus making the offer irrevocable. The mail box rule states that the acceptance is valid the moment it is dispatched by mail, or other method specified by the contract. Although the CISG uses a notice provision for a valid acceptance, the acceptance is deemed valid when the offeror receives an indication of assent by the offeree. Therefore, there is a period of time during which the acceptance is not valid under the CISG, from the point of dispatch to the point of receipt of assent to the offer. This allows the offeree to send an acceptance and then a day later, before the offeror receives the acceptance, call and notify the offeree that there is no acceptance.

Caveat Nota: If the purchaser is the one who is sending the acceptance and he or she wants the option to change, the CISG is more advantageous. On the other hand, if it is likely that the foreign seller will change or withdraw the offer in the next several days, the UCC may be more advantageous for the purchaser.

For example, the mail box rule is beneficial for the offeree, under the UCC, in circumstances where he or she knows that a good deal has been made and the person does not want the offeror to be able to back out of the deal. By validating the acceptance upon dispatch, the offeree is locking in the offeror to the deal that was offered.

However, under the CISG, the mail box rule is not effective because the acceptance is not effective until indication of assent to the offer reaches the offeror. Therefore, the offeree, wishing to effectuate the mail box rule under the CISG must indicate in a clause that the acceptance will be effective upon dispatch; this is assuming the offeree wants to lock himself or herself into the present offer. The following is an example of a clause that might be used by the offeree when dealing with an offeror:

> The following acceptance will be deemed valid and enforceable upon offeror when dispatched by mail by the offeree. No other method of acceptance will be enforceable against offeree.

To avoid the problem of when an acceptance is valid, the offeror may state within the offer how a valid offer may be accomplished. These special contractual clauses can change the outcome under either the UCC or CISG.

What is a Firm Offer?

A firm offer is defined in Article 16(2) of the CISG. This Article makes any offer irrevocable if it merely states a period for which acceptance will be valid. This is a simplified approach in contrast to that used by the UCC. The UCC requires certain criteria to be present before a firm offer will be held to be present.

The only similarities between the UCC and CISG is that the offer must give assurances it will be held open. As stated above, this may be done under the CISG by merely stating that the acceptance must be within a certain period of time. The offeror merely must state a period of time in which the offer may be accepted. The offer is irrevocable and firm for that period of time. On the other hand, if the offeror is merely attempting to state a time in which an acceptance must be received and not create a firm offer, the UCC is advantageous.

Caveat Nota: If the offeror wishes to have a firm offer, the CISG is more advantageous than the UCC.

The differences between the UCC and CISG may be overcome by special contractual clauses. For example, purchasers should be wary of what types of forms and statements they use when they are requesting a quote from a seller. The following is a sample clause that could be used by the purchaser:

> The supplier is required to submit this proposal to the buyer as a firm offer to sell. Supplier will complete the following statement:
>
> Supplier agrees that this is a firm offer to sell and that it will be held firm and not be revocable until _____(date)_____.
>
> Buyer has until and including that date to notify supplier of acceptance.
>
> _____
>
> (signed)

If the supplier is insisting on making the offers on letterhead, and does not purport to create a firm offer, the buyer should request in writing whether it is a firm offer. This is a means of protecting the buyer, and forces the supplier to commit to an offer as firm.

Rejection of a Firm Offer

The UCC does not address the issue of rejecting a firm offer, however, the CISG does. Article 17 states that an irrevocable offer is terminated when a rejection by the offeree reaches the offeror. Therefore, if a firm offer stated that it will remain open until January 1, and rejection reaches the offeror on December 1, the offer is rejected and cannot thereafter be accepted by the offeree. Under the UCC, there is no such discussion, however, one would be required to apply general contract law. Under the common law, there is no such thing as a firm offer, unless consideration passed from the offeree to the offeror. Under that aspect, it might possibly be argued that the offer would have remained open until January 1, unless the offeree signed a release, or the offeror returned the consideration and the offeree accepted the return.

Therefore, when a purchaser or seller decides to revoke its firm offer, it should determine what law will be applicable to the transaction, and take the necessary steps to effectuate the rejection of the firm offer.

Without knowing what law is applicable, the parties may not rely on anything they do in attempting to reject the firm offer.

Conclusion on Offers

Caveat Nota: The main reason for selecting the UCC would be that it favors the conclusion that a valid contract is formed from the time of dispatch of the acceptance, while the CISG does not. The other reason, is that the UCC will determine the price, if it is not included in the contract and it is not deemed an essential term, while the CISG will not find a contract valid unless price is specified. Nevertheless, as long as the domestic parties have carefully written their contracts with special clauses, the UCC and the CISG will yield similar results. The domestic parties must keep in mind that they can control the methods of offering, as well as the acceptance terms between themselves and foreign parties, as long as they are the offerors. If not, they should draft a clause making their offer the one that is to be accepted.

ACCEPTANCE

When is an Acceptance Effective?

Article 18 defines what is an acceptance, and ways in which it may be accomplished. The CISG assumes that there will be some positive expression of acceptance, coming from the offeree to the offeror. There is also an indication that there will be some kind of notice given to the offeror that there has been an acceptance.

Article 18(2) begins to affirm this notion of notice. It states: "An acceptance of an offer becomes effective at the moment the indication of assent reaches the offeror." Therefore, the acceptance is not valid until some notion of notice indicating assent to the offer reaches the offeror.

This Article is different from the UCC's approach to acceptance. The UCC states that an acceptance is valid from the moment it is dispatched in a manner not inconsistent with the offer. The offeror is the "master of the offer" and can define a method by which the acceptance may be valid. The CISG does not follow this approach.

Caveat Nota: The UCC is advantageous for the parties wishing to have enforceable contracts as quickly as possible if mail is used. If fax or E-mail messages are used, it makes no real difference. Because the UCC with supplemental caselaw follows the mail box rule, unless otherwise specified, it is much easier for an offeree to accept the offer and form a valid contract. But under the CISG, some notice of assent must reach the offeror before a valid acceptance will be accomplished.

Because both purchasers and sellers can be the offeror the sample clauses in this section may be used by either, as long as they are in the offeror's position.

Caveat Bene: The offeree can change the positioning of the parties, from offeree to offeror, by using special contractual clauses. However, he or she run the risk of losing the deal, if they do not follow the offeror's methods.

Acceptance by Performance

Under the UCC, an acceptance may be valid by the performance of one of the parties to the contract. The CISG, on the other hand, does not specifically state that acceptance can be accomplished in such a manner. Article 18(3) is not as clear as it could be. However, it is an attempt to include an acceptance by performance, or other acts of assent. It states: "by virtue of the offer, or as a result of past practices which the parties have established between themselves or of usage, the offeree may indicate assent by performing an act." It then goes on to give two examples of when such acts will be acceptable, an act " . . . relating to the dispatch of the goods or the payment of the price, without notice to the offeror, the acceptance is effective at the moment the act is performed. . . ." The CISG imposes a limitation of use for these acts for an acceptance: first, there must be a specific invitation for acceptance by delivery, or, second, the parties must have established a practice of accepting in this manner, or, third, by usage between the parties, or usage as well-known in the trade. Satisfaction of the first and or of the next two will constitute an acceptance.

Caveat Nota: The UCC is advantageous to the party desiring a valid contract to be formed, or a valid acceptance by performance.

The UCC specifically states that an acceptance may be accomplished by performance, unless otherwise specified. The CISG imposes many restrictions in order to accomplish what the UCC specifically allows by the mere performance by one of the parties. However, if the parties have been dealing with each other for many years or it is a custom in the trade or industry to accept by performance, then there will be no difference between the application of either law to this situation.

Under the UCC, there is no doubt that the acceptance may be through performance, or acceptance of delivered goods. The following is a sample clause that may be used to disallow acceptance by performance:

> This offer remains irrevocable until acceptance has reached the (purchaser's or seller's) hands on or before (give a specific date), unless otherwise agreed in writing, notwithstanding Article 16(1) of the CISG, or by the acceptance of goods delivered (for the seller); or by the payment of the purchase price, or a part thereof (for the buyer).

This clause may not be valid for those parties that have had a past practice of accepting by performance, or where it is a well-known custom in the trade or business. To overcome this hurdle, the offeror may wish to include the following clause:

> This offer remains irrevocable until acceptance has reached the (purchaser's or seller's) hands on or before (give a specific date), unless otherwise agreed in writing, notwithstanding Article 16(1) of the CISG, and *notwithstanding any past practices or customs in the industry or trade;* or by the acceptance of goods delivered (for the seller); or by the payment of the purchase price, or a part thereof (for the buyer).

The following is a sample clause that would allow the parties to accept the offer by specifically performing, or otherwise, even if it is not a past practice between the parties, or it is not a custom in the industry under either the UCC or CISG:

> The following offer can only be accepted by the Seller through a written acceptance to the Buyer, or by the delivery of goods described within this contract.

Conclusion to Acceptances

Caveat Bene: The offeror is the master of his or her offer, and can allow a party to accept in any manner it desires under either UCC or CISG. The offeree may also do the same when contracting out. The offeree may state in its acceptance that this is not an acceptance, but a counter-offer, and the only method of acceptance is under the following conditions. Therefore, under either the UCC or CISG, the offeror should be careful in writing their contracts, and always include methods of acceptance.

THE BATTLE OF THE FORMS

UCC v. CISG

The UCC and the CISG treat the battle of the forms differently. The UCC will find a contract between the parties if there is some general agreement that there is a contract, and then decide what the terms are between the parties. The CISG, on the other hand, will not normally find a contract, and instead will determine that a counter-offer had been attempted, and not force a contract between the parties. This counter-offer approach is the codification of the common law rule of the mirror image doctrine. The UCC favors parties attempting to avoid the last shot doctrine. It is advantageous for the offeror because he will be the party in control of the offer and any additional or different terms will be either excluded from the contract, or those terms that are not materially different will be added to the contract. The UCC will shield the offeror from the offeree's firing the last form in response to the offer, thus, becoming the offeror and having its terms control.

The mirror image doctrine states that for an acceptance to be valid, the terms must mirror those terms of that offer. Therefore, any deviation from the offer will be considered a counter-offer. The mirror image doctrine is also considered to be a last shot doctrine. The person who fires the last shot (i.e., sends the last offer), will get his or her terms in the contract, assuming performance begins thereafter. The UCC has abandoned this doctrine.

For example, if the purchaser sends his or her order form, and the supplier sends back an acknowledgment form with somewhat different material terms, under the CISG this would not create an enforceable contract. Under the UCC, there would be an enforceable contract, that consisted of those terms not in conflict. The purchaser must determine how much risk it wants to take when deciding whether to have the UCC or CISG applied in the formation of their contracts. It is also important for the purchaser to determine how important it will be to have their terms control the relationship. The difference will be the difference between a contract and a counter-offer.

1. Material v. Non-Material Different Terms. The UCC and the CISG treat these two types of terms differently. When dealing with materially different terms, the UCC and CISG are in accord, they will not become a part of the contract. However, the CISG will treat the contract with the materially different terms as a counter-offer and hence no contract results. The CISG lists those terms that are material to the contract and must be in accordance with each other on the forms from purchaser and seller for there to be a valid enforceable contract. This Article is fairly inclusive, which has led commentators to conclude that any different term in the acceptance will be material, thus constituting a counter-offer under Article 19(1).

The UCC does not purport to create a list of materially different terms but leaves the decision to the courts to determine the issue. Some examples given by commentators in the UCC are: 1) " . . . a clause negating such standard warranties as that of merchantability or fitness for a particular purpose in circumstances in which either warranty normally attaches, 2) a clause requiring a guaranty of 90% or 100% deliveries in a case such as contract by cannery, where the usage of the trade allows greater quantity leeway; or 3) a clause reserving to the seller the power to cancel upon the buyer's failure to meet any invoice when due." This list does not mean to be exhaustive, but merely be an example of such materially altering terms.

Under the UCC, there will generally be a contract even though there are some differences in the forms. The materially differing clauses in the acceptance do not prevent a contract. The non-materially different terms, in the offers and acknowledgments between merchants, will become a part of the contract. The CISG does not differentiate merchants from non-merchant, when dealing with non-materially altering terms. The CISG will regard non-materially altering terms as a valid acceptance as long as the offeror does not object to the additional or different non-material terms.

Purchaser's and Seller's Clauses to Avoid the Battle of the Forms

It is important for either one of the parties to have their standard terms a part of the contract. Each party will draft terms that will best afford them protection from anything that may go wrong. However, both parties may not have their terms be a part of the contract—it is not possible. Therefore, the parties must negotiate to determine the applicable terms in their contract. This is not a perfect world, and many times the parties are unable to meet face to face and negotiate all the terms. This is where the difficulty arises.

The two parties start sending forms back and forth, and on the back of the forms are the standard terms of contracting that they say must be adhered to, or no contract will be made. In reality, the parties very seldom read these terms, and the offeree then sends an acknowledgment of either receipt of terms, or a previous acknowledgment, on his form which contains different terms on the reverse side. The parties feel that there is a contract, and one party begins performance. When something goes wrong, the result is litigation. What are the binding terms in the contract?

The binding terms under the CISG will be the terms on the back of the offeree's form. If the purchaser sends in an order, he or she is the offeror; the acknowledgment is sent by the seller who is the offeree. Because the seller/offeree was the last party to send a form before performance, that form controls. Also, the original offeror's offer had been rejected, because of the materially different terms on the offeree's return form, thus constituting a counter-offer; assuming some materially different term. The parties began performance, and thus, the offeree's terms are controlling. This is an application of the "last shot" principle. In this example, the CISG appears to work best for the seller/offeree and against the purchaser/offeror.

Most parties want to know how to effectively avoid this situation. It can be found on both the seller's and purchaser's side of the bargaining table. The CISG seems to favor those who are the offerors. A purchaser who is making an order from a listing or catalog of products offered by a seller is an offeror. This assumes that the catalog was an invitation to make an offer, as previously discussed. A sample clause for the purchaser to avoid the battle of the forms problem would be the following:

> The supplier may only accept this offer to buy in writing or by delivering the goods ordered. By doing so the supplier accepts all of the terms and conditions set forth on the face and reverse side of this purchase order. Any additional or different terms you may propose are rejected, unless they are accepted by the buyer in a separate writing.

This clause is attempting to accomplish the following: 1) it is attempting to make this offer the only "offer," 2) it is rejecting, ahead of time, any different or additional terms, unless specifically agreed to by the purchaser evidenced by a separate writing, 3) it is limiting the acceptance, and 4) it is specifically stating when an acceptance will be deemed valid. A valid acceptance may be accomplished in one, or both, of the following manners: 1) by the offeror receiving a written acceptance by the offeree, and/or 2) when there is performance on the part of the seller/offeree. A full explanation of when an acceptance is valid will be discussed later in this section.

The other side of the transaction is when the purchaser is the offeree. To avoid the problem, the purchaser may include the following clause to turn the offer to sell into an offer to buy, thus being the offeror in the transaction.

> Notwithstanding any prior negotiations, this is an offer to buy which you may accept only in writing or by delivering the goods ordered. By doing so the supplier accepts all of the terms on the face and reverse side of this purchase order. Any different or additional terms you may propose are rejected, unless they are accepted by the buyer in a separate writing.

The purchaser must remember that by inserting the above clause into its offer, it runs the risk of losing the deal that the supplier has offered. This is a factor that must be weighed when each party is dealing with each other, and determining which terms it can or cannot live with.

For each purchaser example given above, there is a reverse for the seller's position. The same factors must be considered when the seller decides to force seller's terms upon an unwilling buyer; the result, a potential for loss of business.

Conclusion on the Battle of the Forms

The CISG favors the offeror in the battle of the forms where there is a completed contract, otherwise there may be no contract and the offeree may become the offeror. The purchaser will be the offeror if he or she is responding to an invitation to make an offer, such as a catalog, or is the first person to seek out sellers for a particular product, with the price it will pay included. The purchaser may also deem himself or herself an offeror in the original offer form. A seller will be considered an offeror when it is the person sending out offers to sell at specific prices to purchasers, and also when it is deeming itself the offeror.

However, this battle can be overcome by the parties through careful draftsmanship of the contract terms. If an American purchaser is an offeree, it must be aware that this problem is present under the CISG and not become complacent when negotiating a contract. The American offeree must weigh the factors in being the offeree and decide whether they are comfortable in that position, if not, they must return a form purporting to be a counter-offer, and not an acceptance, and include within the contract a clause that purports to address the problems of the battle of the forms (i.e., stating that the terms within this form contain the only terms that will be binding upon the parties, and any additional or different terms will be disregarded under the ensuing contract).

Caveat Nota: Under the UCC, the parties are mor apt to have a contract and then have the additional or different terms either become a part of the contract or not, depending on the interpretation of §2-207. The UCC has eliminated the "last shot" doctrine that the CISG still recognizes. If the purchaser views certainty of having a binding contract as paramount, the UCC may be the most advantageous. Conflicting terms in the forms of the two parties who deem the terms controlling may cancel each other out under the UCC. Non-material terms not objected to remain and material terms are not part of the contract under the UCC.

CONSEQUENTIAL DAMAGES

Consequential damages under the UCC are those that result from the seller's breach; they include the following:

a. any loss resulting from general or particular requirements and needs of which the seller at the time of contracting had reason to know and which could not reasonably be prevented by cover or otherwise; and

b. injury to person or property proximately resulting from any breach of warranty

They can include any damages, to the buyer, that the seller had *reason to know* in advance of the breach, at the time of contracting. Some include: 1) delayed production by the purchaser of a piece of machinery, 2) down time of the purchaser past the time of performance, and 3) loss of profits by seller for down time, or lack of full performance. This law is favorable to the purchaser. The seller may seek to exclude such damages when a seller is negotiating with a purchaser since they can be very detrimental and costly for the seller. The purchaser will want to oppose such exclusion if possible.

Excluding Consequential Damages

The CISG does not specifically mention consequential damages, but it has been stated in Article 74 that the CISG seems to cover consequential and incidental damages, when it discusses "losses." This language is very similar to the UCC, however, not identical.

The UCC has a specific section allowing the exclusion of consequential damages, while the CISG does not. Some commentators feel that this is a question of the validity of the contract, which is excluded from the CISG under Article 4, and therefore others view it as a question of interpretation under Article 8(2) and therefore it is this author's opinion that it may well be a question of both.

However, Article 74 allows the parties to derogate from the Convention, as they wish. There are exceptions, however, they are not applicable here. Thus, the following clauses are examples of excluding consequential damages for the seller:

> The Seller is not liable for any consequential damages as a result of any breach by him. Seller shall have the right to cure any defect in the contract and the Purchaser shall give the Seller a reasonable amount of time to effect such a cure. Should the Seller not be able to cure the defect, the Purchaser's exclusive remedy is limited to the refund of the purchase price less any reasonable expenses by the seller on Purchaser's behalf.

or;

> The remedies of the Buyer set forth herein are exclusive, and the total liability of the Seller with respect to this Contract or the Equipment and services furnished hereunder, in connection with the performance or breach thereof, or from the manufacture, sale, delivery, installation, repair, or technical direction covered by or furnished under this Contract, whether based on contract, warranty, negligence, indemnity, strict liability or otherwise, shall not exceed the purchase price of the unit of Equipment upon which such liability is based.

Therefore, if the seller uses such clauses it does not matter whether the UCC or CISG is used when dealing with consequential damages, as long as a tribunal is willing to concede that it is not a question of validity, under the CISG.

Incidental Damages and their Exclusion

Incidental damages are meant to cover all reasonable expenses in connection with the handling of rightfully rejected goods. The UCC and CISG are not different in their interpretation and application of incidental damages. Both include the recovery of damages, unless otherwise specifically excluded, incidental to the breach. Under the UCC they include:

> expenses reasonably incurred in inspection, receipt, transportation, and care and custody of goods rightfully rejected, any commercially reasonable charges, expenses or other commissions in connection with effecting cover and any other reasonable expenses incident to the delay or other breach.

This list is not intended to be exhaustive, but is merely illustrative of the types of damages recoverable. They are present to make the purchaser whole again. These damages are not as important to exclude, for the buyer, as they are for the seller. However, they are substantial enough that the seller should attempt to have them excluded also. The following is an example of a clause that may be used to exclude incidental damages for the seller:

> The Seller is not liable for any incidental damages as a result of any breach by him or her. The Purchaser's exclusive remedy is the return of the purchase price less any reasonable expenses incurred by the Seller on Purchaser's behalf.

This clause also attempts to limit the purchaser's remedies in case of a breach.

Purchasers may agree to exclude incidental damages as well in the contract; however, they are more likely to wish to include incidental damages for recovery for seller's breach. The main reason for allowing the exclusion of incidental damages, for purchaser, is to further the contract along; the seller may have a price that is worth taking the risks, along with excluding incidental damages for seller's breach. However, a majority of the purchasers will attempt to have some sort of clause dealing with incidental damages. The following is an example:

> Seller shall be liable for those damages that are a result of the seller's failure to perform under this contract. The Seller shall not attempt to

exclude incidental damages, all exclusions are void under this contract unless specifically agreed to in writing by purchaser.

Conclusion as to Consequential Damages

Caveat Nota: Consequential and incidental damages are desired by the buyer. They are a form of damages that have a wide range of applicability when the seller does not perform under the contract. They are allowed specifically under the UCC and this would seem to be advantageous.

Because these damages can be very detrimental, the seller wishes to have these eliminated from the contract. This will avoid any unnecessary expenses in performing or from being held liable for damages beyond their control. These can be successfully excluded from the contracts by sellers, if they take the precautions outlined above. The purchaser may decide to allow the exclusion as long as it has some other remedy against the seller. Sellers normally include language to the effect of allowing the return of the purchase price, or repair or replacement of any defective parts. If this is an acceptable form of compensation for the purchasers, then there is little problem. But sometimes it is not. If the purchaser has the upper hand in bargaining, it should oppose exclusionary clauses such as these and let the general law of the UCC apply. Even if it is decided that the CISG is to control, the purchaser will want to exclude such clauses if possible.

PURCHASER'S REMEDIES UNDER THE CISG AND THE UCC AND THEIR LIMITATION

The CISG is more advantageous for the breached party. It allows the breached party to accomplish just about anything it wishes, from canceling the contract completely to obtaining specific performance of the contract. Although the UCC only allows the breached party to cover its losses from either receiving the items from another vendor or receiving the difference between the contract price and the market price. Under the UCC the breached party is held to only monetary damages.

The purchaser's remedies in a contract all depend upon what types of exclusions are in the contract. However, absent any exclusionary provision in the contract, under the UCC the general remedies for the seller are: 1) withhold delivery of the goods, 2) stop any delivery by any bailee as provided under §2-705, 3) proceed under §2-704, 4) resell and recover damages as provided for under §§2-706 & 2-709, and 5) cancel the contract. These remedies are not inclusive, there are other remedies as specified in §2-703. The purchaser's remedies under the UCC are: 1) "cover" and have damages under §2-712 as to all the goods affected whether or not they have been identified in the contract, 2) recover damages for non-delivery under §2-713, 3) where the seller fails to deliver or repudiates the contract buyer may also, (i) in a proper case obtain specific performance or replevy the goods as provided in §2-716, or (ii) if the goods have been identified recover them as provided under §2-502.

The purchaser, however, has a myriad of remedies available under the CISG. Some include: 1) rejection of the non-conforming goods or revoking acceptance, this is known as having the "contract avoided," 2) specific performance by the seller (not available under the UCC), 3) notifying the seller that he or she has an additional reasonable amount of time to perform under the contract, and 4) reduction in price by the value of the goods delivered as to the conforming goods.

The CISG favors the party that has not breached the contract by creating a greater number of remedies available to the non-breaching party than under the UCC. For example, specific performance is generally not available under the UCC, because specific performance has been held to apply to only items that are specific and cannot be replaced—unusual items. The CISG does not differentiate between unusual items and items that can be obtained from other sources.

Many of the mentioned purchaser's remedies may be limited by the party's contract. In many contracts the purchaser's remedies are exclusive, and stated in the warranties section of the contract, or are stated in the limitation of liability clause in the contract.

Limiting Purchaser's Remedies through a Limitation of Liability Clause

The limitation of liability clause, for a seller, is extremely important. It is as important to him or her as excluding consequential and incidental damages from the contract. By contrast, the purchaser's best interest is served by not having such a clause; it is imperative that they retain the full range of remedies allowed by law. Whether such a clause will be part of the contract may depend on the bargaining leverage and skill of the purchaser.

If such a clause is included in the contract, in determining whether a limited liability clause is valid is a question of validity that commentators feel is not governed by the convention pursuant to Article 4, thus, bringing into the equation domestic prohibitions against limiting liability. Examples include domestic prohibitions limiting liability for gross negligence, or the consequences of intentional acts.

The UCC makes the limitation a little more complicated when determining whether the limitation is valid. The factors to consider when determining the validity are: 1) the business sophistication each party brings into the negotiations, 2) the relative bargaining power of the parties, 3) whether the limited remedy has failed in its essential purpose, and 4) whether the limitations of damages clauses are unconscionable. Also, caselaw applies as to disclaiming for own negligence or intentional acts. The UCC is more favorable to both parties because it allows the modification of contracts to fit the parties' needs. Therefore, should the parties so desire to include a limitation of liability clause in the contract they may do so. Either party may insist on such an inclusion or not, again depending upon the factors discussed above. The CISG, on the other hand, could be interpreted just as favorable as the UCC; however, it is this author's opinion that such clauses are a part of the validity of the contract not governed by the CISG.

Therefore, when a seller is attempting to limit the purchaser's remedies, through a contractual clause as the one mentioned above, they should keep in mind that if the UCC is applicable, they must follow those standards when drafting such clauses. There are other remedies available to the purchaser when the Seller breaches the contract; they will be discussed later in this article under remedies.

This clause is an example setting forth the exclusion of certain damages, and including other remedies as an exclusive remedy for the seller's breach:

A. If circumstances occur which may give rise to claims for damages (or the right to any other form of relief) based on contract, warranty, indemnity (including patent indemnity), negligence or otherwise, the claiming party shall take all necessary measures to mitigate the damages or loss, provided that this can be done without unreasonable cost or inconvenience. Notwithstanding any other provision of this Contract: (1) such claims or relief shall be limited to direct damages which at the Effective Date of the Contract could be reasonably foreseen as a natural consequence of such circumstance; (2) the total liability of the Seller, including its subcontractors or suppliers, on any and all claims shall not exceed the purchase price allocable to the

Product or service which gives rise to the claim; (3) except as to title and patent indemnity, any such liability shall terminate upon the expiration of the warranty period specified in Article 9; (4) in no event shall the Seller or its subcontractors or suppliers be liable for any special, consequential, incidental, indirect or exemplary damages, including but not limited to, loss of profit or revenues, loss of use or increased expense of operation of the Products or any associated equipment, impairment of other goods, cost of capital or modifications to or substitutions for Products or goods, facilities or services, downtime costs or their increased expense of operation, or claims of Buyer's customers due to added costs or losses, service interruption or failure of supply. Subject to the foregoing, Buyer's exclusive remedies and Seller's sole obligations with respect to delays, defects or nonconformities in or damage to or resulting from the Products or services shall be those respectively provided in Article 4 (Liquidated Damages), Article 9 (Warranties) and Article 10 (Patent Indemnity).

B. The provisions of this Article shall apply to the full extent permitted by law and regardless of fault and shall survive either termination or cancellation of this Contract.

This clause asserts that there will be no other remedy except for those provided for under this clause, or negotiated between the parties.

Conclusion as to Damages and Limitations

This is one of the most important clauses to have in the contract, next to the exclusion of incidental and consequential damages, for the seller. By specifically stating the exclusive remedies for the buyer, the seller is limiting its exposure to unlimited damages, and a possibility that the courts will not find the exclusion of the incidental and consequential damages clause valid. If there is no other appropriate remedy (i.e., the remedy fails its essential purpose), the exclusion clause will not be held valid under the UCC. However, under the CISG, it may be deemed as a validity problem excluded by the CISG under Article 4. Therefore, it is imperative that the seller includes a clause that states what the exclusive and sole remedy of the buyer will be. The limitation of liability clause will serve such a purpose.

The buyer, on the other hand, should attempt to have all remedies available at law at its disposal. To properly protect itself from unscrupulous sellers, the buyer should attempt to negate any exclusion or damages or limitation of remedies clauses in its contracts. However, should the buyer be in a weaker bargaining position it should carefully look at the remedies available to it and decide whether they will properly protect it from any losses; this should be done on a contract-by-contract basis.

WARRANTIES

Warranties are important for purchasers so that they may protect themselves from the problems the goods present to the buyer. The seller wishes to have them excluded, because it does not want unlimited liability for defective goods, or even goods that are not defective but have been mishandled or misused by the buyer. Therefore, the seller attempts to exclude them from the contract. Some buyers will not object to these clauses either, as long as they have some recourse against the seller for defective goods that are the seller's fault. The buyer may accept this limited liability and write the warranties to cover only those problems that are a direct result of the seller's defective goods.

The clauses stated shortly are a good example of the seller excluding most warranties but covering those damages or goods that are a direct result of their breach of performance. Again, under the CISG, this may be deemed a problem of validity of a clause, thus the UCC form of excluding the warranties should be followed.

The buyer, on the other hand, may object to such an exclusion of warranties and limitation of damages. He or she may see the disclaimer as a warning that the seller is not as reliable as once thought. The buyer may then be wary to conduct business with such a seller and take its business elsewhere. Disclaimers must be used cautiously by buyers because of the effect they have upon the reader of such terms. The seller must also be aware that such buyers do attempt to disclaim all remedies and warranties.

Whether the CISG Allows the Exclusion of Warranties

The CISG does not specifically allow the exclusion of warranties as does the UCC under §2-316, nor does it state the word warranty. The CISG uses the term "obligations of the seller." However, the CISG does have a clause which purports to give the purchaser the same rights, as under the warranties in the UCC, which has a preamble stating: "Except where the parties have otherwise agreed. . . ." This is the language that comes closest to the UCC regarding the disclaimer of warranties, in the CISG.

Caveat Nota: Neither the UCC nor the CISG is more favorable than the other, in regard to warranties, with the exception that the UCC has more caselaw interpreting its provisions.

Some commentators state that disclaiming warranties are questions of validity not covered by the CISG pursuant to Article 4. Another interpretation is that it is a question of interpretation under Article 8(2). Still another interpretation stated that the resolution of this conflict should be governed by the international character and the goals of the CISG, that of transnational uniformity of the law. The reason for the international standard on the validity of contracts and exculpatory clauses, is to enhance the predictability of the outcomes for planning purposes. The international trader could make contracts and agreements, knowing that a certain term will not be subject to some foreign country's determination on whether the clause is valid, and subject to their public policy.

Caveat Nota: The modern trend is to allow the parties to disclaim warranties, and determine their validity according to the international standards and usages. The goal of the CISG is to promote uniformity in the international arena, and to promote predictability of outcomes for the international trader.

Excluding the Warranties in International Contracts

Caveat Bene: With this in mind, the American purchaser should be aware that it makes no difference whether they are under the UCC or CISG, any disclaimer of warranties could potentially be detrimental in the long run.

For American sellers however, it will be beneficial to include the disclaimers in their contracts. When disclaiming the warranties, with foreign purchasers, they should still abide by the UCC rules regarding effective disclaimers in each warranty. The following is a sample clause that could be placed in a Sellers standard terms for contract:

> The Seller's obligations under Paragraph B [where there is a paragraph B stated before this paragraph stating the warranties/obligations of the seller] above shall not apply to any Product, or part thereof, which (1) is normally consumed in operation, or (2) has a normal life inherently shorter than the warranty period specified in Paragraph A, or (3) is not properly stored, installed, used, maintained or repaired, or is modified other than pursuant to Seller's instruc-

tions or approval, or (4) has been subject to any other kind of misuse or detrimental exposure, or has been involved in an accident. With respect to any Products not manufactured by seller (except for integral arts of Seller's Products, which the warranties set forth above shall apply), Seller gives no warranty, and only the warranty, if any, given by the manufacturer shall apply. Subject to Article 11, this article sets forth the exclusive remedies for claims based upon defects in or noncomformity of the Products, whether the claim is in contract, warranty, tort (including negligence) or otherwise. Except as set forth in article 10, the foregoing warranties are in lieu of all other warranties, whether oral, written, express, implied or statutory. NO IMPLIED OR STATUTORY WARRANTIES OF MERCHANTABILITY OR FITNESS FOR A PARTICULAR PURPOSE SHALL APPLY.

As one can see, the basic UCC provisions, for excluding warranties, are followed as a precaution from discovering the disclaimer's invalid, should the UCC apply as the gap filling law. Thus, any seller should still follow the guidelines set by the UCC disclaiming their warranties, since the CISG is silent on the matters of how to properly disclaim them. This clause goes beyond that of disclaiming warranties, by also limiting the purchaser's remedies when there is a breach. Such a clause should be specifically explained and negotiated with the buyer if the seller is to preclude it from later attack.

Should the seller be unable to exclude all warranties, it will want to ensure that it has sculpted a well-written clause regarding the warranties. It should also be noted, as stated above, that the CISG does not specifically refer to "warranty" in its language. However, it does give the same remedies under a clause of obligation of the seller. Thus, it would be beneficial for the seller to include, in its definition section, a definition of "warranty." The following clauses may be used where there is no exclusion of warranties:

A. Seller warrants that Products manufactured by Seller shall be free from defects in material, workmanship and title and shall be the kind and quality specified or designated by Seller in this Contract. Seller's obligations, set forth below, shall apply only to failures to meet the foregoing warranties (except as to title) occurring within fifteen (15) months from date of delivery pursuant to Article 3, of which Seller is given written notice within thirty (30) days of such occurrence and provided the Product or part thereof is made available to Seller as specified by Seller.

B. If any product or part thereof fails to meet the foregoing warranties (except as to title), Seller shall repair same or, at its option, replace same in either case F.O.B. factory on the same basis described in Article 2. Any such failure shall not be the cause for extension of the duration of the warranty specified in this Article. If such failure or defect cannot be corrected by Seller's reasonable efforts, the parties shall negotiate an equitable adjustment.

C. Seller's obligations under paragraph B above shall not apply to any Product, or part thereof, which (1) is normally consumed in operation, or (2) has a normal life inherently shorter than the warranty period specified in Paragraph A, or (3) is not properly stored, installed, used, maintained or repaired, or is modified other than pursuant to Seller's instructions or approval, or (4) has been subject to any other kind of misuse or detrimental exposure, or has been involved in an accident.

D. With respect to any Products not manufactured by Seller (except for integral parts of Seller's Products, to which the warranties set forth above shall apply), Seller gives no warrant, and only the warranty, if any, given by the manufacturer shall apply.

E. Subject to Article 11, this Article sets forth the exclusive remedies for claims based upon defects in or non-conformity of the Products, whether the claim is in contract, warranty, tort (including negligence), or otherwise. Except as set forth in Article 10, the foregoing warranties are in lieu of all other warranties, whether oral, written, express, implied or statutory. NO IMPLIED OR STATUTORY WARRANTIES OF MERCHANTABILITY OR FITNESS FOR A PARTICULAR PURPOSE SHALL APPLY.

CONCLUSION

The CISG should be thought of as a good alternative for the American buyer because of the ability to change the contractual language to form to the UCC. Although it has many aspects that may be deemed as concerning contract validity not covered by its article, it has many aspects that are favorable and can be discerned. It differs from the UCC in such aspects as contract formation by mere words alone, and by allowing the last shot doctrine to continue. However, American sellers and purchasers can eliminate these problems by carefully drafting their contracts to conform to the interpretation of the UCC, even though not specifically governed by the UCC.

For the American seller, the CISG, is also a good substitute for the UCC because of the ability to change the contractual language to fit within the UCC language. However, it should be noted that not all the conclusions reached in this section will necessarily happen in a court of law when interpreting the CISG. As stated many times, there are commentators that feel that there are certain areas within the CISG that are questions of validity not covered by the CISG.

Foreign sellers and buyers may deem the use of the CISG as a good faith effort on the part of the American parties to put them on equal ground when negotiating a contract. Because the CISG is a compilation of many nation's desires as to what laws should be used, it may be deemed sufficient in the eyes of businesspersons from those countries that have historically been abused by the stronger negotiating parties. It is being adopted by many countries around the world and will be a force to be reckoned with in the future.

There are few cases interpreting the CISG and its applicability; however, this is due to its recent inception and understanding in the communities that have ratified it. Therefore, it lacks the clarity and uniformity that the UCC enjoys.

It is this writer's conclusion that the CISG should be most seriously considered by the American parties as the law designated to govern the contract, no matter at which side of the bargaining table they sit. Nevertheless, each must consider what it needs to be assured of most. Also, each must be careful of the terms that they are going to include in their contracts, and the methods they use to negotiate contracts.

The following sources were used in writing this section, and may be referenced for additional information:

1. Allen E. Farnsworth and Alfred McCormack, *Review of Standard Forms Under the Vienna Convention.*

2. Helen E. Hartnell, *United Nations Convention on Contracts for the International Sale of Goods,* The Bar Association of St. Louis (1988).

3. Kluwer, "International Contract Manual," *International Sales Law Reporter,* April 1994.

4. Albert H. Kritzer, *International Contract Manual: Contract Checklist— Limitation of Liability,* (1991).

5. The Uniform Commercial Code.

6. The United Nations Convention on Contracts for the International Sale of Goods (CISG).

Cultural-Legal Problems in Foreign Purchasing

The purchasing manager who purchases goods from abroad will readily discover that not only is it wise to understand the law of that country, but also some of its culture. These cultural aspects may affect the negotiation, forming, and carrying out of the contract. While this is true of many cultures throughout the world, a particularly good illustration is found in the Chinese laws and culture. It may be well to first consider some general matters, and then proceed to a consideration of some other pragmatic considerations.

NEGOTIATING AND CONTRACTING IN THE PEOPLE'S REPUBLIC OF CHINA*

Major reforms have been carried out to transform the Chinese economic and legal system to adapt to the international standards and practice. As a result of its "open door" policy, China has established trade relations with most Western trading nations and has become one of the key trading partners of the United States.

With its enormous population and low cost labor, China possesses the possibility of becoming America's major supplier of goods, and the supplier for many American companies. It thus becomes most important

*By Shukang Zhu, Juris Doctor.

for purchasing managers. Yet the purchasing manager may be dealing with someone who sees business transactions and legal obligations very differently.

While the Chinese emphasize "friendship" as a precursor to a business relationship, Westerners use explicit forms such as the external procedures provided by laws and courts. Westerners approach everyone as a stranger, and, hence, use the short-term and fall-back reliance on the formalism of contract and law. Western businessmen build relationships on complementary interests. They begin with nothing personal, but, rather, an assumption of mutual interests: you have something I want or need and I have something you want or need. Interaction depends not on you or me as individuals, but on my ability to meet your needs. If there is to be a relationship, it will develop over our interaction meeting each other's needs.

Since implementing the open door policy, China has placed a high priority on the codification of its law. China enacted economic, trade, and investment legislation covering contracts, trademarks, patents, joint ventures, wholly owned foreign enterprises, taxation of foreign enterprises, and also promulgated miscellaneous related regulations. The Law of the People's Republic of China on Economic Contracts Involving Foreign Interest ("Foreign Economic Contract Law," hereinafter "FECL") is one of the most significant laws in this series.

Foreign Economic Contract Law

While Chinese domestic Economic Contract Law governs contracts concluded between domestic enterprises, individuals or enterprises, and other individuals, FECL only governs contracts concluded between Chinese corporations or enterprises and foreign companies or individuals, provided Chinese law applies to such contracts. (The FECL may also govern contracts concluded between foreign companies if the parties decided to apply the FECL or the law applies because of private international law rules.) Otherwise, it should be remembered that China also has adopted the Convention on the International Sale of Goods.

The Scope of the FECL

Except for international transportation contracts, all other international economic or commercial contracts will generally be governed by the FECL. Joint ventures (including the exploration and development of natural resources), the sale of goods, insurance, processing and assembling arrangements, and compensation trade are within the FECL's scope. It also extends to other contracts including leasing, co-production, technology transfer, licensing, engineering projects, provision of credits, consignment sales, agency cooperative research, and storage.

The FECL has seven chapters containing forty-three articles. The provisions are written in broad terms and are quite flexible, leaving the parties to their creative abilities to form or fashion contracts to fit the transactions. All the basic concepts and principles of contract normally used in the West are firmly embedded in the FECL, such as contract formation, performance and remedy consideration, contract assignment, contract modification, contract termination, dispute settlement and statute of limitations. While exposition of each of these concepts contained in the FECL would require a whole book, the major provisions regarding contract formation, performance and remedy consideration, contract assignment and contract modification and termination are briefly explained below.

Contract Formation under the FECL

The first issue concerning contract formation is contract validity. The FECL provides that if the contract is entered into without the requisite authority, then the Chinese contract law would invalidate it. The FECL will also invalidate foreign economic contracts if they: violate Chinese law; are contrary to the public interest of Chinese society; or are concluded by means of fraud or duress.

Contract validity is inherently intertwined with choice of law problems. Although Article 5 of the FECL provides that the parties may select the law to be applied to the settlement of disputes arising from the contract, parties to the contract must also decide whether Chinese law and public policy will determine the contract validity. Nonetheless, contract validity under China's new economic laws and regulations is not yet clear, and the application of such rules and policies to foreign economic contracts is still in the early stages of development, and there is an insufficient body of legal precedent, case law, to fill the gap.

Performance, Breach and Remedies

Consistent with the American common law and the Uniform Commercial Code (UCC), the FECL provides for the suspension of performance in anticipation of another party's breach—the doctrine of anticipatory breach or repudiation. The party suspending performance without a proper basis must notify the other party and is liable for damages for breach of contract.

Like other legal systems all over the world, China's law recognizes the principle that parties impeded in their performance of contractual obligations by unpredictable and unpreventable events—force majeure— may be exonerated to an appropriate extent from liability for breach of contract.

> Article 24:   When a party cannot perform all or part of its contractual obligations because of an event of force majeure, it shall be fully or partially relieved from liability.
>
> When a party cannot perform in accordance with the contractually agreed time periods because of an event of force majeure, it shall be relieved of liability for delayed performance during the period of continued influence of the effects of the event.
>
> An event of force majeure means an event that the parties could not foresee at the time of conclusion of the contract and the occurrence and effects of which cannot be avoided and cannot be overcome.
>
> The scope of events of force majeure may be agreed to in the contract.
>
> Article 25:   When one party cannot perform all or part of its contractual obligations because of an event of force majeure, it shall promptly inform the other party in order to diminish the losses that might be caused to the other party, and it must within a reasonable period provide evidence issued by the relevant agency. . . .
>
> Article 29:   In any one of the following circumstances, a party shall have the right to inform the other party of the rescission of the contract:
>
> (1) The other party has breached the contract, to the extent that such breach has seriously affected the economic benefits expected when concluding the contract;
>
> (2) The other party has not performed the contract during the period agreed to in the contract, and has still not performed within a reasonable time period allowed for delayed performance;
>
> (3) An event of force majeure has occurred, with the result that none of the contractual obligations can be performed; or
>
> (4) The conditions agreed on in the contract for rescission of the contract have arisen.[1]

[1]FECL, *supra* note 95, arts. 24, 25, 29.

Thus, the FECL defines an event of force majeure in Article 24 as an event that is (1) unforeseeable as of the time when the contract was executed; and (2) the effects of which are (a) unavoidable and (b) insurmountable by the party or parties to the contract. Furthermore, the parties may stipulate the scope of force majeure events in the contract to suit their particular requirements.

However, neither the scope of events of force majeure nor the mechanism by which this principle may actually be implemented is explicitly set forth in the FECL, and neither Chinese arbitration tribunals nor Chinese courts of law have expanded on these issues in their published opinions. The FECL leaves to the contracting parties the task of spelling out detailed provisions on force majeure in their contracts.

With regard to damages, the FECL does not include a provision for specific performance as a remedy. But, reference to losses or damages in many situations is made in Chapter 3. Thus, the FECL basically intends to conform to Western common law and international practice.

Choice of Law Provisions and Dispute Settlement

Historically, China has shown reluctance to apply Western law to commercial transactions. Given the past Chinese practices, the FECL has made a major concession for the foreign party in choice of law rules.

Article 5 provides for party autonomy in selecting the law to govern the contract. The same article applies the law of the country with the most significant contacts, a practice consistent with private international conflict of laws rules. However, the FECL prohibits the parties from selecting the governing law if the transaction is a joint venture contract, or a contract for Chinese-foreign cooperative exploration and development of natural resources.

It appears that Chinese law will apply to a substantial number of foreign trade transactions, but in the absence of a relevant provision of Chinese law governing a specific contractual dispute, the FECL provides that "international practice" shall apply.

Consistent with prior and current Chinese practices, the FECL encourages informal dispute settlements as opposed to arbitration or litigation.

While China has recently made significant progress in codifying economic laws, it is still in the initial stages of developing a uniform system to protect foreign creditors' rights. As China's FECL is still relatively new, its interpretation by domestic courts and domestic and foreign arbitration tribunals presents both uncertainties and opportunities for the international transactions practitioners.

Legal Dispute Resolution

The Chinese are generally loath to resort to legal proceedings. They feel the relationship between the parties involved should prevent any insoluble confrontations from arising. Although adjudication is becoming more acceptable to the Chinese, precipitous lawsuits involving Chinese defendants may result in a potential loss of friendship or advantageous business relationships.

China's foreign economic laws offer several alternative dispute resolution options in an effort to discourage courtroom litigation. First, if possible, the parties should attempt to settle differences through "friendly consultation or mediation." Only when this proves unachievable should the parties turn to arbitration or to the courts.

A Western investor may better understand Chinese dispute resolution by envisioning a system utilizing a continuum of methods of increasing formality and coercion: friendly consultation, then friendly consultation with outside help, non-binding conciliation, arbitration, and finally, litigation.

The Chinese abhor compulsion or coercion and do not rely upon it. Instead, Chinese culture orders society by standards called "li." Good people aspire to conform to Confucian "li"; no honest person behaves so badly that "fa," or law, limits action. In addition to "li," Buddhist-Taoist doctrine requires the Chinese to choose compromise over conflict. As a result, the Chinese ideally resolve all disputes by understanding the needs of the other party, taking their own needs into consideration, and agreeing on an equitable solution. Third party arbitration and litigation are anathema to orderly society, and signal hostility and rejection.

Accordingly, solving disputes by conciliation or arbitration in civil cases, as well as in commercial and maritime cases, has long been a tradition in China. The country's history of arbitration also makes it largely preferable to litigation because of the risks of facing court-appointed officials lacking experience in solving sophisticated economic disputes.

Arbitration is not the only, nor is it necessarily the best, method of resolving disputes with Chinese business partners. Conciliation provides a cheaper, quicker, more flexible, and more friendly means to settle problems than arbitration or litigation. Moreover, the Chinese see the settlement of a dispute either in the courts or through arbitration as a failure of the relationship which reflects badly on both sides.

Most commercial contracts with the Chinese do not mention conciliation directly; instead, it is usually considered an optional step between "friendly negotiations" and "arbitration"—both of which are usually mentioned explicitly in contracts. According to an investor in China, "[i]n arbitration you have to accept the tribunal's decision, which from a businessman's point of view, may not be the best solution, while in conciliation you are free to work out your own."

The process of conciliation or mediation, closely identified with traditional Chinese culture, is considered to be a particularly good method for resolving China-related disputes. When disputes arise, Chinese firms will normally be the first to initiate consultation with their foreign counterparts so as to solve them in a friendly manner. If consultation is unsuccessful, a third party is sometimes asked to mediate. However, in most cases in which consultations fail, a third party will not be invited to mediate and the concerned parties directly seek arbitration or bring the case before the court.

Arbitration is resorted to only when negotiation, consultation, conciliation, or mediation fails or when they are inappropriate to the settlement of a dispute. Infrequently, the parties may choose to resolve their dispute exclusively by arbitration.

Most contracts signed by the Chinese and their foreign counterparts contain arbitration clauses. This illustrates the Chinese preference for arbitration over litigation. Arbitration cases do not necessarily have to be conducted in China. Arbitration may be carried out either in China or in other countries, as decided by the contracting parties through consultation. This is clearly affirmed in the FECL. Cases conducted in China are handled by the Foreign Trade Arbitration Commission (FTAC) and the Maritime Arbitration Commission (MAC). The FTAC deals with disputes in Sino-foreign economic and trade cooperation. Most of the cases are in the area of business contracts, such as product quality, late delivery, and nonperformance. Disputes arising from joint venture contracts are fewer in number, and are mainly grounded on failure to discharge the obligation of making the pledged investment, shortage of circulation funds, poor quality of equipment contributed in lieu of cash, and procurement matters. The MAC deals with Sino-foreign marine disputes. Cases in marine transport are primarily disputes concerning ship leasing contracts and bills of lading, remuneration for salvage work, and collisions. There are also cases concerning freight losses from foreign ships in Chinese harbors, debts, and other trading cases, sometimes in which both parties are foreign.

Over the 1980s, China's FTAC and MAC have made fair and equitable settlements of many cases, contributing to China's enjoyment of a good reputation in the world.

Contract Administration and Enforcement vs. Government Red Tape

While it is not too difficult to nail down detailed agreements on all aspects of a business transaction through persistent negotiation, such as shareholding structure, product, technology transfer, local content, whether products are to be exported, marketing, finance, tax, access to foreign currency, recruitment and training, the resulting contract does not have the weight that it would have in the West because China lacks the necessary body of law as well as an adequate judicial system. Virtually anything is negotiable. Topics which had been closed can be reopened, although there could be seeking of redress for breaches of contract through the courts.

Despite China's establishment of active judicial and arbitration systems and many laws regulating commercial contracts with foreigners, in practice contracts concluded with Chinese entities lack legal enforceability. China's inability to provide contract security to potential investors has hindered its efforts to attract the steady inflow of the much-needed hard currency. Foreign businessmen accustomed to Western standards of legal protection have found Beijing's inconsistent attitude toward contracts among the most frustrating aspects of investment.

Implementing contracts in China is not a simple process, either. In implementing the investment contracts, foreign investors that are not familiar with the importance of personal relationships in China especially encounter all sorts of bureaucratic hurdles after the conclusion of their contracts.

Sometimes, government agencies will directly interfere with the performance of the contract by imposing new rules, conditions or fees that affect the profitability of the venture. The sources of supply of raw materials or other Chinese inputs may be selected by the department-in-charge of the venture, preempting what should normally be a commercial decision by the venture itself. Or the costs of local inputs may be arbitrarily increased if the official hierarchy thinks that the venture is making too much profit.

Perhaps the most baffling and irritating aspect of the administration of contracts concluded with China is the frequency with which either the Chinese parties or Chinese officials insist that signed and approved contracts later be renegotiated. Because of this it is frequently said that contract negotiation never ends in China, and this unenviable reputation is a deterrent to prospective investors.

Caveat Bene: To the Chinese, a signed contract merely marks the end of the initial stage of negotiations, and will be followed by more discussions. More compromises and more concessions are to be expected, as nothing is ever set in stone. Westerners, in particular, are often caught unprepared for frequent Chinese requests to continue negotiations that have supposedly already concluded.

Obtaining a Binding Contract

Careful and studied consideration of legal issues should be prominent on the agenda of any companies interested in doing businesses in China. Within the context of the FECL, as well as other general considerations involved in doing business with China, the following recommendations must be considered for negotiation purposes.

Get a good contract including a reasonable amount of detail. Even though Chinese and Western views of a contract may differ, the Chinese are likely to treat it as a framework for discussion in the event of problems.

In an effort to insulate their contracts from any changes in the legal regime, many foreign companies have even attempted to negotiate clauses that "freeze" the law applicable to the contract as of the date of signature. Such a practice is guaranteed by the FECL which provides that where there is a conflict between the provisions of laws promulgated after an investment contract's approval and those of the contract, the contract "may" continue to be implemented according to its terms.

Resolve problems through negotiation. There is little point in pursuing a claim through courts in China, and few cases in which a judgment in a foreign court or arbitration tribunal have been enforced in China.

Use litigation only as a last resort. Unless the foreign party has no choice or no concern about ending the relationship, addressing problems through the courts should be last on the list of possible solutions.

Use experts and retain legal counsels. A growing number of foreign consultants, law and accountancy firms have established offices in China and can provide considerable expertise as well as access to Chinese contacts. When a contract with the Chinese parties is concluded, the foreign investor should consider consulting lawyers working for Chinese law offices to review for possible conflicts with Chinese rules or regulations. In negotiating a commercial transaction in China, an attorney should be prepared to assume a secondary role, allowing the business parties to negotiate face-to-face as is customary in Asian countries.

A DETAILED APPROACH TO ROLES AND CONTRACTING WITH THE CHINESE*

Although there is some writing on contracting generally with Chinese businessmen, negotiation skills and role playing in the contracting process have not received sufficient emphasis. An international business negotiation involves style, procedure, and substance. A good plan for style and procedure will be determinative.

International business negotiators should decide upon a plan for general negotiating style and procedure in advance and for different roles assigned to members of the negotiating team. The negotiators should also consider alternative plans to adjust to changing circumstances or needs during the negotiation process. There is, of course, no "one-size-fits-all" negotiation plan. Different cultures and contexts require different styles and plans.

In negotiating with the Chinese counterparts, Western business negotiators should keep in mind three facts: 1) the Chinese usually value a long relationship, either business or personal, with their business counterparts, rather than just a transient one; 2) the Chinese are proud of their culture and at the same time resentful of the past invasions of China by the Western "imperialists;" and 3) the Chinese are resilient negotiators and Western negotiators should have sufficient patience during the negotiation.

Place

The place of negotiation is usually determined by the following factors: 1) the subject matter of the negotiation; 2) the intended choice of law; and 3) other cultural considerations.

*Xiaoxue Zhao, Juris Doctor, Attorney-at-Law, St. Louis, Missouri

The Subject Matter of the Negotiation. This may involve pre-negotiation inspection of the subject matter. In case of a sale of goods, the negotiating parties may want to investigate the quality and quantity of goods, the manufacturing facility and work force, and the access to ports and other means of transportation. In case of a joint venture project, the parties also need to carry out on-the-spot inspection of the proposed work site, availability of competent work force and management personnel, access to market and highways and railroads, and sufficient power supply. Because these are essential aspects of the negotiation, it is hard to imagine that the negotiation should be held in another country away from the subject matter.

The Intended Choice of Law. The Uniform Commercial Code (Sec. 1-105) permits the parties to choose the law governing the contract, as long as the transaction bears "a reasonable relation" to the jurisdiction providing the governing law. One factor usually considered in determining the reasonable relation to a jurisdiction is the place of negotiation.

The Convention on International Sale of Goods permits unlimited party autonomy. Both the U.S. and China are member states under the Convention. Therefore, the merchants in the U.S.-Chinese transaction can choose U.S. law, Chinese law, the law of a third country, or simply remain under the law of the Convention. The place of negotiation is always a factor to be considered in choice of law questions. Thus, to achieve more predictability and to avoid confusion on the choice of law issue, the negotiating parties are well-advised to take it into account when choosing the place of negotiation.

Other Cultural Considerations. If the parties are negotiating a long-term project like a joint venture, the first negotiation is usually a good opportunity for the parties to better understand each other and each other's culture. The place of negotiation should depend on the respective parties' knowledge about the other's culture. It should appear to be necessary for the party who has less knowledge of the other country or culture to offer to go to that country to hold the negotiation there. This will be a good opportunity to personally investigate not only the conditions of the project site but also the cultural and political environment of that country.

Finally, an agreement between the parties is always needed on the place of negotiation because a consensus on this very first issue may set the general tone of the start of the negotiation.

Styles

Negotiating styles differ from culture to culture and person to person. The styles can be categorized into two: 1) the adversarial standoff style (or confrontational style); and 2) the consensus-building style. Each style is effective for its own purpose and in its own context.

Confrontational Style.   This style is often counterproductive when negotiating an international business transaction with the Chinese. This style is extracting the most from the other party by using bluffs, threats, procedural manipulations, purposeful ambiguity, and repetitive demands, with little or no desire for interpersonal relations. All of this occurs in the broader context of attempts to extract as much information as can be gained while revealing no information before agreement is reached on any point.

This style's emphasis upon pressing maximum advantage to the point of conquest is often inappropriate when measured against other, more important factors. These factors include the efficient use of time, political and cultural differences, the volatility of international markets, currency exchange fluctuations, and expenses that must be paid by a client along the way to shaping a satisfactory international agreement.

In addition, the ill will engendered by this style may prejudicially color the opponent's judgment, in some cases "killing" the deal. Because the style places parties in unequal positions, it very often reminds the Chinese of their ancestors' humiliating experiences at negotiating tables where they had to pay for the costs of foreign invading armies. The negative connotations of confrontational style is counterproductive, particularly in countries of oriental cultures.

A Chinese attorney witnessed a negotiation where a Western negotiation team was negotiating a joint venture with a Chinese factory. The Western company would provide technology to the joint venture and the Chinese factory would provide facilities. The Western negotiators tried repeatedly to raise the estimated price of their technology and to keep down the valuation prices of Chinese equipment and facilities. They also threatened again and again to unilaterally end the negotiation if their demands were not satisfied.

The Chinese negotiators did not expressly object to the Westerners' demands. In the end, the parties agreed to discuss the details further through fax and the Western negotiators left thinking that a tentative agreement had been reached. However, the moment they left the negotiation room, their Chinese counterparts dumped all documents and memoranda of negotiation.

The Western company soon sent numerous follow-up fax messages requesting further discussion, but got no response at all from the Chinese factory.

The Chinese negotiators later recounted that during the negotiation they had come to regard their counterparts as insincere and difficult to get along with and that they did not raise any objections because they saw no point in continuing the negotiation, but did not want say so expressly so that both sides could save face.

This is an example of adversarial negotiation style killing a business deal that would otherwise have been viable. The Western negotiators neglected a very crucial aspect of Oriental Culture in general and Chinese Culture in particular: the importance of saving one's face. To allow the other side "to save one's face" does not mean giving them whatever they want, but it does require some efforts and considerations to leave them enough space to make concessions or enough grounds upon which they can make such concessions. They should not hesitate to make their demands if they think they are justified, but they should use facts to support their demands, instead of threats to end the negotiation. With statistics to support their demands, it would make it easier for the Chinese negotiator to justify his concessions to his superiors.

There is also considerable cultural diversity about the meaning in international negotiations of silence and delay. The common law rule that, under appropriate circumstances, "silence is acceptance" is not shared in many countries, certainly not in China. In China, people are particularly reluctant to say "no" in front of the person making a request, while in other countries periods of silence are an acceptable and common occasion during which thoughts are arranged and rearranged. In the above example, the Chinese negotiators went as far as agreeing to negotiate in the future to avoid saying "no" during the negotiation while their silence after the negotiation was an unequivocal "no."

The Westerners mentioned above have made every mistake possible in the negotiation. Confrontational style is the best way to break, not to make, a deal.

Consensus-Building Style.   The consensus-building style emphasizes finding some kernels of agreement and expanding upon those areas with a view to building a momentum toward complete agreement. For example, in the first phase of the negotiation, the parties should concentrate on such points of consensus as the mutual willingness to mutually seek opportunities, to develop a business relation and cooperation between each other. Such emphasis upon common ground helps to finesse such pitfalls as a "hidden dimension" in a negotiation.

Of course, one problem is that there may be no initial consensus about the reason for negotiating at all. In such a situation, the Western negotiators should prepare for the upcoming negotiation by making a plan for different stages of the negotiation.

Preparations for the Negotiation. Although in the West, the market is usually dictated by demand and supply, doing business with the Chinese is not so impersonal and has an added aspect of personal relation. The Chinese value continuing personal relation not only in social contexts but also in business contexts. There is a Chinese saying, "Strive for friendly relation even when business negotiation fails." A good personal relation will not only give you a friendly starting point but will also help the mutual understanding throughout the negotiation.

There are numerous ways to build a rapport but several are most effective. The first and most common is the exchange of gifts or souvenirs. The Chinese usually present gifts to the other party if they are serious in building a continuing relation with their counterparts. It is not just a ceremonial routine, but a meaningful message and should be reciprocated by the other side.

In China, the guest should always present his or her gift to the host first. Then the host presents his or her gift to the guest. The host should always be notified in advance of the presentation of the gift so as to avoid the possible embarrassment where the host is not prepared with a gift.

The second way to build a rapport, less common than the first but also very important, is to have dinners together so that both sides can know each other better. It is an unwritten rule that the host should give a welcome dinner to show respect to the guest and the guest should later give a thank-you dinner to show respect to the host and appreciation of the host's hospitality regardless of the outcome of the negotiation.

Even when there seems no possibility that the two sides will do business with each other in near future, the guest should reciprocate with a thank-you dinner. It is not necessary for the host to give the guest an advance notice of the welcome dinner because the two dinners do not take place on the same day.

The advantages of exchanging gifts and giving dinners are: 1) a more reliable relation has been established and the relation will bring benefits with it; 2) a good reputation has also been built among the host's trade or industry, which will bring more customers. The last point is especially true in China where everyone judges each other not only by their business ability but also by their social behavior.

It is important to note a cultural difference that in China, people do not share a meal and split the bill as is common in the U.S. Anyone who does so in China would appear too impersonal and unwilling to develop a continuing relationship. Therefore, it may be all right to have no meals together with the counterparts at all, but it will be absolutely destructive to "go Dutch" with them at a restaurant in China.

The Negotiation Stage.　If, for any reason, Western negotiators fail to do the above preparations before the negotiation, they will have to build a rapport during the first 10 minutes of the negotiation. They should always remember it is courteous to tell people what they want to hear to start building consensus at the negotiation table. They can start with minor subjects like the most favorite Chinese relics or ancient buildings to show their knowledge and appreciation of Chinese culture so as to build up personal rapport, which can lead to more common ground to build more consensus.

Of course, having a pleasant personality and knowledge of Chinese culture alone will not accomplish everything you want. The personal and cultural aspects of negotiations are emphasized because they have not received sufficient attention. Sufficient knowledge of the management structure in China is also important.

The Chinese economy is still very much centralized. The government still has the last word on the finality of many contracts, especially in imports and joint ventures in basic industries.

Normally, a chief Chinese negotiator would be an upper-middle or middle management officer with a considerable amount of discretion, but who does not have unlimited power to finalize the deal. This will have three advantages for the Chinese: 1) they have someone well-informed and experienced leading the negotiation team; 2) there is sufficient guard against abuse because the chief negotiator does not have all the power to make the deal right on spot; 3) a flip side of 2) is the chief negotiator can always be ambiguous or say "sorry" when he or she wants to, by saying he or she would have to "get the approval from bosses upstairs," so as to create more space and time for them to maneuver.

W. Averell Harriman pointed out from his negotiating experiences that "You have to put yourself in the other fellow's shoes. . . . You also have to consider how to make it possible for him to make a concession. . . . But the idea that you can whip your negotiating opposite into agreeing with you is nonsense. . . . If you call a hand, you must recognize that you may lose it."

The same applies to negotiations with the Chinese. The consensus building style is most productive. The key to the consensus building style is an advance determination of: 1) what your negotiating opposites really want; 2) what they really must have; 3) what they may offer in return; 4) what they really cannot offer either because they lack authority to do so or because it would be unacceptable for enterprise, national or international reasons.

Negotiating Teams and Role Playing

The Negotiation Team.   Negotiation teams are most often used with direct foreign investments, joint ventures, and large licensing or sales transactions because these involve complex legal issues. Knowing in advance what minimum *quid pro quo* a negotiating opposite really must have to join in an international business agreement makes it easier to decide upon the necessary members of the negotiating team.

One should appreciate all of the personal, cultural, and linguistic meanings in any conversation, quite apart from the substance of whatever subject matter is under discussion. For example, a team too big may be intimidating and suggest "imperialist" overtones; a team too small can be insulting and also suggest "imperialist" overtones.

The best way to determine the size of a negotiation team is to measure these factors: 1) the complexity of issues involved in the negotiation; and 2) the status and importance of possible members on the opposite team.

This is in fact a balancing test between legal and cultural needs. If the negotiation involves complex issues in securities law, merger or licensing, legal need outweighs cultural need and any necessary number of legal, accounting, and engineering experts should be suitable. On the other hand, if the negotiation involves only a small sales transaction, a single negotiator should suffice. Generally, a negotiation team of three is the most appropriate size in most situations.

Of course, if the formation of the opposite negotiation team is known, it is important to staff your own team with members of equal status and importance so as to avoid offending the opposite side. The higher the status of the chief negotiator, the smaller the number of extra team members he or she may need because presumably he or she has enough power and knowledge to finalize the transaction. In any case, the team should have one member with enough status or importance to convey a sufficient impression of sincerity of purpose and of respect for the dignity of those who will be the negotiating opposites.

In China, lawyers are not welcome at the negotiation table because "transaction lawyers," as opposed to "litigation lawyers," are a new phenomenon in China. At the very mention of lawyers, the Chinese would have an image of the litigators ready to fight in a dispute. A lawyer's presence on a negotiation team, therefore, symbolizes a "hired gun" and may thus indicate a lack of sincerity and trust on the part of the negotiation team. So when a lawyer is absolutely necessary on the team, he or she can participate as "consultant" so as to avoid misunderstanding.

Role Playing. All team members must know about and agree upon the negotiating strategy. However, it is inevitable that at some point during the negotiation an unplanned decision will have to be taken extemporaneously. Therefore, it is essential that team members agree in advance upon the person who will be the team's "voice" to make that decision. If the situation fits one of the alternative plans pre-determined, the "voice" of the team will announce that decision. If the situation goes beyond the imagination of the negotiators, the "voice" of the team should also make a decision either to call a recess or adjourn the negotiation.

Other roles, such as the "compromiser" or the "diplomat," should also be preassigned so as to avoid confusion in the course of the negotiation. As mentioned above, the Chinese are resilient negotiators and are familiar with such role assigning. At a point where the negotiation seems to stall, a compromiser would try to reconcile by shifting the subject to more pleasant ones. In tough moments during a negotiation, courtesy alone may keep a consensus momentum going, especially in China. Enduring courtesy is the essential lubricant of international negotiations. Many negotiations have been saved by this old trick.

Such procedures that are flexible enough to allow time to work out such problems may cultivate ego, avoid a loss of "face" and continue participation in the negotiations. On a negotiation team, a person playing the role of compromiser is a must.

Conclusion

The above thoughts should give some practical guidelines to follow and correct approaches to take while negotiating with the Chinese. Of course, as China opens more and more to the outside world, its culture and legal system are bound to change. But while Western influence is strong in China and is still growing, the Chinese culture and thinking is still present.

Caveat Bene: No matter how drastic the changes may be in China, some of the fundamental traditional philosophy will endure for a long time. Therefore the basic principles mentioned here will continue to be useful.

The following sources were used in writing this section, and may be referenced for additional information:

1. Ralph H. Folsom, Michael W. Gordon, and John A. Spanogle, *International Business Transactions,* (1992).

2. The Uniform Commercial Code.

Regional Country and GATT Purchases

In recent times, countries have been uniting on a regional basis for trade purchases. These regional developments have implications for the purchasing manager, since they lower or eliminate tariffs and may thereby lower the price of goods purchased. Therefore this new chapter has been added. In addition, Appendix A may be consulted for additional NAFTA materials.

NORTH AMERICAN FREE TRADE: SOME OBSERVATIONS*

Recently, the passage of the North American Free Trade Agreement, known as NAFTA, has brought the possibility of even greater contact between United States businesses and those of Mexico and Canada. The purchasing manager may be buying more products from sellers in those countries, and should be familiar with both the general aspects of NAFTA and some of the more particularized tariff categories and phase-out of them.

Purchasing managers should have a general knowledge of NAFTA and its nature, and affects eliminating tariffs, prohibiting discrimination and harmonization.

In regard to some of the specifics of NAFTA, the legislation itself should be consulted. However, it is too extensive to set forth here. Still it may be useful to point out the general planned phase-out of tariffs.

Immediate Elimination—Tariffs on Some Products

Five Years Elimination of Tariffs on Some Products

Ten Years Elimination of Tariffs on Other Products

Fifteen Years—All Tariffs Eliminated

In terms of classification of goods, some within a class may be phased out of tariffs at different points. Some general classifications are:

Automotive and Motor Vehicle Goods, including parts. Phase out immediately, five, or ten years.

Textiles and Apparel. Phase out immediately or over ten years.

Agricultural Goods. Phase out over ten to fifteen years.

Land Transportation. Cross-border truck and bus service. Phase out over ten years.

Other matters are also covered. By the year 2000, Mexico will eliminate almost all restrictions on banks, securities firms, and insurance companies, and liberalize entry of factoring, leasing, warehousing, and bonding companies. There will be no discriminatory access to telecommunications. There is to be no discrimination against service providers from another NAFTA country, though with some exceptions. Harmonization efforts also are to be made in transportation and technical standards.

Some of the basic facts about NAFTA are summed up in the following Administration statement:

- NAFTA will create the biggest market in the world right at our doorstep—a $6.5 trillion market with 370 million people.

- NAFTA will level a playing field that remains—despite recent Mexican market openings—substantially tilted in Mexico's favor. Mexico's tariff barriers to U.S. goods are still 2.5 times greater than our own. All tariffs will be phased out under NAFTA.

- NAFTA will expand benefits the United States has enjoyed since Mexico began to open its markets in 1986. U.S. merchandise exports to Mexico have risen by 228% since 1986, reaching $40.6 billion in 1992.

- U.S. jobs supported by these merchandise exports rose from 274,000 in 1986 to an estimated 700,000 in 1992—these jobs are in all 50 states. (Merchandise exports to Canada support another 1.5 million U.S. jobs.)

- NAFTA will create an estimated 200,000 additional high-wage jobs related to exports to Mexico by 1995.
- NAFTA will increase opportunities for American firms to sell to Mexico. Those opportunities are especially important for small- and medium-size businesses that cannot readily overcome high Mexican border barriers.
- Mexico is already our second largest market for manufactured exports, beating even the more affluent Japan. NAFTA will further increase opportunities for U.S. manufactured exports in Mexico.
- NAFTA will help us promote sustainable development in North America—economic growth with enhanced environmental protection.
- NAFTA will gradually ease many of the pressures in Mexico that currently contribute to illegal immigration across our border.

It is further pointed out that NAFTA will create a huge market where goods may be sold and purchased:

With NAFTA, the United States, Canada and Mexico will create the biggest market in the world—a combined economy of $6.5 trillion and 370 million people:

- Our competitors are expanding their markets in Europe and Asia. NAFTA is our opportunity to respond and compete.
- By increasing our export opportunities, NAFTA will enable us to take advantage of U.S. economic strengths and remain the world's biggest and best exporter.

In addition, Mexico's trade barriers are much higher than ours. This levels the "playing field" which had been heavily tilted in Mexico's favor. The biggest changes are being made by Mexico. As a result:

- Half of all U.S. exports to Mexico will be eligible for zero Mexican tariffs when NAFTA takes effect on January 1, 1994.
- U.S. exports eligible for tariff-free entry into Mexico include some of our most competitive products:
  —Semiconductors and computers
  —Machine tools
  —Aerospace equipment
  —Telecommunications equipment
  —Electronic equipment
  —Medical devices

- Within the first five years after NAFTA is implemented, two-thirds of U.S. industrial exports will enter Mexico duty-free.
- Under NAFTA, Mexico will open its market significantly to U.S. manu-factured exports. For example, for automotive parts, Mexico will elimi-nate 75% of its duties over five years and phase out the rest over ten years.
- NAFTA also will require Mexico to open its market to U.S. service ex-ports (U.S. service exports to Mexico were $8.9 billion in 1992). This will benefit such industries as enhanced telecommunications services, insur-ance, banking, accounting, and advertising.
- Under NAFTA, our access to Canada's service market also will be more open than it is under the existing U.S.–Canada Free Trade Agreement.

In regard to the affect on workers, it is hoped that NAFTA will on balance create more jobs in the United States because of the greater mar-ketplace for them. The phase-outs of tariffs within five, ten, and fifteen years also is viewed as giving workers a chance to adjust to the change. Worker adjustment training programs also are envisioned. Since United States businesses can already establish themselves in Mexico or other countries with even lower priced labor, it is not viewed as creating any added threat to jobs here.

Supplemental Agreements between the United States, Canada, and Mexico are planned to deal with problems of Environment, Labor, and Import Surges. All three countries are members of GATT and although NAFTA is not inconsistent with it, NAFTA prevails in the event of any conflict.

NAFTA AND FREE TRADE—A MIXED BAG

During the first half of 1994, supporters of the North American Free Trade Agreement, a controversial trade pact between the United States, Mexico, and Canada, were jubilant. Early returns showed that U.S. ex-ports to Mexico had risen 16% during the first six months of NAFTA, and Mexican exports to the U.S. were up more than 20%. The dire predictions about massive U.S. layoffs and environmental doom had subsided, and it seemed as if the U.S. had tapped a vast new mine of resources. Numerous American businesses began expanding their operations to Mexico to take full advantage of the agreement, which essentially elimi-nates trade tariffs and forces countries to trade by the same rules.

As 1995 and the pact's one-year anniversary approached, however, the bloom was definitely off the rose. Two political assassinations, and—more importantly—a massive devaluation of the peso sent the Mexican economy into a free fall. Early on in 1995, President Clinton agreed to send an emergency aid package that consisted of several billion dollars, and the situation appears to have stabilized. Still, many companies and investors have put the brakes on, and the yellow caution flag is out.

Nevertheless, free trade and a global economy remain prominently on the agenda. The wave started in April 1994 with 124 countries signing the General Agreement on Tariffs and Trade, or GATT. The premise behind GATT was to lower trade tariffs and increase world trade.

In December of 1994, the U.S., Canada, and 32 countries from Latin America agreed to what will essentially be a larger version of NAFTA. This western hemisphere free trade zone is scheduled to be in place by 2006.

If Mexico can survive the peso crisis, the possibilities for free trade south of the border seem good. Latin America is the only region where the U.S. currently has a trade surplus, and by the end of the century, the U.S. believes it will send more exports to Mexico than Japan. It is, however, important for the purchasing agent to be sure of the point of origin of the goods if he or she is to get the maximum advantage of NAFTA, as explained shortly.

DOING BUSINESS UNDER NAFTA: POINT OF ORIGIN RULES AFFECTING PURCHASES*

The North American Free Trade Agreement (NAFTA) entered into force January 1, 1994, after being ratified by the governments of the U.S., Canada and Mexico. For the first time in history, a trade agreement became the most talked about and debated trade agreement ever. Never before has there been so much public interest and prediction, at least in a trade agreement in which the U.S. was involved. This is not a surprising thought, for NAFTA's economic impact is enormous. It is one of the most labor and environmental comprehensive, regional free trade agreements ever negotiated, and the first between an industrial and developing country.

The agreement is long and detailed and divided by sectors that in

---

* By Elisa Robinson, Juris Doctor, and Attorney-at-Law

and of themselves require intense study and analysis. The purpose of this section will be to focus on only a small but essential part of the agreement as a whole, this is, how the process and procedures of Rules of Origin and Customs Administration under the Agreement will effect U.S. business. Knowing the process and procedures and how they will affect a business helps to maximize NAFTA's benefits and the overall business under NAFTA. Knowing how it is likely to impact businesspeople in all three countries will assist business and legal planning. To better understand, an overview of the NAFTA is provided.

Overview of NAFTA History, Goals and Objectives, and Importance

Before an adequate discussion of NAFTA's Rules of Origin and Customs Administration can be understood, one must first understand exactly what NAFTA is. Its history, goals and objective as well as its importance will be viewed.

Caveat Nota. Under NAFTA, the three member countries will still exist as separate countries, there will still be boarders, custom formalities, immigrations and separate laws. NAFTA, therefore, is not a common market. NAFTA essentially is an agreement to remove barriers to trade and investment, namely tariffs, in an effort to promote economic growth and increased jobs in the three NAFTA countries.

NAFTA was conceived in and around other multinational trade agreements, the Canada-U.S. Free Trade Agreement (CFTA), and the General Agreements on Tariffs and Trade (GATT), as well as the Uruguay Round of multilateral trade negotiations. Article 101 of NAFTA states that, "the Parties to this Agreement, consistent with Article XXVI of GATT, hereby establish a free trade area," that would eliminate trade barriers in the area, but not raise barriers to trade in goods outside the three countries. Setting up NAFTA in that manner consistent with GATT avoids having to extend NAFTA benefits to other non-NAFTA countries, because of the Most Favored Nation provisions in GATT. Therefore, certain provisions and obligations under GATT are assumed. Many of CFTA provisions were incorporated into or modeled after NAFTA; the original negotiations were with Mexico, as the U.S. already had an agreement with Canada, but then later included Canada and incorporated much of the CFTA in the final NAFTA version. Because NAFTA was negotiated during the Uruguay Round, it provided that the Parties should be in no worse position under NAFTA than under agreements concluded pursuant to the Round.

Countries like those in Latin America, the Caribbean, and East Asia feel that NAFTA is inconsistent with GATT, because it takes trade and investment from them, and promotes regionalism. But NAFTA is an extension of GATT overall, although some provisions could be seen to be protectionist, it promotes multilateral trading systems, which creates and increases trade. However, it does not seem to provide for additional members, although each country is free to make its own agreement with other countries and this appears to be in line with European regionalism.

Finally, NAFTA is consistent with GATT because GATT allows exception to MFN treatment as the agreement covers "substantially all" trade among the partner countries and the agreement does not raise barriers to the trade of third countries, which NAFTA does not.

The negotiations between the U.S., Mexico, and Canada began in June 1991 and were concluded in August 1992. U.S. and Canada trade was already supplemented with the CFTA, and while trade between Canada and Mexico is small, to the U.S.'s third highest trading partner, while the U.S. is their leading trading partner. Although basically, trade between the U.S. and Mexico was already tariff free, the agreement stood to benefit the parties in other ways as well as the eventual complete elimination of tariffs.

After negotiations, in September 1992, President Bush notified Congress of his intent to sign NAFTA. In October 1992, presidential candidate Clinton stated his support for NAFTA. He stated that it was acceptable in its present form, although he felt there needed to be some sort of supplemental agreements on the environment and labor and on safeguard powers to combat extreme import surges. After several months of debate, the House of Representatives and the Senate approved NAFTA in November 1993 and the agreement was set on fast-track implementation. The implementation legislation was signed into law on December 8, 1993, and all three governments having completed their required legislation for implementation, NAFTA went into effect on January 1, 1994. The three Supplemental Agreements relating to the environment, labor and import surges also went into effect.

All of this was to reduce trade barriers with two of the U.S.'s most important trade partners, to promote economic and investment opportunities, and to increase jobs. With this purpose in mind, Canada, Mexico, and the U.S. created the largest and richest trading market in the world.

The importance of NAFTA is the dramatic changes it will have for

U.S. goods. The mere size of the free trade area is further evidence of its importance and impact on the whole world and the global economy. The importance of NAFTA is also shown through its goals and objectives. Its purpose is to create the biggest market in the world, which will "level tariff barriers making the game equal for all the players." Its goals are that by doing this, we will create higher wages and more U.S. jobs, increase opportunities to export to Mexico, create economic growth for all three countries, and finally enhance environmental protection. By expanding the field from which U.S. firms and worker can choose, this will increase U.S. competitiveness worldwide.

As President Bush stated in 1992, "By bringing together the largest free trading region in the World, Mexico, the U.S. and Canada are working to ensure that the future will bring increased prosperity, trade and new jobs for the citizens of each of our countries. And as President Clinton said in 1993, "The truth of our age is this and must be this, open and competitive commerce will enrich us as a nation . . . and so I say to you in the face of all the pressures to do the reverse, we must compete, not retreat."

The content of the Agreement includes the preamble to the NAFTA, which states the principles and objectives of the members, they are to promote sustainable developments to protect, enhance and enforce workers' rights, and to improve working conditions in each country.

The remaining opening provisions which set out the objectives of the Agreement are to eliminate barriers to trade, promote conditions of fair competition, increase investment opportunities, protect intellectual property rights, and other objectives aimed at establishing effective procedures for the implementation of the agreement, dispute resolution and further cooperation. It also established the supremacy of the agreement over other conflicting rules, but does create some exceptions. The rest of the agreement addresses specific concerns and provisions to fulfill the above objectives.

Some of these key provisions deal with tariffs and how they will be eliminated, investment barriers and how they will be removed, services, intellectual property, and certain industry-specific provisions and how they will be affected. Specific provisions also deal with safeguards, dispute resolution, government procurement, and rules of origin and customs administration. The Agreement itself is very large and divided in several sections in which the issues relevant to those sections are discussed. Since 1986 when trade barriers began to be lowered between the

U.S. and Mexico, exports to Mexico doubled and added many export related jobs in the U.S., cutting our trade deficit with Mexico. The agreement could lower these trade tariff barriers even further and without it Mexico could raise the tariffs back to previous levels.

NAFTA can raise productivity and wages by increasing economic growth and all countries would win, especially if Mexico, for example, increases its purchasing power, because "for each dollar Mexico spends on imports, seventy cents is spent on U.S. goods." The U.S. goods will be better able to compete in price in Mexico, and integration amongst North America will make U.S. goods more competitive globally. Efficiency can mean lower consumer prices and more consumer choice in North America and even price advantage outside of North America. All this increase in exports means an increase in jobs and better paying jobs, because wages in export-related jobs pay 17% more than the average U.S. wage.

The greatest economic effect however, is the combination of U.S. and Canadian capital, skills, technology, and natural resources with Mexican labor, which will offer new competitive strategies in areas where the U.S. has been losing market share. As non-tariff trade barriers are lowered by opening investment opportunities, trade increases.

The economic effects on specific U.S. industries and consumers varies with each industry and as such, these specific industries' effects, some good and some bad, are beyond this discussion.

One of the main adverse economic effects that is argued is that NAFTA will result in an enormous loss of jobs in the U.S., because jobs will move into Mexico. The Administration has dismissed these predictions because it says that study indicates otherwise. The size of Mexico's economy will not support this mass exodus of jobs and the Mexican market has been relatively open and no such exodus has occurred. Furthermore, as the difference in wages decreases, the benefits of lower labor costs that Mexico brings will decrease, therefore, eliminating any adverse effect. And finally, NAFTA will ease the causes within Mexico that contribute to illegal immigration and drug trafficking across the borders.

Although most of the attention and consideration of the effects of NAFTA have been on Mexico, Canada is also an important factor, because NAFTA has incorporated much of the CFTA. These effects include a significant increase in exports, increase in investment, lower prices in certain products, and more jobs for Americans.

Overview of How the Process and Procedures of Rules of Origin and Customs Administration Will Effect U.S. Business

One of the major issues and areas of concern is that of Rules of Origin and how the NAFTA process and procedures of Rules of Origin, as well as its Customs Administration, will effect U.S. business. NAFTA is structured around lowering tariffs on NAFTA members goods to give these goods a better advantage in the trade zone as well as the global economy, yet not favoring member's states to the discrimination of non-members, consistent with GATT. These rules therefore, are the most important area of NAFTA for they are the lifeline of the Agreement; they determine when goods qualify as NAFTA goods—which allows the system to work. The rules are very long and complex and are designed to benefit only NAFTA member's products and are used to determine when products receive the benefits of lower tariffs under the Agreement. Most importantly, and an area of much concern during the drafting of the agreement, was the designing of rules to determine the origin when material and goods from non-NAFTA member countries are incorporated into an otherwise NAFTA product. Special rules have been designed to protect certain industries like textiles and apparel and automobiles.

To achieve the benefits of NAFTA, the objectives of the Rules of Origin must therefore be strict so that these benefits will go to NAFTA countries and not to products of non-member countries that are only part of NAFTA products. This ensures that Mexico will not become a platform for third countries' exports. It is for this reason that restrictive rules are important. However, they must not be too restrictive or else would require products to use materials solely of NAFTA countries; this would violate GATT. By designing fair and workable rules, ones that can be easily applied, that are clear, certain, and transparent, will enable manufacturers to properly make business decisions and planning. These are the goals and objectives to the rules. Only when these rules are in place can we allow products that use non-member materials but which have been substantially transformed by significant processing operations to qualify as NAFTA goods. This prevents non-members from using NAFTA member's countries as a drop off or "pass-through" of their materials.

Caveat Nota.   The importance of Rules of Origin is in the fact that they define which goods are eligible for this preferential treatment.

The background and history behind the Rules of Origin as well as Customs Administration is parallel to that of the overall NAFTA agreement—much was learned from the strict rules in the CFTA. Because of problems associated with content requirement in automobiles coming in through Canada, drafters were prompted to look into specific industries and strengthen the Rules of Origin in those specific industries.

The main problems with the Rules of Origin is how to get them to work. What is the best standard by which to judge product's eligibility as NAFTA goods that will fulfill the purpose of allowing this benefit only to NAFTA members goods, and fulfilling the goal of lowering tariff barriers to increase economic efficiency and competition.

The process and procedure of Rules of Origin and Customs affect U.S. business because they are the first steps that must be taken for a business to qualify for benefits under NAFTA. For businesses to plan properly, they must be intimately familiar with the rules so that the products they plan to manufacture, to export, to compete against, or to import can be assessed to determine whether they qualify for the benefit of reduced tariffs. The reduced costs can also be taken into account, which may affect price or the potential and profitability of a product in a specific industry.

Note Bene. One of the major things that purchasers should be ascertaining in considering purchase from a NAFTA account is the basic origin of the goods.

Once the process of determining whether a product qualifies for preferential treatment under NAFTA has been completed, this fact must be documented in a Certificate of Origin. This is where it is important that a business has a clear understanding of Customs Administration and procedures because the goods will not qualify if not documented properly and proved they qualify. Under NAFTA, the U.S., Mexico, and Canada have agreed to many uniform customs procedures and regulations. The purpose and benefit is to promote transparency and predictability in the exporting process, to make the process work more efficiently and smoothly, so that the process will not have to be repeated at each border, to help companies understand and deal with sometimes complex procedures, and finally, to promote certainty in the process.

Another problem that can occur in implementing such increase in trade that will result under NAFTA is dealing with different customs processes at each border, even though many of the procedures and regulations will be uniform. Even with uniform tariff and preferential treatment on the base level, if the implementation of the process is too complex or costly in the interpretation and determination of whether the goods comply at the borders, no one will benefit.

Content of the Rules of Origin: The Process of Qualifying Under the Rules of Origin

Determining where a product originated was once an easy problem, but as trade on a global level increased and regional trade agreements became more common, the problem is now no longer so simple. With a need to rid "free riders" and the problem of so many component parts being assembled in various nations, somewhat restrictive rules are needed. In addition, the need to protect certain industries that are susceptible to these problems has brought about specific Rules of Origin related to, for example, automobiles and textiles and apparel. Whether very restrictive specific rules really promote free trade is of course questionable, because the more limitations you impose, the more you move away from free trade. Thus, despite possibly lowering tariffs, you may be increasing other non-tariff barriers to trade. There is of course a danger to using Rules of Origin as a protectionist device, but of course the goal of totally free trade with no quotas or tariffs worldwide is not politically feasible. The goals instead should be to make Rules of Origin as transparent as possible so that they are not hidden barriers to trade. Making them easy to apply, although restrictive, will mean greater business certainty and predictability.

To determine if a business product qualifies for preferential treatment under NAFTA is the first question that someone doing business needs to know to assess the effects or benefits NAFTA will have on their product. Turning then to the Agreement itself, a product is a product of North American origin if it meets one of the following tests:

1. If the product is wholly obtained or produced in the territory of one or more of the Parties, it is a product of North American origin. NAFTA defines this by examples, which include agricultural goods, (e.g., fruits or vegetables grown and harvested in North American, fish, extracted mineral goods, even waste or trash if produced in North America). Products that contain non-member components or ingredients do not qualify.

2. An extension of the above is, if the product is produced entirely in the territory of one or more of the Parties or exclusively from originating materials, it qualifies for preferential treatment under NAFTA. A good, for example, that is made of part Canadian, part Mexican, and part American material qualifies. However, like the first test, if any component or ingredient from non-members countries is included, it does not qualify.

3. Another test is a change in tariff classification test, which replaces the "substantial transformation," the previous standard of the U.S. It works the following way: if a product contains materials that do not originate in North America, but however, the final product is so changed that it now would be classified under a different tariff scheme under the HTS, then it is still classified as a North American good and qualifies for preferential treatment. However, the change in tariff classification must occur by production that occurs entirely within the three NAFTA members countries. This must be a sufficient transformation; for example, a steak produced in North America from a cow imported from France would qualify—it changes from a tariff classification of live animal to a tariff classification of edible meat.

4. If the parts of a product are not considered independent of the whole product, according to the tariff classification test and the tariff heading, the product still may be able to qualify under the regional value content test. In other words, if the unassembled parts are in the same tariff classification as the final product then there is no change in tariff classification. A good example is a bicycle, because each component part (e.g., the tires, handle bar, chain, and seat) is classified under the same tariff heading; therefore there is no change in classification. To overcome this determination, the regional value content test could be applied. If the goods include a specified percentage of North American content added, they may qualify. This test or calculation of regional value content is discussed later.

   Some products that qualify under the change in tariff classification test may also have to qualify under the regional value content test. An example is shoes made in North America from Brazilian leather. Not only does there need to be a tariff classification change from leather to footwear, but the shoes must also add 55% of its cost from North American materials.

5. A final test is the DeMinimus test where a good that fails the tests above could qualify for preferential treatment if its non-NAFTA material content is less than 7% of the transaction value price or the total cost of the good. There is, however, many exceptions to this

test—certain products do not qualify for this test, and some not only require the less than 7% De Minimus requirement, but also add the tariff classification change test as well.

Because of the fear of loss of jobs and the experience under CFTA with the controversy in the Honda case and the GM-Suzuki case, the Rules of Origin became an important issue under NAFTA. A need to have some restrictions and clearer provisions that made calculations or interpretation easier was apparent. Which leads to one of the main problems in interpretation that was at issue under the CFTA and was under NAFTA improved so that the problems could be resolved. This is the calculations of regional content. It requires two variations of calculation depending on the article covering the product under NAFTA.

The Regional Content test, which requires a product's regional content be calculated to determine if it should receive preferential treatment under NAFTA, has two methods. One is the transaction method, which is based on the price paid or payable for a good. The calculation requires taking the transaction value, minus the value of non-NAFTA member materials used in the production of the products, divided by the transaction value, times 100, and this equals the regional value content as a percentage. Usually, the regional content must be 60% of the good under this calculation. Transaction value can not be used if not acceptable under the GATT Custom Valuation Code.

The second method is the net cost method, which is based on the total cost of a good. Here the regional value content percentage equals the net cost of the goods, minus the value of non-NAFTA member materials used in the production of the product, divided by the net cost, times 100. Usually the regional content must be 50% if calculated this way. Either method can be used, except for certain products (e.g., automotive goods and footwear), which specify which calculation is necessary.

You must know how to determine the Rules of Origin and how your product qualifies under them or you cannot do business under NAFTA or take advantage of its benefits. These tests, however, do not all apply to certain specific industries. In certain cases the Rules of Origin are more strict and certain specific requirements have to be considered, for example, the Rules of Origin for textiles and apparel and the Rules of Origin for automobiles. The rules in these industries are discussed in the following.

Specific Industry Examples

As compared with the General System of Preferences of GATT or the CFTA, the Rules of Origin in NAFTA requires a higher regional content and certain specific rules protect certain industries even more where the trade effects may have had enormous adverse effects by free-riding or circumvention for these industries that have much to lose.

Textiles and Apparel. Rules of Origin for textiles and apparel, exempt them from the regional value-content-added test. The rules apply instead a regional value-content-added test that is more restrictive than the regulate Rules of Origin under NAFTA. The test is a "yarn forward rule," which requires that yarn used in the manufacture of the product is produced in a NAFTA member country. The rules therefore require that for textiles and apparel that "the yarn be produced, the fabric made, and the clothing sewn in the NAFTA area. There are certain exceptions, such as materials that are not produced in abundance in the U.S., or if a material is in short supply. These rules increased the strictness of the Rules of Origin in the CFTA. Canadians feel this is a U.S. defense to the increase of imports of Canadian textiles that occurred under the CFTA, and see it as a protectionist device. By raising non-tariff barriers, the Rules of Origin may increase the price of clothes; thus by protecting the industry the consumer interest is sacrificed.

Automobiles. Automobiles also require very restrictive Rules of Origin and a higher regional value content than other North American products. It uses a net cost method in calculating regional value content, which requires the tracing of the value of inputs of component parts for automobiles from countries where they came, in order to determine a correct regional value content. This tracing and net cost method are very complex and hence costly to perform. Automobile parts require 62.5% North American content to receive beneficial treatment.

The restrictiveness of automobile Rules of Origin shows the influence the industry has and was able to reflect during the NAFTA negotiations to protect their industry. This discriminates against foreign manufacturers and forces domestic companies to manufacture automobile parts within the free trade area. This may not be more efficient, but perhaps costs some manufacturers more and hence consumers pay more. It also gives domestic companies other benefits that allow them to stay ahead. Is this really promoting free trade? Critics have argues this point because the protectionism of these restrictive Rules of Origin runs counter to global trade. They also feel that this threatens the economics of other countries, especially developing countries that lose markets or find it harder to compete with the new NAFTA market. It forces foreign companies to invest in North America, perhaps relocating operations within North America, if they want to compete. However, NAFTA member countries feel this is a benefit and provides jobs. Critics say it circumvents the Agreements goals because although the goods are produced in North America, they may not be more efficient.

Returning now to the Rules of Origin overall, after having determined that a business' product qualifies for the benefit of NAFTA's lower tariff, one must then look to the tariff schedules to determine exactly what lower tariff the product will receive, or for exporting to Canada the tariff schedules of the CFTA need to be looked at. There are three schedules: agricultural goods, textiles and apparel, and manufactured goods. A business's product will fit into one of these categories.

The next major step after determining the product qualifies under NAFTA, and determining what tariff it will receive so that a business knows if it will be profitable for it to export the product, is that the business must next document that the requirements of NAFTA for this product have been met. This is where the process and procedures of Customs Administration becomes very important.

Customs Administration and Procedures

Both importers and exporters must be intimately familiar with the Certificate of Origin and what it requires as far as information proving the product's qualifications. The importance of workable customs laws is evident in the fact that the more difficult the process, the less likely business will want to attempt it. The protective U.S. Customs laws having to lessens their strictness and protectionism, in the name of free trade will probably under NAFTA increase enforcement and punishment of custom regulation violation.

The three member countries will have developed a common certificate of origin. It may have to be put in the language of the area into which the product is being imported. The Certificate is good for 12 months from the initial importation and covers a single importation, or many of the same product. The certificate is good up to 4 years from the time it is signed by the exporter or producer and the certificate is not required for an importation below the value of $1,000. Exporters or producers are required to complete and sign the certificate for exporting of a good for the importer to receive the preferential tariff treatment. The exporter or producer signs signifying or warranting their knowledge that the product qualifies.

The certificate is extremely important for an importer because to get the reduced tariff they need to have possession of the certificate and be able to show it to a customs officer. If the product's lower tariff treatment was not claimed, although it would have qualified, the importer can file for a refund of the duties paid within one year of the importation if they have the certificate as proof.

To receive this treatment, the certificate must be signed by the exporter or producer. However, nowhere in NAFTA does it require the certificate to be signed or even provided by the producer. It is completely voluntary. If the producer of the goods does not sign but another party is the exporter, the exporter must produce and sign the certificate or else the importer cannot claim the benefit of the lower tariff. The exporter, who is not the producer of the product, signs only that to the best of its knowledge, or upon reasonable reliance of the producer's statement, that the good qualifies. So the question remains as to who is at fault, if in fact the product does not comply, although it was represented by either the producer or the exporter in the certificate to qualify. It is extremely important in this regard to keep records to prove what basis you relied upon to find if the goods qualify.

Duty drawbacks that are refunds of Customs duties paid upon entry of the goods, when the goods are later exported, will slowly be phased out under NAFTA. Customs user fees will also be slowly eliminated.

Enforcement

NAFTA will create a system in which groups, with members of each NAFTA country, will monitor application of the rules and consider disputes. Disputes not settled will be resolved through non-binding dispute resolution procedures.

It is important to know the customs regulations and how they work, because a violation of the regulations will enable a NAFTA member country's customs to impose penalties. Article 508 of the treaty states that each country shall maintain measures imposing criminal, civil or administrative penalties for violations of its laws and regulations relating to this chapter. Not knowing the law is not a defense for violation.

The penalties can include fines or even jail, or the products can be seized by customs officials if not documented properly, and each country can conduct an investigation to verify the origin.

For a business, a better way to handle the whole process, and one that is highly recommended, is to get an advance ruling, especially if a business is uncertain whether a product will qualify under NAFTA.

Each member of NAFTA must provide procedures to enable a business to obtain an advance ruling through its customs service, including the process and information required. They must provide this to any importer within their own country or an exporter or producer in another NAFTA member country who plans to import into their country. Therefore, an importer needs to obtain an advance ruling from the country it produces in, and an exporter or producer must get the ruling from the country it plans to export to. For U.S. exporters, this requires rulings from Mexican and Canadian customs. This shows how important it is for U.S. business to know these customs systems.

There will still be customs clearance procedures at each border. But the process and much of the procedure and the law to this point and some beyond will be uniform, which will make the system easier to perform. There is, however, inevitable going to be controversy and argument over interpreting tariff classifications, especially if the product being imported hurts a domestic industry. But this process impact and its consequences on the state of customs law, and the benefits of NAFTA, will remain to be see because it will be a slow process. This is especially so because there is a phase-out period for most tariff duties and quotas that will last several years. Furthermore, so that the process is not undermined, there will need to be much enforcement and investigation, or verification of the origin of products, and increased level of penalties, to safeguard U.S. trade. But there will also have to be cooperation in the verification and enforcement process between the countries to keep third countries' products from benefitting. Much of the procedure has yet to be established but the probable effect is clear. It will be very important for businesses to clearly know the process or else be penalized, because the customs services, of the U.S. especially, are sure to increase their efforts to protect trade and make sure that it is fair, as well as try to safeguard against non-NAFTA products from benefitting. The danger of course, is that too much enforcement against other NAFTA member countries will again be a barrier to trade. Hopefully the NAFTA rules and customs procedures' clarity will eliminate this danger.

Overview of Parties Affected

NAFTA affects not only NAFTA members but also other countries. Within the NAFTA countries, exporters and importers are not the only ones affected. NAFTA's implications are far reaching. Some of these effects are as follows: As has been seen, the Rules of Origin and Customs process affects foreign and domestic manufacturers or producers, exporters, as well as importers the same way. Both producers and exporters will be limited in what kinds of products they will be able to produce and export. They must look closer at the makeup of their products and estimate their costs through tariffs. As a business, the goals are to reduce costs and take advantage of opportunities to export at the lowest possible duty rate. This will affect the types of goods offered. It will also affect importers because they may not be able to import the goods they have or want.

NAFTA also affects consumers in that ultimately, increased job and lower prices will result for consumers. The most intriguing effect, however, is the effect NAFTA has on countries outside NAFTA. Clearly the rules make it more difficult for other trading partners in Europe and the Far East to benefit, because NAFTA requires that significant changes or significant value is added in one of the NAFTA countries, especially with regard to automotive products and textiles and apparel. They may have to go to other markets, because they will lose some access to NAFTA ones by a loss of lower tariff benefits and a loss of production and profitability.

Third-party countries will not be excluded from trading with NAFTA countries; they just won't be able to receive the better and reduced tariffs, which means they won't be able to compete as well, and their products may cost more to consumers. However, each country will maintain its own tariffs on imports from non-NAFTA countries. In this way third-party countries will not be affected, but they will not be able to take advantage of the benefits of the reduced trade tariffs between NAFTA countries, and hence these producers will use less of their product. Although tariff levels and trade barriers on importing for third-party countries cannot be increased and will not be affected. Countries that deal in automotive parts and textiles and apparels will be affected the most. The result is that they may have to locate operations in NAFTA countries, no matter what the costs, if they want to compete.

Conclusion of Effects on Business and Trade

The benefit to U.S. workers and business, by requiring that duty-free goods contain substantial North American content, is that the incentive to use North American goods will increase as companies are rewarded by using North American parts and labor.

Because the rules only benefit NAFTA products, they prevent free riders from benefitting by circumventing the rules by minor changes or shipment through Mexico and Canada into the U.S. on non-NAFTA member products. NAFTA strengthens and simplifies the Rules of Origin, lessons learned in the CFTA. NAFTA uses simpler formulas and simple, predictable tariff classification principles, and finally uniform customs provisions that improve procedures for verification, documentation, advance ruling, review, and appeal of determination, all done with an aim towards cooperation. Furthermore, joint or uniform administrative groups, customs procedures, and regulations provide transparency and predictability in the exporting process, which benefits business from having to spend the cost of figuring out complex customs procedures. Uniform customs procedures also allow exporters to have to deal with just one customs procedure instead of several customs regulations of each country at the different borders.

Without NAFTA, business in North America would be as it is now, high tariffs from Mexico and a lack of access to the opportunities, investments, economic market, and no increase in jobs. Without it there would be no improvement to CFTA—there would be no incentive for North American production or labor and materials. To receive no duty treatment on tariff reductions during its phase-out, materials must be North American or processes must take place in NAFTA member countries. NAFTA is facing the challenge to prepare all three markets for the competition that they face ahead in the global market; without NAFTA we could just not compete.

For businesses to be prepared they need to know if their products qualify for reduced tariffs under NAFTA, whether tariffs will be lowered for their products and how low, and who may be available to help them in their exporting. The greatest impact will be on small and medium businesses that before could never have competed in Mexico or Canada because of high trade barriers, costs, and complex rules and regulations. These companies will not be able to export much more easily, which increases exports overall.

To determine these things, the business needs to know the number for its product, which is determined by looking to the Harmonized Commodity Description and Coding System (HS). Exporters can contact the Census Bureau Foreign Trade Division or the Commerce Department for help. Once this is known, the tariff rate and phase out schedule for the products under NAFTA can be consulted. When exporting to Canada, the CFTA tariff schedule, which was not changed by NAFTA, needs to be consulted.

To determine if non-NAFTA countries' goods or materials in your product qualify, the NAFTA Rules of Origin provision must be consulted. These are included in Volume II of the Agreement, which can be obtained through the government printing office in U.S. Customs Services. Consulting the Rules and Customs process, procedures and regulations before you export will bring certainty, so one knows if their goods qualify beforehand. This system keeps non-NAFTA countries' product from being shipped between NAFTA countries to escape a higher tariff.

Then of course, the exporter must fill out the Certificate of Origin. The U.S. Customs or the Commerce Department can help in this process. And finally, a business should research completely the markets they plan to export to first, to determine profitability. Certain trade publications and departments, as well as special exporting programs can help assist in this regard.

THE EUROPEAN COMMUNITY (E.C.)

Another major regional country development that has existed for some time, the European community, is suddenly expanding. New applications for membership are still being filed. In addition to the European Community, there is an affiliated Free Trade Association of some other countries which further expands this vast marketplace.

The purchasing manager should be generally aware of the development. While such a free marketplace without customs and tariffs is not available to United States businesses, some have set up subsidiaries there. It would seem at first that such a closed region might make prices higher for goods being purchased by United States businesses, since customs and tariffs are still applicable. However the purchasing manager should keep in mind the fact that the overall effect of the EC may be to create within it more efficiencies and thereby make prices for goods lower than previously. So the United States purchaser may still come out ahead on price despite the fact that this nation is not a member and goods are still subject to customs.

The following excerpts from the publication "One Grand Market Without Frontiers" is brief but gives a general understanding of the

European Community. Their vision of the treaty establishing the European Community has been described:

The idea of creating a European economy based on a common market is not a new one. The opening lines of the Treaty of Rome signed in 1957 spelled this goal out in specific terms:

"The Community shall have as its task, by establishing a common market and progressively approximating the economic policies of Member States, to promote throughout the Community a harmonious development of economic activities, a continuous and balanced expansion, an increase in stability, an accelerated raising of the standard of living and closer relations between the States belonging to it."

The Treaty clearly envisaged that the Community's prosperity and, in turn, its political and economic unity would depend on a single, integrated market. And to bring that about it set out specific provisions for the free movement of goods, services, people and capital. It also foresaw that this would need to be backed up by action in other related spheres, such as establishing freedom of competition and developing common legislation where necessary.

It also is seen as a way to compete in the worldwide economic market against other major competitors like the United States and Japan.

To facilitate these goals the E.C. Commission published a White Paper in June 1985 setting out the necessary program together with a clear timetable for action. It noted that:

Unlike previous initiatives, the White Paper aims to be completely comprehensive. It seeks to create, step by step, an integrated and coherent economic framework. It does not tackle only one economic sector or area which favors only one particular Member State. Nor does it simply concentrate on minimal proposals that would be easily acceptable to the Member States. It attempts to identify all the existing physical, technical and fiscal barriers which justify the continuing existence of frontier controls and which prevent the free functioning of the market, and it puts forward over 300 legislative proposals required for their removal.

It is this comprehensive approach that is the key to this bold and ambitious set of proposals. Only by tackling all the genuine and relevant barriers that exist is it possible to create a real common market in all aspects, a real "Europe without frontiers." Every single one of those barriers has got to go. The continued presence of one single reason for the maintenance of frontier controls could be enough to require controls at internal frontiers and defeat the whole exercise.

The Commission believes that this single market will only work efficiently if it is expanding and flexible so that resources, both of people and materials, capital and investment, flow to areas of greatest advantage. This is essential if the integrated economy is to cope with changing circumstances.

In 1987, the Single Europe Act became effective. That Act contains the first major amendments to the Treaty of Rome of 1957 and has been described as follows:

This Act has replaced the original Treaty requirement for decisions to be taken by unanimity with a qualified majority requirement as regards certain measures which have as their object the establishment and functioning of the internal market. The unanimity requirement has, in the past, made any decision making a complex and lengthy process and meant that progress was often slowed to the pace of the most reluctant Member State.

Another major aspect of the Single Act is the new "cooperation procedure" which allows the European Parliament a greater input to the Community legislative process, in relation to those areas where the procedure applies. The procedure demands closer liaison between both the Commission and the Council with the European Parliament, through the first and second reading of proposals, as they pass from the stage of Commission initiative to Council adoption.

While the timetables set down for the operation of this more complex legislative procedure should stimulate quicker decision making by all of the institutions involved, it does not guarantee the adoption of a legislative act at the end of it all. Much will still depend on the political will of the institutions.

The Single Act also sets out a number of amendments to the original Treaties covering such diverse subjects as economic and social cohesion, environment, cooperation between the institutions and political cooperation between the Member States.

The importance of the Act for the achievement of the internal market lies in the fact that it provides the necessary political impetus and legal framework to achieve a truly unified market by 1992. Above all, the adoption of the Single Act reflects the renewed political will of the Community to halt the economic fragmentation of the Community and to complete, within a given time frame, the aims of the original Treaties.

Not only are some of the frontier controls and tariffs barriers to trade, but some of the other technical regulations on goods as well. This has been effectively described:

As far as goods are concerned, barriers are caused by the fact that different product regulations and standards—safety standards, health or environmental standards, standards for consumer protection—operate from one Member State to another. The welter of apparently petty restrictions which this causes is endless: for example, cars or televisions have to be altered in innumerable ways to meet all sorts of different national standards. British chocolate simply cannot be sold in some Member States because they use a different definition of chocolate. German law for years prohibited the sale on its territory of beers brewed in other Member States because the additives they contain contravened German national 'purity laws'. Such regulations not only add extra costs, because of separate research, development and marketing costs, but they also distort production patterns. They increase unit costs and stockpiling costs and discourage business cooperation. Where they do not actually forbid it, they at least discourage and penalize attempts to operate on a European scale.

Different national production standards and regulations mean that many products are separately manufactured to separate standards for each separate country. In itself the development of national standards and regulations has been constructive and helpful in guaranteeing that products provide a minimum level of safety for the consumer and they protect the environment. The fact is, however, that they can often act as a disguised form of national protection against similar goods imported from other Member States where different standards are in force.

Thus, for example, a forklift truck manufactured in the UK to British standards and regulations may not meet those applied in Germany. So if a British manufacturer wants to sell his forklift truck in Germany, he may have to alter it to meet German requirements.

It is ironic that such standards and regulations should do such damage when they have the same entirely desirable purpose: the protection of human life and health and the environment: ironic, and it must be said, necessary. It is a goal of the European Community to eliminate these barriers as well.

However, the European Community goes far beyond removing barriers to trade and goods. Persons, services, and ideas also are to be allowed to go freely over the boundaries. A common currency, hopefully, may be developed. In addition to the economic realm, there is to be integration in the political and social realms as well.

GATT—URUGUAY ROUND

In addition to the NAFTA elimination of tariffs in the United States, Mexico, and Canada Region, there is a general lowering of tariffs as to goods produced around the world. This is of general interest to the purchasing manager because it lowers the price of imports generally. This agreement is called the General Agreement on Tariffs and Trade or GATT. The latest agreement was concluded December 15, 1993 by 117 countries in Uruguay. Negotiations had gone on for a number of years there to modify and improve the original GATT, so that this latest agreement is known as GATT—The Uruguay Round. A good description of it by the Office of the United States Trade Representative is set forth in Appendix B.

CUSTOMS PROCEDURE

An importable item must "pass customs." Usually, the passage through customs and physical entry into a country occur simultaneously. An exception occurs when goods enter a "free trade zone" within a country. Goods in a free trade zone are exempt from tariffs while they remain there. Such zones serve as distribution centers, encourage assembly of certain manufactured items for export, provide local employment, and may lessen overall tariffs that must be paid before the goods cross the zone for routine importation into the country.

Most countries in the world, except the U.S. and Canada, classified imports according to the Brussels Tariff Nomenclature (BTN), which identifies items along a progression from raw materials to finished goods. The United States had its own system of classification set out in the Tariff Schedule of the United States (TSUS).

In 1982, the U.S. initiated efforts to convert the TSUS into a Harmonized Commodity Description and Coding System (HS) of Classification, in common with the classification system used by most other countries and developed by the Customs Cooperation Council in Brussels. The U.S. adopted the Harmonized System as the Harmonized Tariff Schedule (HTS) for classification of all imports by enactment of the Omnibus Trade and Competitiveness Act of 1988, starting on January 1, 1989. About forty other nations have adopted HS and use it for U.S. exports.

The U.S. Customs Service normally examines at least one package per invoice and at least ten percent of the packages of merchandise. However, the customs may examine either more or less than this. The purpose of customs examinations is to determine, first, whether goods accurately conform with the description and quantity, second, the dutiable status of the goods and the proper amount of customs duty owed, third, whether the required "country of origin" markings appear, and finally, whether the packages contain any prohibited articles.

The importer is liable for all import duties. It is liable even if the customs service releases the goods in error without payment, or if the importer pays its agent the customs broker, but the customs broker fails to pay the U.S. Customs Service. The liability for customs duty constitutes a "lien" on the goods, and the government's claim for unpaid duties takes priority over other creditors in bankruptcy.

If the importer and the U.S. customs officials disagree about the proper classifications of an imported item, the U.S. Court of International Trade (CIT) has exclusive jurisdiction to resolve their dispute.

For decades, U.S. customs valuation of an imported item was gauged by the American Selling Price (ASP) of the item—i.e., the usual wholesale price at which the same item manufactured in the U.S. was offered for sale.

After the 1979 Tokyo Round of GATT, the GATT approach was incorporated into the U.S. Trade Agreements Act of 1979. United States customs valuation is now calculated by the "transaction value" of the imported item and, if that cannot be determined, by certain fall-back methods which are, in descending order of eligibility for use, the transaction value of identical merchandise, the resale price of the merchandise with allowances for certain factors or the cost of producing the imported item. "Transaction value" is "the price actually paid or payable for the merchandise when sold for exportation to the U.S." plus "certain amounts reflecting packing costs, commissions paid by buyer, any assist, royalty or license fee paid by buyer, and resale, disposal, or use proceeds that accrue to seller."

The Generalized System of Preferences (GSP), 19 U.S.C. Sections 2461–2465, uses a rule of origin in accordance with certain trade preferences to products from developing countries without demanding reciprocity. Under the U.S. GSP, goods are admitted duty free if both the product and its country of origin meet the statutory requirements.

The GSP rule of origin requires that the product be shipped directly into the beneficiary developing country to the U.S. Where goods are produced from material imported into the developing country, the GSP rule of origin requires that at least 35% of the value of an item be added within a developing country for the item to be considered as "originating" in that developing country. The President can remove sufficiently competitive imports from the GSP list when they have reached the level of 25 percent of total U.S. imports of such goods or $25 million in value of imports.

The following sources were used in writing this section, and may be referenced for additional information:

1. Leslie Alan Glick, *Understanding the North American Free Trade Agreement: Legal and Business Consequences of NAFTA,* (1993).
2. Andrew W. Shoyer, *Trade in Goods Under the North American Free Trade Agreement,* Commercial Law & Practice Course Handbook Series, (1993).
3. Clinton Administration Statement on the North American Free Trade Agreement, ISBN #0–16–041871–2, July 1993.
4. Patricia Raiken, "Business Guide to Planning for NAFTA," *Business America,* 1991.
5. Joseph A. LaNasa, "Symposeum on NAFTA: Rules of Origin Under NAFTA: A Substantial Transformation into Objectively Transparent Protectionism," Harvard International Law Journal, 1993.
6. Various issues of *Mexico Trade & Law Reports.*
7. Various issues of *Business America.*

Sales Reform

SUMMIT OF THE AMERICAS

The U.S. took another bold move in the international trade area late in 1994 when it—along with Canada and 32 Latin American countries—agreed to become part of a free trade area by 2006. This took place in Miami in December at the Summit of the America's Conference.

Much work remains to be done before this comes to fruition. The nations in the Western Hemisphere are already tied by dozens of trade agreements, which will make creating a free trade pact interesting. Also, the countries will be challenged to create a zone that is not only open to countries in this hemisphere, but in the East as well.

This agreement could be crucial to both the U.S. and its neighbors. Currently, the U.S. enjoys a trade surplus with Latin America—the only region where that is the case—and many of these countries are now privatizing and in need of imports and investments. In turn, some rough estimates have free trade raising income in Latin America by as much as $500 per person.

Only time will tell if this will indeed be a win-win situation, but barring a collapse similar to what felled Mexico, the potential appears to be there for just such an occurrence.

NAFTA Information

NAFTA has a 24-hour automated information system. Simply dial (202) 482–4464, follow the step-by-step instructions, and the information that you request will be automatically faxed to you. "NAFTA Facts" is available 24 hours a day, seven days a week.

Document #0102   **NAFTA FACTS MAIN MENU**
                                Effective February 15, 1994

GENERAL INFORMATION

0101: NAFTA Facts Main Menu (THIS DOCUMENT)
0102: List of New or Updated NAFTA Facts Documents—February 1994

0103: Contact Information for Local International Trade Administration District Offices
0104: U.S. Department of Commerce Industry Specialist and Country Desk Officer Lists
0105: Department of Commerce *Flash Facts* Hotlines
0106: Trade Information Center Contact Information and How to Order the *Export Programs Directory*
0107: *The ABCs of Exporting,* Overview and GPO Order Information

NORTH AMERICAN FREE TRADE AGREEMENT (NAFTA) SERIES:

CONTACTS FOR NAFTA QUESTIONS/ORDER INFORMATION FOR NAFTA DOCUMENTS

2001: U.S. Government Key NAFTA Contacts
2002: Ordering Information for NAFTA Text/Tariff Elimination Schedule/ Supplemental Agreements
2003: List of NAFTA Documents Available from National Technical Information Service (NTIS) and Ordering Information
2004: List of NAFTA Documents Available on the National Trade Data Bank (NTDB) and Ordering Information for NTDB CD-ROM Disks/How to Access NTDB at Federal Depository Libraries
2005: List of Department of Commerce NAFTA Industry Reports and Ordering Information
2006: List of USDA Documents on NAFTA Agricultural Provisions and Ordering Information

BACKGROUND INFORMATION ON NAFTA AND SPECIFIC NAFTA PROVISIONS

3001: General Facts on NAFTA
3002: Key NAFTA Provisions: List of Provision-Specific NAFTA Facts Documents Available
3003: NAFTA's effect on the U.S.–Canada Free Trade Agreement
3004: Background: North American Development Bank (NADBank)/Border Environmental Cooperation Commission (BECC) and Funding of U.S.– Mexico Border Infrastructure
3005: Summary of North American Agreement on Environmental Cooperation
3006: Summary of North American Agreement on Labor Cooperation
3007: Summary of the Understanding on Emergency Action (Safeguards)
3008: Effect of NAFTA on Maquiladores

SPECIAL ANNOUNCEMENTS

4001: Doing Business Under NAFTA: Dates and Locations for "NAFTA Customs Rules for Exporters" Seminar Series
4002: Acceleration of NAFTA Tariff Elimination Schedules (need to find exact document number)

NORTH AMERICAN FREE TRADE
AGREEMENT (NAFTA) SERIES (cont'd)

NAFTA RULES OF ORIGIN
AND CUSTOMS INFORMATION

5000: How to Use the NAFTA Facts to Determine Rules of Origin, and List of Rules of Origin Documents Available

The 5000 submenu includes information on qualifying your product for NAFTA tariff preference, and how to fill out your NAFTA Certificate of Origin. The most commonly requested documents in this series are:

5001: Making the NAFTA Origin Determination
5002: A Copy of the NAFTA Certificate of Origin
5003: Qualifying Your Product for NAFTA Tariff Preference *(includes additional information on completing the NAFTA Certificate of Origin)*

NAFTA TARIFF SCHEDULE FOR U.S.
EXPORTS TO MEXICO

6000: How to Use the NAFTA Facts to Determine Tariff Phaseouts for Mexico. List of specific Tariff Phaseout available by Harmonized System Number

NAFTA TARIFF SCHEDULE FOR U.S.
EXPORTS TO CANADA

7000: How to Use NAFTA Facts to Determine Tariff Phaseouts for Canada. For specific Tariff Phaseouts by Harmonized System Number, call (202) 482-3101

DOING BUSINESS IN CANADA

0100: Menu of documents available on Doing Business in Canada. To order Doing Business in Canada Documents, call (202) 482-3101
0130: Office of Canada Publications, Desk Officers and Customs Information

DOING BUSINESS IN MEXICO

BASIC INFORMATION ON MEXICO
AND THE MEXICAN MARKET

8101: Fact Sheet: Mexico Trade and Economic Statistics Profile

8102: Top 50 U.S./Mexico Imports and Exports by Product Sector

8103: U.S. Manufactured Goods Trade Balance with Mexico

8104: Description of *U.S. Exports to Mexico: A State-by-State Overview, 1987–1992*

8105: Best Prospects for U.S. Exports to Mexico

8106: List of Magazines and Directories on Doing Business in Mexico

8107: Order Information and List of Mexico Documents Available from National Technical Information Service (NTIS)

8108: List of Mexico Documents Available on the National Trade Data Bank (NTDB) and How to Get Copies

8109: Background Notes: Historical and Cultural Information on Mexico

8110: Tips for Travellers to Mexico

8111: Contacts for U.S. Citizens Living in Mexico

8112: Guidelines for Driving Private Vehicles Into Mexico

8113: Sending Gifts to Mexico

OTHER OFFICES TO CONTACT FOR INFORMATION
ON THE MEXICAN MARKET

8201: U.S. Government Mexico Contacts—Interagency List

8202: U.S. Government Contacts for Exporting Agricultural Products to Mexico

8203: Organizations Providing U.S. & Mexican Border Region Commercial Assistance

8204: Importing to the U.S. from Mexico—Mexican Trade Commission Contact Information

MARKETING YOUR PRODUCTS
AND SERVICES IN MEXICO

8301: Market Promotion Services Available from U.S. & Foreign Commercial Service Offices in Mexico

8302: Calendar of 1994 Trade Shows in Mexico

8303: How to Get Lists of Mexican Companies and U.S. Firms in Mexico

8304: List of Major Mexican Retail Chains and Grocery Stores

8305: List of Mexican Advertising Firms and Publications Media

8306: Finding a Distributor: Legal Framework and Practical Guide to Selection

8307: Financing Exports to Mexico

8308: Temporary Entry Visa Requirements for Business Persons Travelling to Mexico

DOING BUSINESS IN MEXICO (cont'd)

PREPARING YOUR PRODUCT FOR SHIPPING AND SALE TO MEXICO

LEGAL AND TAX ISSUES

GATT—Uruguay Round: Jobs for the United States, Growth for the World

A HISTORIC TRADE AGREEMENT

On December 15, 1993, 117 countries concluded a major agreement to reduce barriers blocking exports to world markets, to extend coverage and enhance disciplines on critical areas of trade, and to create a more fair, more comprehensive, more effective, and more enforceable set of world trade rules.

The Uruguay Round agreement is the most comprehensive trade agreement in history. The existing set of trade rules was incomplete; it was unreliable; and it was increasingly unresponsive to major concerns of U.S. exporters.

The United States is uniquely positioned to benefit from the Uruguay Round trade agreement and the new world trade system it will create. U.S. *workers* will gain from significant new employment opportunities and additional high-paying jobs associated with the increased production of goods for export. U.S. *companies* will gain from significant opportunities to export more agricultural products, manufactured goods, and services. U.S. *consumers* will gain from greater access to a wider range of lower priced, higher quality goods and services. As a nation, we will compete, and we will prosper.

This historic agreement will:

- cut foreign tariffs on manufactured products by over one-third, the largest reduction in history;
- protect the intellectual property of U.S. entrepreneurs in industries such

145

as pharmaceuticals, entertainment, and software from piracy in world markets;

- ensure open foreign markets for U.S. exporters of services such as accounting, advertising, computer services, tourism, engineering, and construction;
- greatly expand export opportunities for U.S. agricultural products by limiting the ability of foreign governments to restrict trade through tariffs, quotas, subsidies, and a variety of other domestic policies and regulations;
- ensure that developing countries follow the same trade rules as developed countries and that there will be no "free riders";
- establish an effective set of rules for the prompt settlement of disputes, thus eliminating shortcomings in the current system that allowed countries to drag out the process and to block judgments they did not like; and
- create a new World Trade Organization (WTO) to implement the agreements reached.

This agreement will not:

- impair the effective enforcement of U.S. laws;
- limit the ability of the United States to set its own environmental and health standards and to pass its own laws; or,
- erode the sovereignty of the United States to pass its own laws.

Background

The talks concluded on December 15, 1993 were launched at a meeting of trade ministers from more than 100 countries held in 1986 in Punta del Este, Uruguay. These talks are therefore usually referred to as the Uruguay Round of multilateral trade negotiations. They are the latest and most significant set of negotiations that have been carried out periodically since the late 1940s.

Following World War II, the major economic powers of the world, recognizing that obstacles to trade hindered economic development and growth, negotiated a set of rules for reducing and limiting barriers to trade and for settling trade disputes. These rules were called the General Agreement on Tariffs and Trade (GATT).

While the world has benefitted enormously from the reduction of trade barriers and expansion of trade made possible by the GATT, the GATT rules were increasingly out of step with the rapidly changing world of global commerce. They did not cover many areas of trade such as intellectual property and services; they did not provide meaningful rules for important aspects of trade such as agriculture; and they did not bring about the prompt settlement of disputes. The old GATT rules also created unequal obligations among different countries, despite the fact that many of the countries that were allowed to keep their markets relatively closed were among the greatest beneficiaries of the system.

The successful conclusion of the Uruguay Round negotiations was an important part of President Clinton's strategy for strengthening the domestic economy. The President led the effort to reinvigorate the Uruguay Round and to break the gridlock that had stalled the negotiations despite several years of preparation and another seven years of negotiations.

The final result is a good deal for U.S. workers and companies. It helps us to bolster the competitiveness of key U.S. industries, to create jobs, to foster economic growth, to raise our standard of living, and to combat unfair foreign trade practices. The agreement will give the global economy a major boost, as the reductions in trade barriers create new export opportunities, and as the new rules give businesses greater confidence that export markets will remain open and that competition in foreign markets will be fair.

THE IMPORTANCE OF TRADE
TO THE UNITED STATES

The U.S. economy is now woven into the global economy. Where we once bought, sold, and produced almost entirely at home, we now participate fully in the global marketplace. By expanding our sales abroad, we create new jobs at home and we expand our own economy. The new world trade agreement will enable us to create new jobs in our most competitive industries. Trade (exports plus imports) is now equivalent to about a quarter of the value of what we produce as a nation—up from just 13 percent two decades ago. Trade benefits not only the company that exports, but also the company that produces parts incorporated in exported products, the insurance agency that insures exporters, and the drug store and the coffee shop near the exporter's factory. As a result of past trade negotiations, exports have consistently grown faster than domestic output since World War II. They have been a particularly important source of U.S. economic growth in the past few years.

In 1992, over 7 million workers in the U.S. owed their jobs to merchandise exports. Of those, roughly one-third were employed by industries directly producing merchandise for export; two-thirds were employed in jobs indirectly supported by exports. An additional 3.5 million U.S. workers owed their jobs to U.S. service exports.

Over 3.9 million workers were employed producing items used in the production of exported products, or capital goods needed to produce them. And nearly 1 million jobs were supported by trade in other ways—in a wide range of service jobs such as financing, hauling, wholesaling, and brokerage.

Jobs supported by exports are well paid; wages in export-related jobs are 17 percent higher than the U.S. average wage.

In addition to the more than 7 million U.S. jobs supported by merchandise exports, many other jobs are supported by exports of services. U.S. exports of services have been growing rapidly and have reached about 40 percent of the value of U.S. merchandise exports.

U.S. companies exporting goods and services are often limited by trade barriers that nations construct to protect local industries. Those barriers can be tariffs, which are taxes on goods entering a country, or non-tariff barriers, which are often rules, regulations, subsidies, or other unfair trading practices that distort and limit trade.

To the extent, then, that we reduce trade barriers around the world to U.S. exports of goods and services, we increase economic opportunities here at home for workers in all areas of the economy.

At the same time, increased access to foreign markets and increased competition at home benefit consumers. Lower trade barriers reduce prices, improve quality, and widen the choice of consumer goods. This benefits both families and companies looking for good bargains and high quality.

Major forces of change are sweeping the world. The United States must harness these forces, not hide behind walls. Prosperity is the partner of change, and Americans are at their best when facing new challenges. U.S. workers, the most productive in the world, will be better able to compete as these rules of trade go into effect.

HOW THE URUGUAY ROUND AGREEMENT BENEFITS AMERICANS

1. The Uruguay Round Agreement provides a needed boost to the world economy, which is currently stalled.

Well over 100 countries were engaged in the Uruguay Round negotiations, including the European Union and Japan as well as emerging economies in Latin America and Southeast Asia. The Uruguay Round will increase global trade and give the world economy, which is currently stalled, a major boost. This will in turn help the U.S. economy.

For some years now a global recession has slowed our own growth, leaving our economy performing below its potential. In expectation of the increased exports that will result from increased trade, companies are likely to build new plants and order new machinery. This will create many new jobs even in non-exporting industries such as construction, capital goods, and transportation. Our domestic growth is thus linked to the success—or failure—of the world economy.

2. The Uruguay Round Agreement helps ensure long-term U.S. economic growth.

The Uruguay Round achieved a more than one-third average reduction in tariffs on trade with our GATT partners around the world. Tariffs will be entirely eliminated in several industries in which the United States is highly competitive. In addition, many non-tariff barriers will be eliminated or reduced. This round of global trade negotiations, unlike the seven that preceded it, will expand export opportunities in services as well as goods, and in developing countries as well as in developed economies such as Japan and Western Europe.

The Uruguay Round will reduce barriers to exports in some of our most competitive industries. On average, every billion dollars of merchandise trade exports results in 16–17 thousand new jobs here at home—with higher than average wages.

These reductions in trade barriers and the resulting expansion of trade will have a dynamic effect on the U.S. economy. Both the new export opportunities and the increased competition that flow from lower tariffs will induce businesses to invest more, thus stimulating long-term economic growth. The increased competition will spur technological innovation which, in turn, will further add to growth.

Even before the Uruguay Round was completed, researchers had attempted to quantify its likely effects on the American economy. The existing estimates unanimously conclude that economic effects will be positive. All told, the Uruguay Round, when fully implemented, should add $100 billion to $200 billion to U.S. GDP annually.

U.S. workers will clearly benefit through greater job growth, higher real wages, and increased labor productivity. How these benefits will be apportioned between employment and wage increases is difficult to predict and depends on several factors. One study by DRI/McGraw-Hill, which drew from work done by USTR and the Council of Economic Advisors in 1990, estimated that the net U.S. employment gain (over and above normal growth of employment in the economy) will be 1.4 million jobs by the tenth year after implementation.

These are substantial gains to the U.S. economy, but the benefit could well be higher. The estimate did not take into account the reductions in barriers to trade in services or the improvements in trade rules, including better protection abroad for U.S. intellectual property rights.

3. The Uruguay Round Agreement benefits consumers by effectively raising incomes.

The lowering of tariffs will also result in lower consumer prices for imported products, which, of course, will benefit consumers. In addition, greater global competition will force domestic producers to become more efficient and to lower their prices, further benefitting consumers. And because the expansion of trade that will stem from the Uruguay Round will expand income, Americans will enjoy higher incomes and lower prices.

4. The Uruguay Round Agreement helps to level the playing field for U.S. farmers, businesses, and workers by strengthening trade rules.

The World Trade Organization will have much stronger trade rules than the GATT, thus enabling U.S. workers to compete with their foreign counterparts on more equal terms. Our markets are the most open in the world. We want to make sure foreign markets are as open to our companies as ours is to foreign companies.

5. The Uruguay Round Agreement ensures fair and prompt resolution of trade disputes.

Nations that trade with one another naturally have disputes from time to time. One criticism of the GATT has been that disputes take too long to resolve, and sometimes stay unresolved. Companies or workers injured when a GATT member country has broken a rule often waited in vain for an effective remedy. The new dispute settlement process under the WTO will eliminate the procedural delays that so often frustrated U.S. workers or firms. It sets deadlines for panel decisions and appeals. And it strengthens our ability to combat unfair trading practices by allowing "cross retaliation" when a country fails to modify its laws or regulations in response to a dispute settlement decision. "Cross retaliation" means that if a country is found guilty of committing an unfair practice in a certain sector, the United States can respond with a measure in another sector, allowing us to use the strongest means available to ensure that a country will implement its WTO obligations.

6. The Uruguay Round Agreement addresses environmental issues in international trade.

The Uruguay Round marks a first step toward recognizing the interdependence of economic and environmental goals in world trade rules. The preamble to the new World Trade Organization establishes sustainable development as a goal and recommends a work program to begin to deal with these issues. Moreover, by fostering greater efficiency and higher productivity, increased trade can actually reduce pollution by encouraging the growth of less polluting industries and the adoption and diffusion of cleaner technologies.

7. The Uruguay Round Agreement supports transitions to democracy.

The new trade agreement will support U.S. foreign policy goals by improving the export opportunities of formerly communist or authoritarian governments, thus facilitating their transition to democratic forms of government and market-oriented economic policies. Nations around the world are rejecting centralized political and economic systems. Many of the developing nations are renouncing inward-looking, protectionist policies, and are eager to become full and equal participants in the global trading system. The Uruguay Round agreement will ensure that they will become members of the new World Trade Organization on the basis of an agreed-upon set of rules.

WHAT THE URUGUAY ROUND ACCOMPLISHES IN KEY AREAS

Market Access: Expanding U.S. Exports, Jobs, and Growth

In an economy increasingly reliant on trade, opening up new markets is absolutely essential to creating jobs and growth.

Since World War II, international trade negotiations have lowered tariffs by about 85 percent, resulting in unprecedented export-led economic growth and ushering in an era of prosperity among the trading nations. Before the Uruguay Round, however, significant barriers remained.

The agreement on market access for goods will:

- eliminate tariffs in major industrial markets and significantly reduce or eliminate tariffs in many markets, in the following areas:
  - —Construction equipment   —Distilled spirits
  - —Agricultural equipment   —Beer
  - —Medical equipment   —Pharmaceuticals
  - —Steel   —Paper
  - —Furniture   —Toys
- make deep cuts ranging from 50 to 100 percent on important electronics items (such as semiconductors, computer parts, and semiconductor manufacturing equipment) by major U.S. trading partners;

- harmonize tariffs of developed and major developing countries in the chemical sector at very low rates (0, 5.5, and 6.5 percent); and,
- cut European tariffs on goods imported from the United States by over 50 percent.

Moreover, the Uruguay Round agreement will sharply limit the non-tariff barriers to imports—such as quotas and voluntary export restraints—that have often sprouted to replace falling tariffs.

Strengthened Global Trade Rules: Helping U.S. Companies and Workers Compete

The rules of the new World Trade Organization will help ensure that all WTO members play by the same rules. These new global trade rules will enable our companies and workers to compete on a more level playing field.

Specifically, the World Trade Organization will have more effective rules in the following areas:

- *Dispute Settlement.* A swift, sure, and effective mechanism to resolve trade disputes will ensure that the United States will have recourse to a speedy remedy when foreign countries violate international rules and raise new trade barriers.
- *Dumping.* Under the new rules, the United States retains its ability to take effective action against unfair dumping practices, while U.S. exporters are ensured fair application of anti-dumping laws by foreign countries. The United States was able to achieve these goals despite strong international pressure to weaken U.S. laws. Specifically, the new dumping agreement enhances transparency, permits the United States to discipline circumvention, allows for "cumulation" of imports to determine whether U.S. industry is injured, provides a deferential standard of review so U.S. decisions are not summarily overturned, and recognizes the right of unions to file petitions.
- *Subsidies.* The new agreement strengthens our ability to combat unfairly subsidized foreign products that compete against non-subsidized U.S. products, while preserving our ability to pursue pre-competitive research for initiatives like Sematech.
- *Import Safeguards.* New rules will enable the United States to take temporary actions against surges in imports without having to pay compensation. At the same time, the new rules will ensure that other countries will follow the same kind of objective and transparent procedures that the United States follows.

- *Product Standards*. Stronger, more comprehensive rules will ensure that product standards are not used to keep out imports, while allowing each country to set its own standards for the protection of human life, health, and the environment. The United States will not have to change any of its health and safety standards, because they are based on objective, scientific criteria and are not used as trade barriers.

Developing Countries: Full Participants in the New Global Trading System

Many developing nations, from Latin America to East Asia, have committed themselves in the Uruguay Round to accept more fully the market-oriented global trade rules of the WTO. This helps us, because developing countries buy nearly a third of U.S. exported goods and services—about $235 billion a year—and are our fastest growing export markets. This will also help them, because the more market-oriented policies and the reduced trade barriers will increase economic opportunities and raise income in these countries.

The Uruguay Round will more fully integrate developing countries into the world economy by:

- opening their markets to goods, services, and investment;
- committing them to following the same rules of fair, open trade as all other countries; and
- moving away from a system of obligations in which developing countries enjoy the benefits of the trading system without adhering to the rules.

Intellectual Property Rights: New Rules to Safeguard American Ingenuity

Creativity and innovation are among America's greatest strengths. American films, music, software, and medical advances are prized around the globe. The jobs of thousands of workers are dependent on the ability to sell these products abroad. Royalties from patents, copyrights, and trademarks are a growing source of foreign earnings to the U.S. economy. The U.S. victims of international piracy are a "who's who" of innovative industries: automakers and moviemakers; chemical and aviation companies; songwriters and software-writers; inventors of cellular telephones; and authors of books. The World Trade Organization will establish international rules to protect Americans from the global counterfeiting of their creations and innovations.

Strong intellectual property protection spurs innovation, which creates jobs and increases U.S. competitiveness. Whether you are a rock star, the developer of a new drug to help cure cancer, the author of new database management software, or a person employed to produce or sell such products—as many Americans increasingly are—the World Trade Organization will help ensure that the fruits of your creativity are protected around the world.

The agreement on Trade Related Intellectual Property establishes improved standards for the protection of intellectual property rights and provides for the effective enforcement of those standards.

In the area of copyrights, the new agreement resolves some key trade problems for U.S. software interests by protecting computer programs as literary works and databases as compilations under copyright. It also benefits motion picture and recording interests by giving them the right to authorize or prohibit the rental of their products and establishing a term of 50 years for the protection of sound recordings and motion pictures.

In the area of patents, the new agreement resolves long-standing trade irritants for key U.S. industries by protecting the product and process patents of virtually all types of inventions, including those in pharmaceuticals and chemicals, establishing meaningful limitations on the ability to impose compulsory licensing, and ensuring a patent term of 20 years.

In the area of trademarks, the new agreement requires member countries to register service marks in addition to trademarks and to provide enhanced protection for internationally well known marks. It also prohibits countries from adopting laws that would result in the mandatory linking of marks or the compulsory licensing of marks.

The new agreement also provides rules for protecting trade secrets, integrated circuits, and industrial designs.

Services: International Rules to Bolster a Key Part of Our Economy

The new World Trade Organization will extend fair trade rules to a sector that encompasses 50–60 percent of our economy and 70 percent of our jobs: services. Countries agreed to new rules in more than 150 service sectors and subsectors not previously covered by world trade rules. Industries such as advertising, law, accounting, information and computer services, environmental services, engineering, and tourism are a large and growing component of the U.S. economy. When a company makes a product, it needs financing, advertising, insurance, computer software, and so forth. Competition for these services is now global.

We lead the world in this sector with nearly $180 billion in exports annually. The World Trade Organization will implement new rules on trade in services, which will establish for the first time a set of clear, fair, and non-restrictive rules to:

- expand market opportunities for U.S. service providers by removing barriers to foreign trade in services;
- enable service firms to set up shop overseas and be treated as fairly as local firms;
- prevent governments from interfering in services trade through byzantine regulations that serve as *de facto* trade barriers; and,
- ensure that countries administer their laws and regulations in services in an open manner.

Eighty-nine governments have submitted a schedule of market access commitments in specific sectors, such as professional services (accounting, architecture, engineering), other business services (computer services, rental and leasing, advertising, market research, consulting, security services), communications (value-added telecommunications, couriers, audio-visual services), construction, distribution (wholesale and retail trade, franchising), educational services, environmental services, financial services (banking, securities, insurance), health services and tourism services.

Agriculture: Opening Markets for U.S. Exports

U.S. farmers are the envy of the world, but too often they have not been able to sell the products of their hard labor abroad, because the old GATT rules did not effectively limit agricultural trade barriers. Many countries have kept our farmers out of global markets by limiting imports and subsidizing exports. These same policies have raised prices for consumers around the world.

The Uruguay Round agreements will reform policies that distort the world agricultural market and international trade in farm products. By curbing policies that distort trade, the World Trade Organization will open up new trade opportunities for efficient and competitive agricultural producers like the United States.

The rules of the World Trade Organization will:

- reduce budgetary outlays for export subsidies by 36 percent and reduce the quantity of subsidized exports by 21 percent;
- lower market access barriers by converting all non-tariff barriers to tariffs and reducing these and existing tariffs by an average of 36 percent (with a minimum 15 percent cut for any particular product);
- open markets that had been closed off to U.S. goods. For example, for the first time, U.S. farmers will be able to sell rice in Japan and Korea on a regular basis;
- reduce trade-distorting internal support policies by 20 percent. The U.S. will not have to change any of its internal support programs because of

the substantial reductions made in the 1990 Food, Agriculture, Conservation and Trade Act and the recent budget reconciliation packages; and

- ensure that food health regulations are based on scientific evidence and are not used as trade barriers. This will not in any way force us to reduce our standards, since our regulations are solidly based on scientific research.

Reduced Trade Barriers: Removing Barriers Embodied in Foreign Investment Rules

The Uruguay Round agreement will reduce trade barriers associated with investment (such as local content rules) and prohibit regulations on investment that create new trade barriers. Reducing trade barriers associated with investment will help keep U.S. manufacturing jobs at home. At the same time, the new agreement will help U.S. businesses to expand and sell abroad in the most efficient way possible, by preventing foreign governments from telling them what they have to buy locally or what they have to export.

The Environment: Recognizing the Relationship Between Environmental and Trade Issues

When negotiators began the Uruguay Round discussions in 1986, there was little if any awareness of the link between environmental issues and trade issues. World leaders now agree that we must recognize the interdependence of economic and environmental goals in trade negotiations. Although environmental issues were not originally part of the Uruguay Round negotiations, the United States initiated discussions on the environment in the late stages of the negotiations. This led to new provisions that elevate the importance of the environment in trade negotiations.

Specifically, the new World Trade Organization will embrace the goal of promoting sustainable development; provide a more "transparent" dispute settlement process to protect our own efforts to preserve the environment, and establish a tangible commitment to a new initiative on trade and the environment.

Perhaps most importantly, there will be a comprehensive examination of the interaction between trade rules and environmental objectives. The WTO will create a Committee on Trade and Environment with a broad mandate, including the possibility of recommending changes to trade rules where necessary.

QUESTIONS AND ANSWERS

What Is the Uruguay Round?

In 1986, trade ministers from over 100 countries met in Punta Del Este, Uruguay. They set in motion negotiations aimed at the reduction of trade barriers, which were concluded on December 15, 1993. Specifically, the Uruguay Round agreements include:

- lower tariff and non-tariff barriers for manufactured products and other goods;
- rules to protect the intellectual property of U.S. entrepreneurs, entertainment industries, and software producers;
- new markets for U.S. firms producing services;
- fair competition and open markets in agriculture;
- the full participation of developing countries in the global trading system;
- effective rules on antidumping, subsidies, and import safeguards; and
- a dispute settlement system that will be speedy, cannot be blocked or delayed by the losing country, and will authorize "cross retaliation" retaliation in another country when its decisions are not promptly implemented.

What Is the World Trade Organization?

Following World War II, the major economic powers of the world, recognizing that high trade barriers hindered economic development and growth, created the General Agreement on Tariffs and Trade (GATT), a set of global rules for international trade. As a result of the Uruguay Round, these rules have been substantially expanded and improved, and extended to most trading nations on an equivalent basis. In light of the comprehensive nature of the new rules, responsibility for their enforcement has been given to a new World Trade Organization (WTO). These rules will substantially reduce foreign government practices that restrict trade. The WTO will also provide procedures for negotiating additional reductions of trade barriers and for the prompt and effective settlement of disputes in all of the policy areas covered by the new world trade agreement.

Does the U.S. Lose Sovereignty with the Round?

No. Nothing in the WTO relinquishes our sovereignty. The decision of the United States to enter into an agreement that expands trade and creates jobs is an exercise in sovereignty, not a surrender of it.

What does happen is that workers and companies around the world will compete on a level playing field, using the same rule book—and that will promote American economic growth and help protect American jobs.

How Do the Rules of the World Trade Organization Affect Our Health and Safety Standards?

Not at all. We will remain able to maintain the health and safety standards we believe are necessary. At the same time, the World Trade Organization will ensure that other nations cannot block our exports by using standards not based on scientific evidence.

How Does the World Trade Organization Affect the Environment?

When negotiators began the Uruguay Round discussions in 1986, there was no general awareness of the link between environmental issues and trade issues. World leaders now agree that we must recognize the interdependence of economic and environmental goals in trade policy.

The text establishing the World Trade Organization acknowledges the need to address environmental issues. The United States has proposed major initiatives on trade and the environment as a top priority for consideration by the WTO.

Thus, the World Trade Organization, which will create a Committee on Trade and Environment, will assist our efforts to protect our environment, and it will assist efforts to reach international agreement on environmental issues that affect the entire world, such as ozone depletion, global climate change and biodiversity.

Will There Be Job Loss as a Result of Increased Trade? What Will Happen to Workers That Lose Their Jobs?

Increased trade will result in *more* jobs for Americans. The new trade agreement will result in substantial job creation for the United States, but there will be some job dislocations. We must help those men and women who lose their jobs for whatever reason (defense conversion, corporate downsizing, etc.) The President is working to establish a program of worker retraining and adjustment, which is an essential element of his economic strategy.

How Will the New World Trade Agreement Affect Consumers?

The agreement will be a big plus for consumers. The substantial reductions in trade barriers will result in lower prices and greater variety of goods. From tropical nuts to French wines to Japanese stereo equipment, U.S. consumers will enjoy the benefit of greater availability of foreign products. At the same time, greater competition will lower prices on domestic products. This will benefit not only individual consumers buying clothing or food, but also businesses buying parts. That, in turn, will make those companies more competitive and help protect U.S. jobs.

How Is the New World Trade Agreement Different from the North American Free Trade Agreement (NAFTA)?

The NAFTA completely eliminates tariff and non-tariff barriers between the United States, Canada and Mexico over a 15-year period.

The new world trade agreement will lower trade barriers and eliminate some tariffs among well over 100 countries, including major U.S. trading partners, like the European Union and Japan. Unlike the NAFTA, it will not completely eliminate all barriers. Because so many more countries were involved, the new global trade agreement is more complex than NAFTA, but offers much greater potential to stimulate U.S.—and global—economic growth.

What Will Happen Next?

The agreement was signed in mid-April 1994. Once the United States and the other governments have ratified the agreements, they will go in effect, most likely in early 1995.

FOR MORE INFORMATION

Individuals interested in a more detailed summary of the Uruguay Round can obtain a copy of *The Executive Summary of the Uruguay Round of Multilateral Trade Negotiations* from the Office of the U.S. Trade Representative, 600 17th Street, N.W., Washington D.C., 20506, or by calling the Commerce Department's "Uruguay Round Hotline" at (800) USA-TRADE.

Seller and Purchaser Clauses for Foreign Trade

EXPORT CONTRACT TERMS AND CONDITIONS OF SALE*

1. GENERAL:

All quotations, offers to sell, proposals, acknowledgments and acceptances of orders by Seller are subject to the following terms and conditions, and acceptance by buyer is expressly limited to them.

2. CONTRACT OF SALE:

A binding contract of sale shall be entered into between buyer and seller, and shall become effective, upon the happening of any of the following:

(a) Buyer's written acceptance of a firm written proposal submitted by the seller;

(b) Seller's separate written acceptance of buyer's purchase order or other document furnished by purchaser;

*Courtesy of Bryan Sandler. This was taken from the Terms and Conditions of Sale for the Barry-Wehmiller Company, St. Louis, Mo., reprinted with their approval.

(c) Seller's acceptance of a sales agreement form prepared by Seller's authorized sales representative and executed by Buyer.

The contract of sale shall include all of the following terms and conditions. When the contract of sale is entered into by Seller's written acceptance of Buyer's purchase order or the document furnished by Buyer, Seller's acceptance is expressly limited to these terms and conditions, and any matters contained in any purchase order or other document furnished by Buyer which state terms additional to or which conflict with the following are deemed proposals for addition to the contract of sale, and do not become part of the contract of sale unless expressly and separately agreed to by Seller.

3. PRICES AND SPECIFICATIONS:

Prices and specifications quoted are valid for the stated period. Price quotations do not include any federal, state, local or other taxes, and Buyer agrees to pay or collect on account of the manufacture or sale of goods and performance of any services under this agreement. All licenses or other approvals required shall be obtained by Buyer, at Buyer's expense. Buyer shall promptly ship prepaid and without charge to Seller, for Seller's approval, Buyer's specified samples of containers and products to be handled by Seller's products. After the contract of sale becomes effective, specification changes requested by Buyer will be made only by separate written agreement, in which event the prices quoted in connection with the original specifications will be subject to change. Unless otherwise specified, Underwriters Laboratories approved electrical fixtures and electrical wiring are used, and wiring practices conform to the National Electric Code. Wiring to local standards will be furnished only if expressly incorporated in specifications and price quotations, accompanied by a copy of such local code.

4. SUPPLIES FOR DESIGN TESTING:

Buyer shall promptly ship prepaid and without obtaining Buyer's charge to Seller, for seller's approval, to make changes in the design and specifications of the Buyer's specified samples of containers, products sold hereunder, or of any component part, which changes do not affect the performance of the goods sold, and materials to be handled by Seller's products and other engineering information of Buyer required by the Seller for design and testing purposes.

5. NOTICE OF NON-CONFORMITY; BUYER'S REMEDIES:

Buyer shall give seller written notice of any claim for shortage, error, or other non-conformity of the products within thirty days after receipt at customer's designated delivery point, or be barred from any claim or remedy for such shortage, error, or other non-conformity. Except for warranty claims (which are governed exclusively by Section 8 below), Buyer's exclusive remedies for all claims arising out of the contract of sale shall be the right to return non-conforming products to Seller and, at Seller's option, to receive repayment of the purchase price or repair or replacement of non-conforming products or components.

6. WARRANTY

Seller warrants that the products sold hereunder are free from defects in material and workmanship when used in the manner and for the purposes for which designed, and in accordance with all instructions and directions for installation, operation and maintenance furnished by Seller, for a period of one year from receipt at customer's designated delivery point, or 2,000 hours of operation, whichever occurs earlier, subject to the following conditions:

(a) Buyer shall notify Seller in writing promptly upon discovery of facts giving rise to any claim under this warranty, stating specifically the nature of the claim, the date of the discovery of same and identifying by serial number and invoice the product involved. Failure to so notify Seller within ninety to one hundred eighty days after discovery of facts giving rise to the claim shall fully and completely relieve seller from any obligation under this warranty.
No claim under the terms of this warranty will be accepted by Seller unless and until the nature of the claim shall have been established to the satisfaction of an authorized representative of Seller, and no return of any product claimed to be defective will be accepted unless accompanied by a Returned Materials Authorization supplied by Seller. If a claim is accepted, Seller will issue a credit to Buyer against the invoiced price of repair or replacement. All returns shall be at Buyer's expense.

(b) Seller's obligations under this warranty are expressly limited to the repair replacement, at seller's option, of any defective products or components determined by Seller as aforesaid to be defective under the terms of this warranty, and do not extend to any damages arising from any alleged act or omission of Seller, beyond the invoiced price of any product or component that is found by Seller to be defective under the terms of this warranty. All other remedies are expressly excluded.

(c) This warranty applies only to products properly used and maintained and is expressly non-applicable to any products or components which have been repaired, altered or changed other than in accordance with instructions and directions furnished by Seller and its authorized representatives or to any product which has not been operated or utilized in accordance with instructions or directions furnished by Seller, or which has been operated or treated in any matter which, in the reasonable judgment of Seller, adversely affects its reliability and performance.

(d) This warranty does not apply to normal wear or consumable parts. This warranty also does not apply to any product or component not manufactured by the Seller, and Buyer's sole warranty with respect to such items shall be that of the manufacturer, if any.

(e) THIS WARRANTY COMPRISES THE ENTIRE AND SOLE WARRANTY PERTAINING TO THIS PURCHASE AND PRODUCTS SOLD HEREUNDER. SELLER MAKES NO OTHER REPRESENTATIONS, WARRANTIES OR GUARANTEES OF ANY KIND, INCLUDING BUT NOT LIMITED TO, MERCHANTABILITY AND FITNESS FOR PURPOSE, WHETHER EXPRESS, IMPLIED OR ARISING BY OPERATION OF LAW, TRADE USAGE OR COURSE OF DEALING EXCEPT AS SET FORTH HEREIN. ANY OTHER REPRESENTATIONS, STATEMENTS OR PROMISE WARRANTIES OR GUARANTEES MADE BY ANY PERSON ARE UNAUTHORIZED AND ARE NOT BINDING UPON SELLER UNLESS SEPARATELY SET FORTH IN WRITING. Any descriptions of the products and any specifications, samples, models, drawings, diagram, engineering sheets or similar material used in connection with this are for the sole purposes of identifying the products not to be construed as warranties, either express or implied.

7. REMEDIES OF SELLER:

The contract of sale shall be governed by the law of the State of Missouri, and Seller retains all rights under the applicable law in addition to those expressly provided for herein. Buyer agrees to execute any documents at Seller's request with respect to creation and perfection of a security interest in the goods sold. If Seller is required to employ attorneys or engage in any legal proceedings to enforce its rights hereunder, buyer agrees to pay Seller's reasonable attorney's fees, cost and expenses incurred in connection with such enforcement.

8. REMEDIES OF BUYER:

Buyer shall give Seller written notice of any claim for shortage or error within ten days after receipt at customer's designated delivery point, which is agreed to be a reasonable time for discovery and the giving of such notice, or be barred from any claim or remedy for such shortage or error. Other than as expressly provided herein, Buyer's exclusive remedies for all claims arising out of the contract of sale shall be the right to return non-conforming products to Seller, at Buyer's expense and, at Seller's option, to receive repayment of the purchase price or components.

9. APPLICABLE LAW

This contract shall be governed by the law of the State of Missouri and the Uniform Commercial Code.

EXPORT CONTRACT TERMS
AND CONDITIONS *OF PURCHASE**

1. GENERAL:

All quotations, offers to sell, proposals, acknowledgments and acceptances of orders by Buyer are subject to the following terms and conditions, and acceptance by buyer is expressly limited to them.

2. CONTRACT OF SALE:

A binding contract of sale shall be entered into between buyer and seller, and shall become effective, upon the happening of any of the following:

(a) Seller's written acceptance of a firm written proposal submitted by the Seller;

(b) Buyer's separate written acceptance of Seller's purchase order or other document furnished by purchaser;

(c) Buyer's acceptance of a sales agreement form prepared by seller's authorized sales representative and executed by Seller.

The contract of sale shall include all of the following terms and conditions When the contract of sale is entered into by Buyer's written acceptance of Seller's purchase order or the document furnished by buyer, seller's acceptance is expressly limited to these terms and conditions, and any matters contained in any purchase order or other document furnished by Buyer which state terms

*This was taken from the Terms and Conditions of Sale for the Barry-Wehmiller Company, St. Louis, Mo., reprinted with their approval.

additional to or which conflict with the following are deemed proposals for addition to the contract of sale, and do not become part of the contract of sale unless expressly and separately agreed to by Buyer.

3. PRICES AND SPECIFICATIONS:

Prices quoted are valid for the state period. Price quotations do include any federal, state, local and other taxes, and seller agrees to pay or collect on account of the manufacture or sale of goods and performance of any services under this agreement. After the contract of sale becomes effective, specification changes requested by seller will be made only by separate written agreement, in which event the prices quoted in connection with the original specifications will not be subject to change.

4. SUPPLIES FOR DESIGN TESTING:

Seller shall not be responsible for buyer's changes in the design and specifications of the Seller's specified samples of containers, products sold hereunder, or of any component part, which changes do not affect the performance of the goods sold, and materials to be handled by Buyer and other engineering information.

5. SELLER'S REMEDIES FOR NON-PERFORMANCE:

Seller's exclusive remedy for non-performance by the Buyer is the return of the goods then shipped, or the price thereof for such goods shipped, or the difference between the purchase price and the cover price incurred by Seller. This is the exclusive remedy for Seller, no other remedies will be available to Seller for breach by the buyer, including those given under the UCC and the Convention.

6. WARRANTY

Seller shall not be able to exclude any warranties or obligations under the UCC or the Convention, without the prior agreement, in writing signed by both parties, for the exclusion of any warranties. Any attempt to exclude any warranty or obligation by seller shall not be given effect.

7. REMEDIES OF BUYER:

The Buyer's remedies include but are not limited to those that are incurred because of Seller's breach, for seller's non-performance and all consequential and incidental damages, including, but not limited to, damages incurred by any loss in production, sale due to loss of production, and any and all other expenses incurred by Buyer due to Seller's non-performance. Any attempt to limit Buyer's remedies by the Seller shall not be given effect and will be considered a material term and a counter-offer under the Convention. Buyer shall also be allowed to determine that the contract is void upon its sole determination. Buyer shall also be able to have Seller specifically perform if Buyer so wishes.

8. APPLICABLE LAW

This contract shall be governed by the law of the State of Missouri and the Uniform Commercial Code.

United Nations Convention on Contracts for the International Sale of Goods: Official English Text

The following is the official English text of the United Nations Convention on Contracts for the International Sale of Goods. For a detailed legal analysis of the provisions, see Appendix E.

[Public Notice 1004]

U.S. Ratification of 1980 United Nations Convention on Contracts for the International Sale of Goods: Official English Text

On December 11, 1986 the United State deposited at United Nations Headquarters in New York its instrument of ratification of the 1980 U.N. Convention on Contracts for the International Sale of Goods. The United States did so jointly with China and Italy. The Convention will enter into force on January 1, 1988 between the United States and the following countries: Argentina, China, Egypt, France, Hungary, Lesotho, Syria, Yugoslavia and Zambia.

The Convention sets out substantive provisions of law to govern the formation of international sales contracts and the rights and obligations of the buyer and seller. It will apply to sales contracts between parties with their places of business in different countries bound by Convention, provided the parties have left their contracts silent as to applicable law. Parties are free to specify applicable law and to derogate from or vary the effect of provisions of the Convention. Certain types of sales and sales of certain types of goods are excluded from the

Convention's scope, and the Convention is not concerned with the validity of the contract. Part I of the Convention sets out its sphere of application and general provisions. For the Convention to be applicable the contract of sale need not be concluded in or evidenced by writing unless one of the parties has its place of business in a country that has made a reservation in this regard. The United States did not make this reservation. Article 100 deals with the Convention's applicability to sales contract formation and sales contracts themselves in relation to its entry into force.

United States ratification was coupled with a declaration that the United States would not be bound by Article 1(1)(b), which will have a narrowing effect on the sphere of application of the Convention.

Traders and their counsel are advised to study the Convention carefully in light of international sales and purchases involving parties in the above-mentioned countries and additional countries for which the Convention will eventually be entering into force.

The legal analysis that accompanied the Convention to the Senate and that relates its provisions to the corresponding provisions of the Sales Article of the Uniform Commercial Code may be found in 22 *International Legal Materials* 1368–80 (1984) (a bi-monthly publication of the American Society of International Law). A complete bibliography with citations to publications that reproduce the Convention text and legislative materials concerning the Convention, as well as secondary literature including books, symposia and law review articles, is to be published by Professor Peter Winship, Southern Methodist University School of Law, in the Spring 1987 issue of *The International Lawyer,* the law review published by the Section of International Law and Practice of the American Bar Association.

For the most current information about countries that have ratified or acceded to the Convention, write or phone the United Nations, which was designated as the depositor for the Convention: United Nations, Treaty Section, New York, N.Y. 10017 (212) 754 or 958/5048.

The Office of Treaty Affairs, Department of State, maintains records on multilateral treaties such as the 1980 Sales Convention that are based, in part, on information provided it by the United Nations. It updates that information and, on a monthly basis, publishes information in the *State Department Bulletin* about developments concerning treaties and conventions to which the United States is a party. The Department of State publication "Treaties in Force" annually lists all states parties to treaties and conventions to which the United States is a party, with the status as of January 1 of any given year, noting also whether a state may have made reservations when becoming a party.

The Department understands that a number of legal publications will be printing the text of the Convention and materials that accompanied it to the Senate, some listing countries becoming parties and any reservations or declarations to which their ratification may have been subject. These include: United

States Code Annotated, 1987 pocket part to 15 U.S.C.A. Appendix; Uniform Laws Annotated, Appendix to Uniform Commercial Code, with a reference to the Convention in connection with Article 2; United States Code Service in an Appendix at the end of Title 15; Martindale-Hubbell Law Directory in Volume VIII, Part VII: Selected International Conventions to which the United States is a party.

There is reproduced below a photocopy of the United Nations-certified English text of the Convention which traders and their counsel are encouraged to use, as typographical errors may be contained in any other published version of the text. It should be noted that the Arabic, Chinese, French, Russian and Spanish Convention texts have equal authenticity with the English text.

Peter H. Pfund,

Assistant Legal Adviser for Private International Law

UNITED NATIONS CONVENTION ON CONTRACTS FOR THE INTERNATIONAL SALE OF GOODS

The states parties to this Convention:

Bearing in mind the broad objectives in the resolutions adopted by the sixth special session of the General Assembly of the United Nations on the establishment of a New International Economic Order,

Considering that the development of international trade on the basis of equality and mutual benefit is an important element in promoting friendly relations among States,

Being of the Opinion that the adoption of uniform rules which govern contracts for the international sale of goods and take into account the different social, economic and legal systems would contribute to the removal of legal barriers in international trade and promote the development of international trade,

Have agreed as follows:

PART I—SPHERE OF APPLICATION AND GENERAL PROVISIONS

CHAPTER I—SPHERE OF APPLICATION

Article 1

(1) This Convention applies to contracts of sale of goods between parties whose places of business are in different States:

(a) When the States are Contracting States; or

(b) When the rules of private international law lead to the application of the law of a Contracting State.

(2) The fact that the parties have their places of business in different States

is to be disregarded whenever this fact does not appear either from the contract or from any dealings between, or from information disclosed by, the parties at any time before or at the conclusion of the contract.

(3) Neither the nationality of the parties nor the civil or commercial character of the parties or of the contract is to be taken into consideration in determining the application of this Convention.

Article 2

This Convention does not apply to sales:

(a) Of goods bought for personal, family or household use, unless the seller, at any time before or at the conclusion of the contract, neither knew nor ought to have known that the goods were bought for any such use;

(b) By auction;

(c) On execution or otherwise by authority of law;

(d) Of stocks, shares, investment securities, negotiable instruments or money;

(e) Of ships, vessels, hovercraft or aircraft;

(f) Of electricity.

Article 3

(1) Contracts for the supply of goods to be manufactured or produced are to be considered sales unless the party who orders the goods undertakes to supply a substantial part of the materials necessary for such manufacture or production.

(2) This Convention does not apply to contracts in which the preponderant part of the obligations of the party who furnishes the goods consists in the supply of labour or other services.

Article 4

This Convention governs only the formation of the contract of sale and the rights and obligations of the seller and the buyer arising from such a contract. In particular, except as otherwise expressly provided in this Convention, it is not concerned with:

(a) the validity of the contract or of any of its provisions or of any usage;

(b) the effect which the contract may have on the property in the goods sold.

Article 5

This Convention does not apply to the liability of the seller for death or personal injury caused by the goods to any person.

Article 6

The parties may exclude the application of this Convention or, subject to article 12, derogate from or vary the effect of any of its provisions.

CHAPTER II—GENERAL PROVISIONS

Article 7

(1) In the interpretation of this Convention, regard is to be had to its international character and to the need to promote uniformity in its application and the observance of good faith in international trade.

(2) Questions concerning matters governed by this Convention which are not expressly settled in it are to be settled in conformity with the general principles on which it is based or, in the absence of such principles, in conformity with the law applicable by virtue of the rules of private international law.

Article 8

(1) For the purposes of this Convention statements made by and other conduct of a party are to be interpreted according to his intent where the other party knew or could not have been unaware what that intent was.

(2) If the preceding paragraph is not applicable, statements made by and other conduct of a party are to be interpreted according to the understanding that a reasonable person of the same kind as the other party would have had in the same circumstances.

(3) In determining the intent of a party or the understanding a reasonable person would have had, due consideration is to be given to all relevant circumstances of the case including the negotiations, any practices which the parties have established between themselves, usages and any subsequent conduct of the parties.

Article 9

(1) The parties are bound by any usage to which they have agreed and by any practices which they have established between themselves.

(2) The parties are considered, unless otherwise agreed, to have impliedly made applicable to their contract or its formation a usage of which the parties knew or ought to have known and which in international trade is widely known to, and regularly observed by, parties to contracts of the type involved in the particular trade concerned.

Article 10

For the purposes of this Convention:

(a) If a party has more than one place of business, the place of business is that which has the closest relationship to the contract and its performance, having regard to the circumstances known to or contemplated by the parties at any time before or at the conclusion of the contract;

(b) If a party does not have a place of business, references are to be made to his habitual residence.

Article 11

A contract of sale need not be concluded in or evidenced by writing and is not subject to any other requirement as to form. It may be proved by any means, including witnesses.

Article 12

Any provision of article 11, article 29 or Part II of this Convention that allows a contract of sale or its modification or termination by agreement or any offer, acceptance or other indication of intention to be made in any form other than in writing does not apply where any party has his place of business in a Contracting State which has made a declaration under article 96 of this Convention. The parties may not derogate from or vary the effect of this article.

Article 13

For the purposes of this Convention "writing" includes telegram and telex.

PART II—FORMATION OF THE CONTRACT

Article 14

(1) A proposal for concluding a contract addressed to one or more specific persons constitutes an offer if it is sufficiently definite and indicates the intention of the offeror to be bound in case of acceptance. A proposal is sufficiently definite if it indicates the goods and expressly or implicitly fixes or makes provision for determining the quantity and the price.

(2) A proposal other than one addressed to one or more specific persons is to be considered merely as an invitation to make offers, unless the contrary is clearly indicated by the person making the proposal.

Article 15

(1) An offer becomes effective when it reaches the offeree.

(2) An offer, even if it is irrevocable, may be withdrawn if the withdrawal reaches the offeree before or at the same time as the offer.

Article 16

(1) Until a contract is concluded an offer may be revoked if the revocation reaches the offeree before he has dispatched an acceptance.

(2) However, an offer cannot be revoked:

(a) If it indicates, whether by stating a fixed time for acceptance or otherwise, that it is irrevocable; or

(b) If it was reasonable for the offeree to rely on the offer as being irrevocable and the offeree has acted in reliance on the offer.

Article 17

An offer, even if it is irrevocable, is terminated when a rejection reaches the offeror.

Article 18

(1) A statement made by or other conduct of the offeree indicating assent to an offer is an acceptance. Silence or inactivity does not in itself amount to acceptance.

(2) An acceptance of an offer becomes effective at the moment the indication of assent reaches the offeror. An acceptance is not effective if the indication of assent does not reach the offeror within the time he has fixed or, if no time is fixed, within a reasonable time, due account being taken of the circumstances of the transaction, including the rapidity of the means of communication employed by the offeror. An oral offer must be accepted immediately unless the circumstances indicate otherwise.

(3) However, if, by virtue of the offer or as a result of practices which the parties have established between themselves or of usage, the offeree may indicate assent by performing an act, such as one relating to the dispatch of the goods or payment of the price, without notice to the offeror, the acceptance is effective at the moment the act is performed, provided that the act is performed within the period of time laid down in the preceding paragraph.

Article 19

(1) A reply to an offer which purports to be an acceptance but contains additions, limitations or other modifications is a rejection of the offer and constitutes a counter-offer.

(2) However, a reply to an offer which purports to be an acceptance but contains additional or different terms which do not materially alter the terms of the offer constitutes an acceptance, unless the offeror, without undue delay, objects orally to the discrepancy or dispatches a notice to that effect. If he does not so object, the terms of the contract are the terms of the offer with the modifications contained in the acceptance.

(3) Additional or different terms relating, among other things, to the price, payment, quality and quantity of the goods, place and time of delivery, extent of

one party's liability to the other or the settlement of disputes are considered to alter the terms of the offer materially.

Article 20

(1) A period of time for acceptance fixed by the offeror in a telegram or a letter begins to run from the moment the telegram is handed in for dispatch or from the date shown on the letter or, if no such date is shown, from the date shown on the envelope. A period of time for acceptance fixed by the offeror by telephone, telex or other means of instantaneous communication, begins to run from the moment that the offer reaches the offeree.

(2) Official holidays or non-business days occurring during the period for acceptance are included in calculating the period. However, if a notice of acceptance cannot be delivered at the address of the offeror on the last day of the period because that day falls on an official holiday or a non-business day at the place of business of the offeror, the period is extended until the first business day which follows.

Article 21

(1) A late acceptance is nevertheless effective as an acceptance if without delay the offeror orally so informs the offeree or dispatches a notice to that effect.

(2) If a letter or other writing containing a late acceptance shows that it has been sent in such circumstances that if its transmission had been normal it would have reached the offeror in due time, the late acceptance is effective as an acceptance unless, without delay, the offeror orally informs the offeree that he considers his offer as having lapsed or dispatches a notice to that effect.

Article 22

An acceptance may be withdrawn if the withdrawal reaches the offeror before or at the same time as the acceptance would have become effective.

Article 23

A contract is concluded at the moment when an acceptance of an offer becomes effective in accordance with the provisions of this Convention.

Article 24

For the purposes of this Part of the Convention, an offer, declaration of acceptance or any other indication of intention "reaches" the addressee when it is made orally to him or delivered by any other means to him personally, to his place of business or mailing address, or if he does not have a place of business or mailing address, to his habitual residence.

PART III—SALE OF GOODS

CHAPTER I—GENERAL PROVISIONS

Article 25

A breach of contract committed by one of the parties is fundamental if it results in such detriment to the other party as substantially to deprive him of what he is entitled to expect under the contract, unless the party in breach did not foresee and a reasonable person of the same kind in the same circumstances would not have foreseen such a result.

Article 26

A declaration of avoidance of the contract is effective only if made by notice to the other party.

Article 27

Unless otherwise expressly provided in this Part of the Convention, if any notice, request or other communication is given or made by a party in accordance with this Part and by means appropriate in the circumstances, a delay or error in the transmission of the communication or its failure to arrive does not deprive that party of the right to rely on the communication.

Article 28

If, in accordance with the provisions of this Convention, one party is entitled to require performance of any obligation by the other party, a court is not bound to enter a judgment for specific performance unless the court would do so under its own law in respect of similar contracts of sale not governed by this Convention.

Article 29

(1) A contract may be modified or terminated by the mere agreement of the parties.

(2) A contract in writing which contains a provision requiring any modification or termination by agreement to be in writing may not be otherwise modified or terminated by agreement. However, a party may be precluded by his conduct from asserting such a provision to the extent that the other party has relied on that conduct.

CHAPTER II—OBLIGATIONS OF THE SELLER

Article 30

The seller must deliver the goods, hand over any documents relating to them and transfer the property in the goods, as required by the contract and this Convention.

Section I. Delivery of the Goods and Handing Over of Documents

Article 31

If the seller is not bound to deliver the goods at any other particular place, his obligation to deliver consists:

(a) If the contract of sale involves carriage of the goods—in handing the goods over to the first carrier for transmission to the buyer;

(b) If, in cases not within the preceding subparagraph, the contract relates to specific goods, or unidentified goods to be drawn from a specific stock or to be manufactured or produced, and at the time of the conclusion of the contract the parties knew that the goods were at, or were to be manufactured or produced at, a particular place—in placing the goods at the buyer's disposal at that place;

(c) In other cases—in placing the goods at the buyer's disposal at the place where the seller had his place of business at the time of the conclusion of the contract.

Article 32

(1) If the seller, in accordance with the contract or his Convention, hands the goods over to a carrier and if the goods are not clearly identified to the contract by markings on the goods, by shipping documents or otherwise, the seller must give the buyer notice of the consignment specifying the goods.

(2) If the seller is bound to arrange for carriage of the goods, he must make such contracts as are necessary for carriage to the place fixed by means of transportation appropriate in the circumstances and according to the usual terms for such transportation.

(3) If the seller is not bound to affect insurance in respect of the carriage of the goods, he must, at the buyer's request, provide him with all available information necessary to enable him to affect such insurance.

Article 33

The seller must deliver the goods:

(a) If a date is fixed by or determinable from the contract, on that date;

(b) If a period of time is fixed by or determinable from the contract, at any time within that period unless circumstances indicate that the buyer is to choose a date; or

(c) In any other case, within a reasonable time after the conclusion of the contract.

Article 34

If the seller is bound to hand over documents relating to the goods, he must hand them over at the time and place and in the form required by the contract. If the seller has handed over documents before that time, he may, up to that time, cure any lack of conformity in the documents, if the exercise of this right does not cause the buyer unreasonable inconvenience or unreasonable expense. However, the buyer retains any right to claim damages as provided for in this Convention.

Section II. Conformity of the Goods and Third Party Claims

Article 35

(1) The seller must deliver goods which are of the quantity, quality and description required by the contract and which are contained or packaged in the manner required by the contract.

(2) Except where the parties have agreed otherwise, the goods do not conform with the contract unless they:

(a) Are fit for the purposes for which goods of the same description would ordinarily be used;

(b) Are fit for any particular purpose expressly or impliedly made known to the seller at the time of the conclusion of the contract, except where the circumstances show that the buyer did not rely, or that it was unreasonable for him to rely, on the seller's skill and judgment;

(c) Possess the qualities of goods which the seller has held out to the buyer as a sample or model;

(d) Are contained or packaged in the manner usual for such goods or, where there is no such manner, in a manner adequate to preserve and protect the goods.

(3) The seller is not liable under subparagraphs (a) to (d) of the preceding paragraph for any lack of conformity of the goods if at the time of the conclusion of the contract the buyer knew or could not have been unaware of such lack of conformity.

Article 36

(1) The seller is liable in accordance with the contract and this Convention for any lack of conformity which exists at the time when the risk passes to the buyer, even though the lack of conformity becomes only after that time.

(2) The seller is also liable for any lack of conformity which occurs after the time indicated in the preceding paragraph and which is due to a breach of

any of his obligations, including a breach of any guarantee that for a period of time the goods will remain fit for their ordinary purpose or for some particular purpose or will retain specified qualities or characteristics.

Article 37

If the seller has delivered goods before the date for delivery, he may, up to that date, deliver any missing part or make up any deficiency in the quantity of the goods delivered, or deliver goods in replacement of any non-conforming goods delivered or remedy any lack of conformity in the goods delivered, provided that the exercise of this right does not cause the buyer unreasonable inconvenience or unreasonable expense. However, the buyer retains any right to claim damages as provided for in this Convention.

Article 38

(1) The buyer must examine the goods, or cause them to be examined, within as short a period as is practicable in the circumstances.

(2) If the contract involves carriage of the goods, examination may be deferred until after the goods have arrived at their destination.

(3) If the goods are redirected in transit or redispatched by the buyer without a reasonable opportunity for examination by him and at the time of the conclusion of the contract the seller knew or ought to have known of the possibility of such redirection or redispatch, examination may be deferred until after the goods have arrived at the new destination.

Article 39

(1) The buyer loses the right to rely on a lack of conformity of the goods if he does not give notice to the seller specifying the nature of the lack of conformity within a reasonable time after he has discovered it or ought to have discovered it.

(2) In any event, the buyer loses the right to rely on a lack of conformity of the goods if he does not give the seller notice thereof at the latest within a period of two years from the date on which the goods were actually handed over to the buyer, unless this time-limit is inconsistent with a contractual period of guarantee.

Article 40

The seller is not entitled to rely on the provisions of articles 38 and 39 if the lack of conformity relates to facts of which he knew or could not have been unaware and which he did not disclose to the buyer.

Article 41

The seller must deliver goods which are free from any right or claim of a third party, unless the buyer agreed to take the goods subject to that right or claim. However, if such right or claim is based on industrial property or other intellectual property, the seller's obligation is governed by article 42.

Article 42

(1) The seller must deliver goods which are free from any right or claim of a third party based on industrial property or other intellectual property, of which at the time of the conclusion of the contract the seller knew or could not have been unaware, provided that the right or claim is based on industrial property or other intellectual property:

(a) Under the law of the State where the goods will be resold or otherwise used, if it was contemplated by the parties at the time of the conclusion of the contract that the goods would be resold or otherwise used in that State; or

(b) In any other case, under the law of the State where the buyer has his place of business.

(2) The obligation of the seller under the preceding paragraph does not extend to cases where:

(a) At the time of the conclusion of the contract the buyer knew or could not have been unaware of the right or claim; or

(b) The right or claim results from the seller's compliance with technical drawings, designs, formulae or other such specifications furnished by the buyer.

Article 43

(1) The buyer loses the right to rely on the provisions of article 41 or article 42 if he does not give notice to the seller specifying the nature of the right or claim of the third party within a reasonable time after he has become aware or ought to have become aware of the right or claim.

(2) The seller is not entitled to rely on the provisions of the preceding paragraph if he knew of the right or claim of the third party and the nature of it.

Article 44

Notwithstanding the provisions of paragraph (1) of article 39 and paragraph (1) of article 43, the buyer may reduce the price in accordance with article 50 or claim damages except for loss of profit, if he has a reasonable excuse for his failure to give the required notice.

Section III. Remedies for Breach of Contract by the Seller

Article 45

(1) If the seller fails to perform any of his obligations under the contract or this Convention, the buyer may:

(a) Exercise the rights provided in articles 46 to 52;

(b) Claim damages as provided in articles 74 to 77.

(2) The buyer is not deprived of any right he may have to claim damages by exercising his right to other remedies.

(3) No period of grace may be granted to the seller by a court or arbitral tribunal when the buyer resorts to a remedy for breach of contract.

Article 46

(1) The buyer may require performance by the seller of his obligations unless the buyer has resorted to a remedy which is inconsistent with this requirement.

(2) If the goods do not conform with the contract, the buyer may require delivery of substitute goods only if the lack of conformity constitutes a fundamental breach of contract and a request for substitute goods is made either in conjunction with notice given under article 39 or within a reasonable time thereafter.

(3) If the goods do not conform with the contract, the buyer may require the seller to remedy the lack of conformity by repair, unless this is unreasonable having regard to all the circumstances. A request for repair must be made either in conjunction with notice given under article 39 or within a reasonable time thereafter.

Article 47

(1) The buyer may fix an additional period of time of reasonable length for performance by the seller of his obligations.

(2) Unless the buyer has received notice from the seller that he will not perform within the period so fixed, the buyer may not, during that period, resort to any remedy for breach of contract. However, the buyer is not deprived thereby of any right he may have to claim damages for delay in performance.

Article 48

(1) Subject to article 49, the seller may, even after the date for delivery, remedy at his own expense any failure to perform his obligations, if he can do so without unreasonable delay and without causing the buyer unreasonable inconvenience or uncertainty of reimbursement by the seller of expenses advanced by the buyer. However, the buyer retains any right to claim damages as provided for in this Convention.

(2) If the seller requests the buyer to make known whether he will accept performance and the buyer does not comply with the request within a reason-

able time, the seller may perform within the time indicated in his request. The buyer may not, during that period of time, resort to any remedy which is inconsistent with performance by the seller.

(3) A notice by the seller that he will perform within a specified period of time is assumed to include a request, under the preceding paragraph, that the buyer make known his decision.

(4) A request or notice by the seller under paragraph (2) or (3) of this article is not effective unless received by the buyer.

Article 49

(1) The buyer may declare the contract avoided:

(a) If the failure by the seller to perform any of his obligations under the contract or this Convention amounts to a fundamental breach of contract; or

(b) In case of non-delivery, if the seller does not deliver the goods within the additional period of time fixed by the buyer in accordance with paragraph (1) of article 47 or declares that he will not deliver within the period so fixed.

(2) However, in cases where the seller has delivered the goods, the buyer loses the right to declare the contract avoided unless he does so:

(a) In respect of late delivery, within a reasonable time after he has become aware that delivery has been made;

(b) In respect of any breach other than late delivery, within a reasonable time:

(i) After he knew or ought to have known of the breach;

(ii) After the expiration of any additional period of time fixed by the buyer in accordance with paragraph (1) of article 47, or after the seller has declared that he will not perform his obligations within such an additional period; or

(iii) After the expiration of any additional period of time indicated by the seller in accordance with paragraph (2) of article 48, or after the buyer has declared that he will not accept performance.

Article 50

If the goods do not conform with the contract and whether or not the price has already been paid, the buyer may reduce the price in the same proportion as the value that the goods actually delivered had at the time of the delivery bears to the value that conforming goods would have had at that time. However, if the seller remedies any failure to perform his obligations in accordance with article 37 or article 48 or if the buyer refuses to accept performance by the seller in accordance with those articles, the buyer may not reduce the price.

Article 51

(1) If the seller delivers only a part of the goods or if only a part of the goods delivered is in conformity with the contract, articles 46 to 50 apply in respect of the part which is missing or which does not conform.

(2) The buyer may declare the contract avoided in its entirety only if the failure to make delivery completely or in conformity with the contract amounts to a fundamental breach of the contract.

Article 52

(1) If the seller delivers the goods before the date fixed, the buyer may take delivery or refuse to take delivery.

(2) If the seller delivers a quantity of goods greater than that provided for in the contract, the buyer may take delivery or refuse to take delivery of the excess quantity. If the buyer takes delivery of all or part or the excess quantity, he must pay for it at the contract rate.

CHAPTER III—OBLIGATIONS OF THE BUYER

Article 53

The buyer must pay the price for the goods and take delivery of them as required by the contract and this Convention.

Section I. Payment of the Price

Article 54

The buyer's obligation to pay the price includes taking such steps and complying with such formalities as may be required under the contract or any laws and regulations to enable payment to be made.

Article 55

Where a contract has been validly concluded but does not expressly or implicitly fix or make provision for determining the price, the parties are considered, in the absence of any indication to the contrary, to have impliedly made reference to the price generally charged at the time of the conclusion of the contract for such goods sold under comparable circumstances in the trade concerned.

Article 56

If the price is fixed according to the weight of the goods, in case of doubt it is to be determined by the net weight.

Article 57

(1) If the buyer is not bound to pay the price at any other particular place, he must pay it to the seller:

(a) At the seller's place of business; or

(b) If the payment is to be made against the handing over of the goods or of documents, at the place where the handing over takes place.

(2) The seller must bear any increase in the expenses incidental to payment which is caused by a change in his place of business subsequent to the conclusion of the contract.

Article 58

(1) If the buyer is not bound to pay the price at any other specific time, he must pay it when the seller places either the goods or documents controlling their disposition at the buyer's disposal in accordance with the contract and this Convention. The seller may make such payment a condition for handing over the goods or documents.

(2) If the contract involves carriage of the goods, the seller may dispatch the goods on terms whereby the goods, or documents controlling their disposition, will not be handed over to the buyer except against payment of the price.

(3) The buyer is not bound to pay the price until he has had an opportunity to examine the goods, unless the procedures for delivery or payment agreed upon by the parties are inconsistent with his having such an opportunity.

Article 59

The buyer must pay the price on the date fixed by or determinable from the contract and this Convention without the need for any request or compliance with any formality on the part of the seller.

Section II. Taking Delivery

Article 60

The buyer's obligation to take delivery consists:

(a) In doing all the acts which could reasonably be expected of him in order to enable the seller to make delivery; and

(b) In taking over the goods.

Section III. Remedies for Breach of Contract by the Buyer

Article 61

(1) If the buyer fails to perform any of his obligations under the contract or this Convention, the seller may:

(a) Exercise the rights provided in articles 62 to 65;

(b) Claim damages as provided in articles 74 to 77.

(2) The seller is not deprived of any right he may have to claim damages by exercising his right to other remedies.

(3) No period of grace may be granted to the buyer by a court or arbitral tribunal when the seller resorts to a remedy for breach of contract.

Article 62

The seller may require the buyer to pay the price, take delivery or perform his other obligations, unless the seller has resorted to a remedy which is inconsistent with this requirement.

Article 63

(1) The seller may fix an additional period of time of reasonable length for performance by the buyer of his obligations.

(2) Unless the seller has received notice from the buyer that he will not perform within the period so fixed, the seller may not, during that period, resort to any remedy for breach of contract. However, the seller is not deprived thereby of any right he may have to claim damages for delay in performance.

Article 64

(1) The seller may declare the contract avoided:

(a) If the failure by the buyer to perform any of his obligations under the contract or this Convention amounts to a fundamental breach of contract; or

(b) If the buyer does not, within the additional period of time fixed by the seller in accordance with paragraph (1) of article 63, perform his obligation to pay the price or take delivery of the goods, or if he declares that he will not do so within the period so fixed.

(2) However, in cases where the buyer has paid the price, the seller loses the right to declare the contract avoided unless he does so:

(a) In respect of late performance by the buyer, before the seller has become aware that performance has been rendered; or

(b) In respect of any breach other than late performance by the buyer, within a reasonable time:

(i) After the seller knew or ought to have known of the breach; or

(ii) After the expiration of any additional period of time fixed by the seller in accordance with paragraph (1) of article 63, or after the buyer has declared that he will not perform his obligations within such an additional period.

Article 65

(1) If under the contract the buyer is to specify the form, measurement or other features of the goods and he fails to make such specification either on the date agreed upon or within a reasonable time after receipt of a request from the seller, the seller may, without prejudice to any other rights he may have, make the specification himself in accordance with the requirements of the buyer that may be known to him.

(2) If the seller makes the specification himself, he must inform the buyer of the details thereof and must fix a reasonable time within which the buyer may make a different specification. If, after receipt of such a communication, the buyer fails to do so within the time so fixed, the specification made by the seller is binding.

CHAPTER IV—PASSING OF RISK

Article 66

Loss of or damage to the goods after the risk has passed to the buyer does not discharge him from his obligation to pay the price, unless the loss or damage is due to an act or omission of the seller.

Article 67

(1) If the contract of sale involves carriage of the goods and the seller is not bound to hand them over at a particular place, the risk passes to the buyer when the goods are handed over to the first carrier for transmission to the buyer in accordance with the contract of sale. If the seller is bound to hand the goods over to a carrier at a particular place, the risk does not pass to the buyer until the goods are handed over to the carrier at that place. The fact that the seller is authorized to retain documents controlling the disposition of the goods does not affect the passage of the risk.

(2) Nevertheless, the risk does not pass to the buyer until the goods are clearly identified to the contract, whether by markings on the goods, by shipping documents, by notice given to the buyer or otherwise.

Article 68

The risk in respect of goods sold in transit passes to the buyer from the time of the conclusion of the contract. However, if the circumstances so indicate, the risk is assumed by the buyer from the time the goods were handed over to the carrier who issued the documents embodying the contract of carriage. Nevertheless, if at the time of the conclusion of the contract of sale the seller knew or ought to have known that the goods had been lost or damaged and did not disclose this to the buyer, the loss or damage is at the risk of the seller.

Article 69

(1) In cases not within articles 67 and 68, the risk passes to the buyer when he takes over the goods, or if he does not do so in due time, from the time when the goods are placed at his disposal and he commits a breach of contract by failing to take delivery.

(2) However, if the buyer is bound to take over the goods at a place other than a place of business of the seller, the risk passes when delivery is due and the buyer is aware of the fact that the goods are placed at his disposal at that place.

(3) If the contract relates to goods not then identified, the goods are considered not to be placed at the disposal of the buyer until they are clearly identified to the contract.

Article 70

If the seller has committed a fundamental breach of contract, articles 67, 68 and 69 do not impair the remedies available to the buyer on account of the breach.

CHAPTER V—PROVISIONS COMMON TO THE OBLIGATIONS OF THE SELLER AND OF THE BUYER

Section I. Anticipatory Breach and Installment Contracts

Article 71

(1) A party may suspend the performance of his obligations if, after the conclusion of the contract, it becomes apparent that the other party will not perform a substantial part of his obligations as a result of:

(a) A serious deficiency in his ability to perform or in his creditworthiness; or

(b) His conduct in preparing to perform or in performing the contract.

(2) If the seller has already dispatched the goods before the grounds described in the preceding paragraph become evident, he may prevent the handing over of the goods to the buyer even though the buyer holds a document which entitles him to obtain them. The present paragraph relates only to the rights in the goods as between the buyer and the seller.

(3) A party suspending performance, whether before or after dispatch of the goods, must immediately give notice of the suspension to the other party and must continue with performance if the other party provides adequate assurance of his performance.

Article 72

(1) If prior to the date for performance of the contract it is clear that one of the parties will commit a fundamental breach of contract, the other party may declare the contract avoided.

(2) If time allows, the party intending to declare the contract avoided must give reasonable notice to the other party in order to permit him to provide adequate assurance of his performance.

(3) The requirements of the preceding paragraph do not apply if the other party has declared that he will not perform his obligations.

Article 73

(1) In the case of a contract for delivery of goods by installments, if the failure of one party to perform any of his obligations in respect of any installment constitutes a fundamental breach of contract with respect to that installment, the other party may declare the contract avoided with respect to that installment.

(2) If one party's failure to perform any of his obligations in respect of any installment gives the other party good grounds to conclude that a fundamental breach of contract will occur with respect to future installments, he may declare the contract avoided for the future, provided that he does so within a reasonable time.

(3) A buyer who declares the contract avoided in respect of any delivery may, at the same time, declare it avoided in respect of deliveries already made or of future deliveries if, by reason of their interdependence, those deliveries could not be used for the purpose contemplated by the parties at the time of the conclusion of the contract.

Section II. Damages

Article 74

Damages for breach of contract by one party consist of a sum equal to the loss, including loss of profit, suffered by the other party as a consequence of the breach. Such damages may not exceed the loss which the party in breach foresaw or ought to have foreseen at the time of the conclusion of the contract, in the light of the facts and matters of which he then knew or ought to have known, as a possible consequence of the breach of contract.

Article 75

If the contract is avoided and if, in a reasonable manner and within a reasonable time after avoidance, the buyer has bought goods in replacement or the seller has resold the goods, the party claiming damages may recover the difference between the contract price and the price in the substitute transaction as well as any further damages recoverable under article 74.

Article 76

(1) If the contract is avoided and there is a current price for the goods, the party claiming damages may, if he has not made a purchase or resale under article 75, recover the difference between the price fixed by the contract and the current price at the time of avoidance as well as any further damages recoverable under article 74. If, however, the party claiming damages has avoided the contract after taking over the goods, the current price at the time of such taking over shall be applied instead of the current price at the time of avoidance.

(2) For the purposes of the preceding paragraph, the current price is the price prevailing at the place where delivery of the goods should have been made or, if there is no current price at that place, the price at such other place as serves as a reasonable substitute, making due allowance for differences in the cost of transporting the goods.

Article 77

A party who relies on a breach of contract must take such measures as are reasonable in the circumstances to mitigate the loss, including loss of profit, resulting from the breach. If he fails to take such measures, the party in breach may claim a reduction in the damages in the amount by which the loss should have been mitigated,

Section III. Interest

Article 78

If a party fails to pay the price or any other sum that is in arrears, the other party is entitled to interest on it, without prejudice to any claim for damages recoverable under article 74.

Section IV. Exemptions

Article 79

(1) A party is not liable for a failure to perform any of his obligations if he proves that the failure was due to an impediment beyond his control and that he could not reasonably be expected to have taken the impediment into account at the time of the conclusion of the contract or to have avoided or overcome it, or its consequences.

(2) If the party's failure is due to the failure by a third person whom he has engaged to perform the whole or a part of the contract, that party is exempt from liability only if:

(a) He is exempt under the preceding paragraph; and

(b) The person whom he has so engaged would be so exempt if the provisions of that paragraph were applied to him.

(3) The exemption provided by this article has effect for the period during which the impediment exists.

(4) The party who fails to perform must give notice to the other party of the impediment and its effect on his ability to perform. If the notice is not received by the other party within a reasonable time after the party who fails to perform knew or ought to have known of the impediment, he is liable for damages resulting from such non-receipt.

(5) Nothing in this article prevents either party from exercising any right other than to claim damages under this Convention.

Article 80

A party may not rely on a failure of the other party to perform, to the extent that such failure was caused by the first party's act or omission.

Section V. Effects of Avoidance

Article 81

(1) Avoidance of the contract releases both parties from their obligations under it, subject to any damages which may be due. Avoidance does not affect any provision of the contract for the settlement of disputes or any other provision of the contract governing the rights and obligations of the parties consequent upon the avoidance of the contract.

(2) A party who has performed the contract either wholly or in party may claim restitution from the other party of whatever the first party has supplied or paid under the contract. If both parties are bound to make restitution, they must do so concurrently.

Article 82

(1) The buyer loses the right to declare the contract avoided or to require the seller to deliver substitute goods if it is impossible for him to make restitution of the goods substantially in the condition in which he received them.

(2) The preceding paragraph does not apply:

(a) If the impossibility of making restitution of the goods or of making restitution of the goods substantially in the condition in which the buyer received them is not due to his act or omission;

(b) If the goods or part of the goods have perished or deteriorated as a result of the examination provided for in article 38; or

(c) If the goods or part of the goods have been sold in the normal course of business or have been consumed or transformed by the buyer in the course of normal use before he discovered or ought to have discovered the lack of conformity.

Article 83

A buyer who has lost the right to declare the contract avoided or to require the seller to deliver substitute goods in accordance with article 82 retains all other remedies under the contract and this Convention.

Article 84

(1) If the seller is bound to refund the price, he must also pay interest on it, from the date on which the price was paid.

(2) The buyer must account to the seller for all benefits which he has derived from the goods or part of them:

(a) If he must make restitution of the goods or part of them; or

(b) If it is impossible for him to make restitution of all or part of the goods or to make restitution of all or part of the goods substantially in the condition in which he received them, but he has nevertheless declared the contract avoided or required the seller to deliver substitute goods.

Section VI. Preservation of the Goods

Article 85

If the buyer is in delay in taking delivery of the goods, or where payment of the price and delivery of the goods are to be made concurrently, if he fails to pay the price, and the seller is either in possession of the goods or otherwise able to control their disposition, the seller must take such steps as are reasonable in the circumstances to preserve them. He is entitled to retain them until he has been reimbursed his reasonable expenses by the buyer.

Article 86

(1) If the buyer has received the goods and intends to exercise any right under the contract or this Convention to reject them, he must take such steps to preserve them as are reasonable in the circumstances. He is entitled to retain them until he has been reimbursed his reasonable expenses by the seller.

(2) If goods dispatched to the buyer have been placed at his disposal at their destination and he exercises the right to reject them, he must take possession of them on behalf of the seller, provided that this can be done without pay-

ment of the price and without unreasonable inconvenience or unreasonable expense. This provision does not apply if the seller or a person authorized to take charge of the goods on his behalf is present at the destination. If the buyer takes possession of the goods under this paragraph, his rights and obligations are governed by the preceding paragraph.

Article 87

A party who is bound to take steps to preserve the goods may deposit them in a warehouse of a third person at the expense of the other party provided that the expense incurred is not unreasonable.

Article 88

(1) A party who is bound to preserve the good in accordance with article 85 or 86 may sell them by any appropriate means if there has been an unreasonable delay by the other party in taking possession of the goods or in taking them back or in paying the price or the cost of preservation, provided that reasonable notice of the intention to sell has been given to the other party.

(2) If the goods are subject to rapid deterioration or their preservation would involve unreasonable expense, a party who is bound to preserve the goods in accordance with article 85 or 86 must take reasonable measures to sell them. To the extent possible he must give notice to the other party of his intention to sell.

(3) A party selling the goods has the right to retain out of the proceeds of sale an amount equal to the reasonable expenses of preserving the goods and of selling them. He must account to the other party for the balance.

PART IV—FINAL PROVISIONS

Article 89

The Secretary-General of the United Nations is hereby designated as the depositary for this Convention.

Article 90

This Convention does not prevail over any international agreement which has already been or may be entered into and which contains provisions concerning the matters governed by this Convention, provided that the parties have their places of business in States parties to such agreement.

Article 91

(1) This Convention is open for signature at the concluding meeting of the United Nations Conference of Contracts for the International Sale of Goods and will remain open for signature by all States at the Headquarters of the United Nations, New York until 30 September 1981.

(2) This Convention is subject to ratification, acceptance or approval by the signatory States.

(3) This Convention is open for accession by all States which are not signatory States as from the date it is open for signature.

(4) Instruments of ratification, acceptance, approval and accession are to be deposited with the Secretary-General of the United Nations.

Article 92

(1) A Contracting State may declare at the time of signature, ratification, acceptance, approval or accession that it will not be bound by Part II of this Convention or that it will not be bound by Part III of this Convention.

(2) A Contracting State which makes a declaration in accordance with the preceding paragraph in respect of Part II or Part III of this Convention is not to be considered a Contracting State within paragraph (1) of article 1 of this Convention in respect of matters governed by the Part to which the declaration applies.

Article 93

(1) If a Contracting State has two or more territorial units in which, according to its constitution, different systems of law are applicable in relation to the matters dealt with in this Convention, it may, at the time of signature, ratification, acceptance, approval or accession, declare that this Convention is to extend to all its territorial units or only to one or more of them, and may amend its declaration by submitting another declaration at any time.

(2) These declarations are to be notified to the depositary and are to state expressly the territorial units to which the Convention extends.

(3) If, by virtue of a declaration under this article, this Convention extends to one or more but not all of the territorial units of a Contracting State, and if the place of business of a party is located in that State, this place of business, for the purposes of this Convention, is considered not to be in a Contracting State, unless it is in a territorial unit to which the Convention extends.

(4) If a Contracting State makes no declaration under paragraph (1) of this article, the Convention is to extend to all territorial units of that State.

Article 94

(1) Two or more Contracting States which may have the same or closely related legal rules on matters governed by this Convention may at any time declare that the Convention is not to apply to contracts of sale or to their formation where the parties have their places of business in those States. Such declarations may be made jointly or by reciprocal unilateral declarations.

(2) A Contracting State which has the same or closely related legal rules on matters governed by this Convention as one or more non-Contracting States may at any time declare that the Convention is not to apply to contracts of sale or to their formation where the parties have their places of business in those States.

(3) If a State which is the object of a declaration under the preceding paragraph subsequently becomes a Contracting State, the declaration made will, as from the date on which the Convention enters into force in respect of the new Contracting State, have the effect of a declaration made under paragraph (1), provided that the new Contracting State joins in such declaration or makes a reciprocal unilateral declaration.

Article 95

Any State may declare at the time of the deposit of its instrument of ratification, acceptance, approval or accession that it will not be bound by subparagraph (1)(b) of article 1 of this Convention.

Article 96

A Contracting State whose legislation requires contracts of sale to be concluded in or evidenced by writing may at any time make a declaration in accordance with article 12 that any provision of article 11, article 29, or Part II of this Convention, that allows a contract of sale or its modification or termination by agreement or any offer, acceptance, or other indication of intention to be made in any form other than in writing, does not apply where any party has his place of business in that State.

Article 97

(1) Declarations made under this Convention at the time of signature are subject to confirmation upon ratification, acceptance or approval.

(2) Declarations and confirmations of declarations are to be in writing and be formally notified to the depositary.

(3) A declaration takes effect simultaneously with the entry into force of this Convention in respect of the State concerned. However, a declaration of which the depositary receives formal notification after such entry into force takes effect on the first day of the month following the expiration of six months after the date of its receipt by the depositary. Reciprocal unilateral declarations under article 94 take effect on the first day of the month following the expiration of six months after the receipt of the latest declaration by the depositary.

(4) Any State which makes a declaration under this Convention may withdraw it at any time by a formal notification in writing addressed to the depositary. Such withdrawal is to take effect on the first day of the month following the

expiration of six months after the date of the receipt of the notification by the depositary.

(5) A withdrawal of a declaration made under article 94 renders inoperative, as from the date on which the withdrawal takes effect, any reciprocal declaration made by another State under that article.

Article 98

No reservations are permitted except those expressly authorized in this Convention.

Article 99

(1) This Convention enters into force, subject to the provisions of paragraph (6) of this article, on the first day of the month following the expiration of twelve months after the date of deposit of the tenth instrument of ratification, acceptance, approval or accession, including an instrument which contains a declaration made under article 92.

(2) When a State ratifies, accepts, approves or accedes to this Convention after the deposit of the tenth instrument of ratification, acceptance, approval or accession, this Convention, with the exception of the Part excluded, enters into force in respect of that State, subject to the provisions of paragraph (6) of this article, on the first day of the month following the expiration of twelve months after the date of the deposit of its instrument of ratification, acceptance, approval or accession.

(3) A State which ratifies, accepts, approves or accedes to this Convention and is a party to either or both the Convention relating to a Uniform Law on the Formation of Contracts for the International Sale of Goods done at The Hague on 1 July 1964 (1964 Hague Formation Convention) and the Convention relating to a Uniform Law on the International Sale of Goods done at The Hague on 1 July 1964 (1964 Hague Sales Convention) shall at the same time denounce, as the case may be, either or both the 1964 Hague Sales Convention and the 1964 Hague Formation Convention by notifying the Government of the Netherlands to that effect.

(4) A State party to the 1964 Hague Sales Convention which ratifies, accepts, approves or accedes to the present Convention and declares or has declared under article 92 that it will not be bound by Part II of this Convention shall at the time of ratification, acceptance, approval or accession denounce the 1964 Hague Sales Convention by notifying the Government of the Netherlands to that effect.

(5) A State party to the 1964 Hague Formation Convention which ratifies, accepts, approves or accedes to the present Convention and declares or has declared under article 92 that it will not be bound by Part III of this Convention shall at the time of ratification, acceptance, approval or accession denounce the

1964 Hague Formation Convention by notifying the Government of the Netherlands to that effect.

(6) For the purpose of this article, ratifications, acceptances, approvals and accessions in respect of this Convention by States parties to the 1964 Hague Formation Convention or to the 1964 Hague Sales Convention shall not be effective until such denunciations as may be required on the part of those States in respect of the latter two Conventions have themselves become effective. The depositary of this Convention shall consult with the Government of the Netherlands, as the depositary of the 1964 Conventions, so as to ensure necessary co-ordination in this respect.

Article 100

(1) This Convention applies to the formation of a contract only when the proposal for concluding the contract is made on or after the date when the Convention enters into force in respect of the Contracting States referred to in subparagraph (1)(a) or the Contracting State referred to in subparagraph (1)(b) of article 1.

(2) This Convention applies only to contracts concluded on or after the date when the Convention enters into force in respect of the Contracting States referred to in subparagraph (1)(a) or the Contracting State referred to in subparagraph (1)(b) of article 1.

Article 101

(1) A Contracting State may denounce this Convention, or Part II or Part III of the Convention, by a formal notification in writing addressed to the depositary.

(2) The denunciation takes effect on the first day of the month following the expiration of twelve months after the notification is received by the depositary. Where a longer period for the denunciation to take effect is specified in the notification, the denunciation takes effect upon the expiration of such longer period after the notification is received by the depositary.

Done at Vienna, this eleventh day of April, one thousand nine hundred and eighty, in a single original, of which the Arabic, Chinese, English, French, Russian and Spanish texts are equally authentic.

In witness whereof the undersigned plenipotentiaries, being duly authorized by their respective Governments, have signed this Convention.

PARTIES TO THE CONVENTION

United Nations convention on contracts for the international sale of goods. Done at Vienna April 11, 1980; entry into force for the United States January 1, 1988.

States which are parties:

Argentina[1]
Australia[2]
Austria
Belarus[3]
Bulgaria
Canada[4]
Chile[5]
China[6]
Czechoslovakia[7]
Denmark[8]
Ecuador[9]
Egypt
Finland[10]
France
Germany, Fed.Rep. of[11]
Guinea[12]
Hungary[13]
Iraq
Italy
Lesotho
Mexico
Netherlands
Norway[14]
Romania
Russian Federation[15]
Spain
Sweden[16]
Switzerland
Syrian Arab Republic
Uganda[17]
Ukraine[18]
United States[19]
Yugoslavia
Zambia

MESSAGE ACCOMPANYING TRANSMITTAL

When the Convention was transmitted to the Senate by the President on September 21, 1983, the following message accompanied it (Treaty Document No. 98–9):

LETTER OF TRANSMITTAL

THE WHITE HOUSE, *September 21, 1983.*

To the Senate of the United States:

With a view to receiving the advice and consent of the Senate to ratification, I transmit herewith the United Nations Convention on Contracts for the International Sale of Goods. This Convention was adopted on April 11, 1980, by the United Nations Conference on Contracts for the International Sale of Goods and was signed on behalf of the United States at United Nations Headquarters on August 31, 1981.

The Convention would unify the law for international sales, as our Uniform Commercial Code in Article 2 unifies the law for domestic sales.

The Convention was prepared, with the active participation of representatives of the United States, by the United Nations commission on International Trade Law (UNCITRAL) and received the unanimous approval of this worldwide body; the Convention was then adopted, without dissent, by the United Nations Conference of sixty-two States. This unanimity attests to the broadly perceived need for the Convention and the value of its provisions.

The House of Delegates of the American Bar Association recommended in 1981 that the United States ratify the Convention, subject to a declaration permitted under Article 95 as to the grounds for applicability. I concur fully in this recommendation for the reasons set forth in the enclosed report of the Department of State.

The report of the Department of State provides a summary of the Convention and describes its approach. Worthy of emphasis is the international deference that the Convention accords to the contract made by the parties to an international sale. The parties may agree that domestic law rather than the Convention will apply, and their contract may modify or supplant the Convention's rules. The uniform international rules play their significant role when, as often occurs, a problem arises that the parties did not anticipate and solve by contract.

International trade now is subject to serious legal uncertainties. Questions often arise as to whether our law or foreign law governs the transaction, and our traders and their counsel find it difficult to evaluate and answer claims based on one or another of the many unfamiliar foreign legal systems. The Convention's uniform rules offer effective answers to these problems.

Enhancing legal certainty for international sales contracts will serve the interests of all parties engaged in commerce by facilitating international trade. I recommend that the Senate of the United States promptly give its advice and consent to the ratification of this Convention.

RONALD REAGAN.

LETTER OF SUBMITTAL

DEPARTMENT OF STATE,
Washington, August 30, 1983.

THE PRESIDENT.
The White House.

THE PRESIDENT: I have the honor to submit to you the United Nations Convention on Contracts for the International Sale of Goods with the recommendation that it be transmitted to the Senate for its advice and consent to ratification. This Convention, adopted without dissent on April 11, 1980, by a United Nations conference of sixty-two States, culminated a half-century of work to prepare uniform law for the international sale of goods.

Sales transactions that cross international boundaries are subject to legal uncertainty—doubt as to which legal system will apply and the difficulty of coping with unfamiliar foreign law. The sales contract may specify which law will apply, but our sellers and buyers cannot expect that foreign trading partners will always agree on the applicability of United States law. Insistence by both parties on this sensitive point can prolong and jeopardize the making of the contract.

The Convention's approach provides an effective solution for this difficult problem. When a contract for an international sale of goods does not make clear what rule of law applies, the Convention provides uniform rules to govern the questions that arise in the making and performance of the contract.

The Convention does not restrict the parties' freedom to settle by contract the full range of their rights and obligations. Instead it provides that its rules yield to the terms of the international sales contract. A major need for the Convention's uniform law arises from the fact that the buyer and the seller do not anticipate every question that might arise or consider it essential to deal with every problem, and it is often inexpedient to hold up the transaction until the parties find a solution for all foreseeable contingencies. In short, the Convention (like modern national systems of commercial law) serves the significant function of providing solutions for problems that the parties have failed to resolve by contract.

The usefulness of the Convention is enhanced by the fact that its rules were specially fashioned to meet the problems and needs of international trade. Our sellers and buyers now must cope with foreign statutes and code that were prepared a century or more ago, and were designed for domestic sales that bear little resemblance to current international transactions. Even when these problems have been ameliorated by case-law, such developments are often unknown or inaccessible to our lawyers.

The present Convention was adopted in six languages; English, of course, is one. The legislative history of the Convention is readily available in English, and most of the explanatory writing about the Convention is in English. Under the Convention our traders will not be forced to rely on foreign advice concerning the implications of the rules of a wide variety of foreign legal systems and often inadequate translations of such advice or rules.

This Convention replaces the Hague Sales Convention of 1964 which, because of defects, has not been widely accepted. (The United States has neither signed nor become a party to these Conventions.) These defects were discussed and resolved during a decade of preparatory work by the United Nations Commission on International Trade Law (UNCITRAL). The thirty-six member States of UNCITRAL provided representation for all major legal systems and regions of the world. United States representatives played an active and influential part in this preparatory work and in the 1980 Conference. UNCITRAL unanimously approved the draft Convention, and the 1980 Plenipotentiary conference of sixty-two States, again without dissent, adopted the final text.

During the eighteen-month period for signing the Convention after the 1980 Conference the following became Signatory States: Austria; Chile; Czechoslovakia; Denmark; Finland; France; German Democratic Republic; Germany, Federal Republic of; Ghana; Hungary; Italy; Lesotho; Netherlands; Norway; People's Republic of China; Poland; Singapore; Sweden; United States of America; Venezuela; and Yugoslavia. Steps for both Signatory and non-Signatory States to become parties to the Convention are now under way. Argentina, Egypt, France, Hungary, Lesotho and Syria have already ratified or acceded to the Convention, which will come into force approximately one year after four more countries have submitted their ratifications or accessions (Article 99(1)). Signature and ratification by the United States were recommended by the House of Delegates of the American Bar Association in 1981.

For the reasons set forth in Appendix B of the Legal Analysis, I recommend that United States ratification be made subject to the declaration permitted under Article 95 that the United States will not be bound by Article 1(1)(b) of the Convention. As a result of this reservation, the Convention will be applicable only when the seller and the buyer have their places of business in different Contracting States. This limitation, also approved by the American Bar Association, provides a clear, fair and adequate basis for the applicability of the Convention.

Enclosed is a Legal Analysis comparing the Convention's provisions with those of the Sales Article of the Uniform Commercial Code (UCC), which has been enacted by every State of the United States except Louisiana. It will be noted that the Convention embodies the substance of many of the important provisions of the UCC and is generally consistent with its approach and outlook.

The Convention is subject to ratification by signatory states (Article 91(2)), but is self-executing and thus requires no federal implementing legislation to come into force throughout the United States. As already indicated, the Convention's effect is limited to foreign commerce of the United States and it will not affect purely domestic contracts of sale.

The Convention is a notable example of world-wide legal cooperation. It provides practical help for sellers and buyers, in our country and abroad, and by adding certainty to law it will facilitate international trade.

The Department of Commerce supports this recommendation and the Department of Justice has no objection to it.

It is hoped that the Senate will promptly give favorable consideration to this Convention and approve ratification by the United States.

Respectfully submitted.

GEORGE P. SHULTZ.

Legal Analysis of the Convention on Contracts for the International Sale of Goods

Although the Convention on Contracts for the International Sale of Goods (see Appendix D) has been discussed both in the main volume and this supplement, it may be helpful for the reader to have the State Department notes interpreting the various provisions. These are set forth herein.

Legal Analysis of the United Nations Convention on Contracts for the International Sale of Goods (1980)

The Convention provides uniform rules to resolve questions that have not been answered by the contracts made by the seller and the buyer in an international sale. The salient features of the Convention were summarized in the Letter of Submittal to the President. To assist in a closer study of these rules, the present statement provides a brief synopsis of the 101 articles of the Convention.

It is not feasible in this brief analysis to provide a thorough commentary on the Convention's uniform rules of law for the sale of goods. Such a commentary calls for a substantial book; detailed studies are provided by books and articles that are listed in Appendix A.

The present document is designed to spot-light the most significant provisions of the Convention, and to indicate the relationship between these provisions and United States law as set forth in Article 2 on Sale of Goods of the Uniform Commercial Code, which has been enacted by virtually all States of the United States.

STRUCTURE OF THE CONVENTION

The uniform rules for sales transactions appear in Parts I–III of the Convention. Part I (Arts. 1–13) defines the Convention's field of application and includes other general provisions. Part II (Arts. 14–24) governs formation of the contract. Part III (Arts. 25–88) governs the rights and obligations of the parties to the contract of sale. Part IV ("Final Provisions": Arts. 89–101) establishes procedures for implementing the Convention and sets out the reservations that a State may make.

PART I: SPHERE OF APPLICATION AND GENERAL PROVISIONS

(Articles 1–13)

INTRODUCTION TO PART OF THE CONVENTION

Part I sets forth rules that apply throughout the Convention. Chapter I defines the Convention's field of application. Chapter II addresses other general questions, notable interpretation of the Convention and the sales contract.

A. The Convention's Field of Application: Chapter I

Article 1 addresses two issues that control the applicability of the Convention: (1) When is a sale "international"? and (2) What contact between the sales transaction and a Contracting State will invoke the Convention? (A "Contracting State" is a country that has become a party to the Convention.) Articles 2 and 3 exclude specified types of *commodities and transactions.* Articles 4 and 5 draw the line between *issues* that are regulated and those that are excluded; the excluded issues include the validity of the contract, the effect of the contract on the ownership rights of third persons (Art. 4) and liability for death or personal injury (Art. 5). The chapter closes with a brief but important provision (Art. 6) yielding overriding effect to the contract made by the parties.

CHAPTER I. SPHERE OF APPLICATION

(Articles 1–6)

Article 1. Basic rules on Applicability

Under Article 1 the Convention will apply only if two requirements are met: (1) the seller and the buyer have their "places of business in different States," and (2) both of these States are Contracting States (i.e. States that have adopted the Convention). This simplified basis for applicability reflects a recommendation that the United States ratify subject to a declaration authorized by Article 95; the reasons for making this declaration and its effect are set forth in Appendix B. Thus, an American court would apply the Convention only to sales with an international character between parties in whose countries the Convention is in force.

Article 2. Exclusions from the Convention

Article 2 provides for six exclusions from the Convention. Three (paragraphs (a)–(c)) are based on the nature of the transaction and three (paragraphs (d)–(f)) are based on the nature of the goods.

Paragraph (a) excludes substantially all consumer purchases by language based on the Uniform Commercial Code (UCC 9–109(1)). The principal impact of the Convention is thus on commercial sales between persons in business.

The remaining five exclusions do not call for discussion in this analysis.

Article 3. Goods to be Manufactured: Services

Paragraph (1) makes it clear that a sale is not excluded from the scope of the Convention merely because it calls for the manufacture or production of goods. On the other hand, it also makes it clear that the Convention does not extend to transactions in which the party receiving a finished product supplies "a substantial part" of the necessary materials.

Paragraph (2) excludes "service" contracts, in which the "supply of labour or other services" comprises the preponderant part of the transaction.

Article 4. Issues Covered and Excluded; Validity; Effect on Property Interests of Third Persons

While Articles 1–3 identify the *contracts* that are subject to the Convention, Article 4 defines the *issues* to which the Convention applies. Article 4 states that the Convention "governs only" the following: (1) "the formation of the contract" (Part II of the Convention) and (2) "the rights and obligations of the seller and the buyer arising from such a contract" (Part III of the Convention). In addition it excludes from the Convention issues with respect to "the validity of the contract or of any of its provisions or of any usage." One example is a rule of national law that prohibits the sale of specified products, such as heroin, and invalidates contracts relating to such illegal sales.

Article 4 also provides that the Convention "is not concerned with . . . the effect which the contract may have on the property in the goods sold." Whether the sale to the buyer cuts off outstanding property interests of third persons is not dealt with by the Convention. This specific provision illustrates the general rule of Article 4 that the Convention is concerned only with the "rights and obligations of *the seller and the buyer*" arising from the sales contract. For the buyer's right, *as against the seller,* to receive goods title, see Articles 41–43, *infra.*

Article 5. Exclusion of Liability for Death or Personal Injury; "Product Liability"

Article 5 makes the Convention inapplicable to the liability of the seller for death or personal injury caused by the goods. This was done lest the Convention collide with rules of national law on product liability.

Article 6. The Contract and the Convention

The dominant theme of the Convention is the primacy of the contract. See, *e.g.,* Arts. 4 and 35. Of the many provisions that develop this theme, Article 6 is the most important. Thus, the parties may exclude the Convention or "vary the effect" of any of its provisions. The breadth of the parties' freedom to contract is emphasized by the one exception stated in Article 6—the privilege of an adhering State under Articles 12 and 96 to preserve its domestic rules that require a writing. (See Art. 12, *infra*).

CHAPTER II. GENERAL PROVISIONS

(Articles 7–13)

Article 7. Interpretation of the Convention

A. *International Character; Uniformity; Good Faith*

Paragraph (1) provides that in interpreting the Convention there shall be regard for two closely-related principles—(a) the Convention's "international character" and (b) "the need to promote uniformity in its application." The latter provision is usual in uniform legislation in the United States. *See* UCC 1–102(2)(c). Paragraph (1) also provides that in interpreting the Convention there shall be regard for promoting "the observance of good faith in international trade." The Uniform Commercial Code states a "good faith" requirement that is broader than the principle of interpretation stated in the Convention. *See* UCC 1–203: "Every contract or duty within this Act impose a duty of good faith in its performance or enforcement." See also: UCC 2–103(1)(b).

B. *"General Principles"*

Paragraph (2) provides that, where possible, questions "are to be settled in conformity with the general principles on which [the Convention] is based"—an approach that was designed to strengthen uniform international interpretation of the Convention. A somewhat similar principle is expressed in the Uniform Commercial Code. For example, section 1–102(1) states that the UCC is to be "liberally construed and applied to promote its *underlying purposes and policies.*"

Article 8. Interpretation of Statements or Other Conduct of a Party

While Article 7 deals with interpretation of the *Convention,* the present Article deals with the interpretation of the statements and conduct of the *parties,* including the provisions of the contract of sale. When there is no common "intent" of the parties, Article 8(2) applies the objective standard familiar to the common law.

Article 8(3) authorizes "due consideration" of conduct subsequent to the agreement as this may shed light on the intentions and expectations of the parties. Similarly, the Uniform Commercial Code states that in some circumstances a "course of performance accepted or acquiesced in without objection shall be relevant to determine the meaning of the agreement" (UCC 2–208). See also UCC 2–207(3) under which "conduct by both parties which recognizes the existence of a contract is sufficient to establish a contract for sale . . ."

Article 9. Practices of the Parties; Trade Usages

One of the important features of the Convention is the legal effect it gives to practices of the parties and to commercial usages.

(1) Practices Established Between the Two Parties

Expectations that have the force of contract can be established by the parties' patterns of behavior. Under Article 9(1) the parties are bound by the "practices which they have established between themselves." The Uniform Commercial Code also gives contractual effect to the "course of dealing between parties"—defined as "a sequence of previous conduct between the parties to a particular transaction which is fairly to be regarded as establishing a common basis of understanding for interpreting their expressions and other conduct." (UCC 1–205)

(2) Usages of Trade

Article 9(2) provides that the agreement embrace a party's expectation that the other party will observe the usages of their trade. Unless the parties have agreed otherwise, effect is given to a trade usage "of which the parties knew or ought to have known" and which "in international trade is widely known to, and regularly observed by, parties to contracts of the type involved in the particular trade concerned." The Uniform Commercial Code also gives contractual effect to a "usage of trade"—defined as "any practice or method of dealing having such regularity of observance in a place, vocation or trade as to justify an expectation that it will be observed with respect to the transaction in question." (UCC 1–205)

Under Article 6, "The parties may . . . derogate from or vary the effect" of the provisions of the Convention, and applicable usage has the same effect as a provision of a sales contract. In short, the provisions of the Convention yield to the expectations of the parties, whether derived from express contract terms, from their established practices or from applicable trade usage.

Article 10. Definition of "Place of Business"

The Convention refers to a party's "place of business" in several articles: 1, 12, 20(2), 24, 31(c), 42(1)(b), 57(1)(a), 69(2) and 96. If a commercial enterprise maintains a central office and one or more branch offices, Article 10 makes applicable the place of business "which has the closest relationship to the contract and its performance. . . ."

Article 11. Inapplicability of Domestic Requirement
that Contract be in Writing

A. Domestic Rules: "Statute of Frauds"

In 1677 the English Parliament (29 Car. II, c.3) enacted a Statute of Frauds which required a signed writing for the enforcement of a wide variety of transactions, including the sale of goods. This requirement was embodied in the United Kingdom's Sale of Goods Act (1893), was closely followed in the (U.S.A.) Uniform Sales Act (1896), and formed the basis for an elaborate statute of frauds included in the Uniform Commercial Code (§ 2–201). In recent decades, however, the tide has been running against such formal requirements. In 1954 Britain repealed this part of the Sale of Goods Act—a step that has been followed by many of the other countries that had adopted this Act. Most civil law countries do not impose such formal requirements for the making of commercial contracts. Formal requirements have generated litigation and uncertainty, and are generally regarded to be of doubtful value for international trade.

B. The Convention

The 1980 Convention rejects such formal requirements (Article 11). This does not, however, bar the parties from imposing formal requirements. An offeror may require that an acceptance be in writing; an oral "acceptance" is not an "assent" to the offer. (See Arts. 18 and 19, *infra.*) In addition, pursuant to Article 29, *infra,* the parties by a contract in writing may require "any modification or termination by agreement" to be in writing.

A Contracting State may protect its formal requirements from Article 11 by making a reservation under Article 96. *See* Article 12, *infra.*

Article 12. Declaration by Contracting State Preserving
Its Domestic Requirements as to Form

Laws of the U.S.S.R. impose strict formal requirements for the making of foreign trade contracts. In the UNCITRAL proceedings, delegates of the U.S.S.R. indicated that preserving these requirements was of great importance to protect its established patterns for the making of foreign trade contracts. Most delegates, however, including the United States, concluded that formal requirements were inconsistent with modern commercial practice—particularly in view of the speed and informality that characterized many transactions in a market economy.

The result was a compromise. In Part IV (Final Provisions), Article 96 authorizes a Contracting State "whose legislation requires contracts of sale to be concluded in or evidenced by writing" to make a "declaration" that Article 11 (and certain other provisions of the Convention affecting formal requirements) "does not apply where any party has his place of business in that State." Article 12 articulates the effect of a declaration under Article 96. A declaration (reservation) under Article 96 would not ensure that the formal requirements of the declaring State would apply to transactions involving its buyers and sellers. Such applicability would result only when conflicts rules point to the formal requirements of the declaring State. However, conflicts rules may point to foreign law, which may have no formal requirements or may impose formal requirements that are unfamiliar to traders in the declaring State. These considerations explain why it is not recommended that the United States make a declaration pursuant to Article 96.

Article 13. Telegram and Telex as a "Writing"

This provision does not call for discussion.

PART II: FORMATION OF THE CONTRACT

(Articles 14–24)

INTRODUCTION TO PART II OF THE CONVENTION

A. Relation Between Part II and other Parts of the Convention

Part II of the Convention, Formation of the Contract, is subject to the rules of Part I (Arts. 1–13) on the scope and interpretation of the Convention, but is independent of Part III (Arts. 25–88) which deals with the obligations of the parties to the contract. Article 92 (Part IV) permits a Contracting State to declare that it will not be bound either by Part II or by Part III.

B. Structure of Part II

The first four articles (14–17) deal with the offer—the minimum criteria for an offer (Art. 14), and the withdrawal (Art. 15), revocation (Art. 16) or termination (Art. 17) of an offer. The next five articles (18–22) deal with acceptance—"acceptances" that do not match the offer (Art. 19), the period allowed for acceptance (Arts. 20 and 21), and withdrawal of an acceptance (Art. 22). The two final articles (Arts. 23 and 24) relate to the time when a contract is concluded.

Article 14. Criteria for an Offer

(1) "Public Offers"

Article 14 incorporates the generally accepted premise that a person may make an offer to as large a group as he wishes. However, a communication addressed to a large group, if construed as an offer, can involve practical difficulties and hazards. These practical considerations are reflected in Article 14(2): If a proposal is not "addressed to *one or more specific persons*," it is not an offer "unless the contrary is clearly indicated by the person making the proposal." See Restatement Second of Contracts § 29.

(2) Definiteness: Unstated Price

Difficult problems arise when the parties neither fix the price, expressly or implicitly, nor agree on a method for fixing the price. The Convention's solution calls for construing Article 14(1) in the light of Article 55, which states that in the above circumstances the parties are considered, in the absence of any indication to the contrary, to have impliedly made reference to the price generally charged for such goods at the time of the conclusion of the contract. The Uniform Commercial Code (§ 2–305) similarly provides that the parties "if they so intend can conclude a contract for sale even though the price is not settled."

Article 15. When Offer Becomes Effective; Prior Withdrawal

Under Article 15 an offeror may withdraw an offer by a communication that reaches the offeree ahead of the offer. The reason supporting Article 15 is that the enforcement of contracts is designed to protect expectations; none can arise until the offer reaches the offeree. *Cf.* Article 18(2), *infra.*

Article 16. Revocability of Offer

Article 16 limits the powers of an offeror to revoke an offer which the offeror has stated or indicated will be "firm" or irrevocable, or on which the offeree has reasonably relied. Compare the provisions giving effect to "firm" offers in the Uniform Commercial Code (UCC 2–205). See Restatement Second of Contracts § 87 and Illustration 6.

Article 17. Rejection of Offer Followed by Acceptance

Under Article 17, an offeree may not accept an offer which he has rejected. The same rule is applied in the United States. See Restatement Second of Contracts § 38.

Article 18. Acceptance: Time and Manner for Indicating Assent

Article 18 states how an offer may be accepted. Its most significant provision is in paragraph (3): under some circumstances, an offeree may accept an offer by performing an act requested by the offeror, such as dispatch of the goods. For a similar rule see Section 2–206(1)(b) of the Uniform Commercial Code.

Article 19. "Acceptance" With Modifications

Article 19 faces the situation in which a reply to an offer purports to be an acceptance but contains modifications of the offer. This situation most commonly results from the routine exchange of the buyer's printed purchase order and the seller's printed acknowledgment of sale form. Under the Convention, no contract results from such an exchange if the purported acceptance contains additional or different terms that materially alter the offer. A list of examples of material alterations makes it clear that most alterations are material. However, an acceptance with an immaterial modification will be effective unless the offeror objects.

The Convention's approach to this difficult problem differs from that of the

Uniform Commercial Code, under which even a material alteration may not prevent the purported acceptance from creating a contract (UCC 2–207). The Convention would thus avoid many of the problems that have arisen under and resulted in criticism of the Code provision.

Articles 20–24

The following articles dealing with various aspects of acceptance do not call for discussion:

Article 20. Interpretation of Offeror's Time-Limits for Acceptance

Article 21. Late Acceptances: Response by Offeror

Article 22. Withdrawal of Acceptance

Article 23. Effect of Acceptance; Time of Conclusion of Contracts

Article 24. When Communication "Reaches" the Addressee

These articles complete Part II: Formation of Contract.

PART III: SALE OF GOODS

(Articles 25–88)

INTRODUCTION TO PART III OF THE CONVENTION

When an enforceable international sales contract has been formed, Part III governs the rights and obligations of the seller and buyer.

Part III has five chapters. Chapter I (Arts. 25–29) contains general provisions that are applicable throughout Part III of the Convention. Chapter II (Arts. 30–52) deals with the obligations of the seller (Secs. I & II) and remedies for the seller's breach (Sec. III). Chapter III (Arts. 53–65), paralleling the structure of Chapter II, states the obligations of the buyer (Secs. I and II) and remedies for the buyer's breach (Sec. III). Chapter IV (Arts. 66–70) is devoted to risk of loss. Chapter V (Arts. 71–88) addresses anticipatory breach (Sec. I), damage measurement and interest (Secs. II & III), excuses ("exemptions") based on serious impediments (Sec. IV), effects of avoidance (Sec. V), and duties to preserve goods that face loss or deterioration (Sec. VI).

CHAPTER I. GENERAL PROVISIONS

(Articles 25–29)

Article 25. Definition of "Fundamental Breach"

A. Introduction

The breach of a sales contract by one party gives the other party a right to recover damages, but Article 25 relates to other remedies—the buyer's right to reject goods and the seller's right to refuse to deliver. In domestic law these remedies may be called "rejection," "revocation of acceptance," "avoidance," "termination" or "cancellation." In the Convention (Arts. 49 and 64) a party's privilege not to perform the contract because of the other party's breach is |called "avoidance of the contract."

In the Convention, as in our legal system, "avoidance" is not available for every breach. Under Articles 49(1)(a) and 64(1)(a), *infra,* a party may avoid the contract when the other party commits a "fundamental breach"—a term that is defined in Article 25.

The role played by "fundamental breach' under the Convention is similar to that played by Section 2–608 of the Uniform Commercial Code, under which a buyer who has accepted goods that turn out to be defective may revoke his acceptance if the non-conformity *"substantially* impairs" the value of the goods to him (UCC 2–612, but *cf.* 2–601). The UCC does not attempt to define "substantial" impairment. The Convention's definition of "fundamental breach" also allows leeway to consider whether avoidance is needed to assure full protection for the aggrieved party.

Article 26. Notice of Avoidance

Article 26 provides that a "declaration of avoidance of the contract is effective only if made by notice to the other party." This is one of the significant advances of the 1980 Convention over the 1968 Hague Convention on Sales (ULIS).

At various points ULIS gave an injured party a remedy called *"ipso facto* avoidance." This type of avoidance occurred automatically with no need to notify the other party (ULIS 25, 26(1)). Consequently, the other party might be led to perform in ignorance of the injured party's decision to refuse performance. At the 1964 Hague Conference the delegations of the United States and other states attempted unsuccessfully to eliminate *ipso facto* avoidance.

In the UNCITRAL proceedings, the delegations of the United States and other countries were able to remove the doctrine of *ipso facto* avoidance, resulting in the simple rule of Article 26. Requiring that notice be given of a remedy as drastic as avoidance is consistent with the Uniform Commercial Code. See UCC 2–602(1) (notice of rejection), 2–608(2) (notice of revocation of acceptance).

Article 27. Delay or Error in Communications

Under Article 26, *supra,* avoidance of a contract is effected "by notice" and in other settings communications have important consequences. *E.g.* Arts 39(1) (notice of lack of conformity) and 43 (notice of right or claim of third party). Article 27 addresses the problems that arise when a notice is sent but, because of a mishap in transmission, is delayed, garbled or lost. Article 27 lays down the general rule that a party satisfies his duty to notify if he dispatches the communication "by means appropriate in the circumstances."

This general rule is subject to exceptions in Articles 47(2), 48(4), 63(2), 65(1) & (2) and 79(4). Nearly all of these exceptions involve a communication by a party who is in breach of contract; the "receipt" principle was used so that a mishap in transmission would not add to the burdens of the aggrieved party.

The Uniform Commercial Code similarly requires the buyer to "notify" the seller of breach or "be barred from any remedy," and provides that one "notifies" another *"by taking such steps* as may be reasonably required to inform the other in ordinary course whether or not such other actually comes to know of it" (UCC 2–607(3) and 1–201(26)). The UCC, like the Convention, states exceptions from this general rule (*e.g.* § 2–616).

Article 28. Specific Performance and the Rules of the Forum

The Convention's system of remedies for breach of contract is based on the premise that a party in breach may be compelled to perform his obligations. On the other hand, restrictions on the right to specific performance appear in Articles 46(2) and 46(3).

Even with the restrictions just mentioned, the Convention grants specific performance on a wider scale than does the common law. As a concession to the common law, Article 28 provides that rules of national law withholding specific performance will prevail over the rules of the Convention. Thus, courts in the United States would still be subject to the limits on such remedies provided in Section 2–716 of the Uniform Commercial Code. *Cf.* UCC 2–709.

Article 29. Modification of Contract; Requirement of a Writing

Sales contracts sometimes provide that they may be modified only in writing. Article 29 gives effect to these private "statutes of frauds." The Uniform Commercial Code is similar (UCC 2–209(2)).

CHAPTER II. OBLIGATIONS OF THE SELLER

(Articles 30–52)

Introduction to Chapter II

Chapter II opens with a brief statement giving the essence of the seller's obligations (Art. 30). The remaining articles of the Chapter are grouped in three sections. Two sections define the seller's most important duties: The time and place for delivering the goods (Sec. I, Arts. 31–34); the quality of the goods and their freedom from third party claims (Sec. II, Arts. 35–44). The final section sets forth the basic remedies that are given to the buyer when the seller fails to perform his duties under the contract (Sec. III, Arts. 45–52).

The brief summary of Chapter II in Article 30 does not call for further discussion.

SECTION I: DELIVERY OF THE GOODS AND HANDING OVER THE DOCUMENTS

(Articles 31–34)

Article 31. Place for Delivery

When the contract, interpreted in the light of practices and usages, does not state where the seller should deliver the goods, the place of delivery is determined by Article 31. See also the Convention's rules on risk of loss in Article 67 and 69, *infra.*

Article 32. Shipping Arrangement

In international sales, the seller usually completes his obligation to deliver by "handing over the goods to the first carrier for transmission to the buyer." Art. 31, *supra,* and Article 67, *infra.* However, the seller also normally makes various arrangements with respect to carriage. Any provision of the sales contract (including usage and any practice between the parties) is decisive as to the seller's obligations in this regard; to the extent that there is no agreement with respect to shipping arrangements. Article 32 fills the gap.

Paragraph (1), requiring the seller to notify the buyer of the shipment, is similar to Section 2–504(c) of the Uniform Commercial Code. Paragraph (2), dealing with transportation arrangements, is similar to UCC 2–504. Paragraph (3) calls for cooperation between the parties with respect to supplying needed information concerning insurance. Similar rules on co-operation are set forth in the Uniform Commercial Code (2–311, 2–319(1)(c) and 2–319(3)).

Article 33. Time for Delivery

This article does not call for discussion.

Article 34. Documents relating to the Goods

Article 34 responds to commercial practice in international sales that permits, and often requires, delivery of the goods to be effected by handing over documents (such as a bill of lading) that control the goods. Accord: UCC 2–310(b). *Cf.* UCC 2–505 and 2–507(2).

Article 34 also provides that the seller's right to "cure" a defective delivery of goods (Art. 37, *infra*) extend to the delivery of documents. The Uniform Commercial Code provides that a seller may cure a "tender or delivery," which may include the tender of documents (2–508(1); 2–504(b)).

SECTION II. CONFORMITY OF THE GOODS AND THE THIRD PARTY CLAIMS

(Articles 35–44)

Introduction to Section II

Articles 35 and 36 define the seller's obligations with respect to the quality of the goods. Articles 37–40 describe procedures that apply when goods are defective—the seller's privilege to cure defects in the goods (Art. 37) and the buyer's obligation to examine the goods and notify the seller of nonconformity (Arts. 38–40). Articles 41 and 42 define the rights of the buyer when the goods are subject to third party claims of ownership (Art. 41) and of rights based on patents, trademarks or other types of intellectual property (Art. 42). Article 43 requires the buyer to notify the seller of these claims; the concluding article (Art. 44) gives grounds for excusing a failure to notify the seller.

Article 35. Conformity of the Goods

Paragraph (1) of Article 35 emphasizes that the seller must supply goods of the quality provided in the contract. As mentioned earlier (Art. 9, *supra*) under the Convention the practices established by the parties and applicable trade usages help to determine the contractual obligations of the parties. Accord: UCC 1–205. The Uniform Commercial Code also emphasizes the importance of the contract. (UCC 2–313).

Paragraph (2) of Article 35, like Sections 2–314 and 2–315 of the Uniform Commercial Code, gives effect to the buyer's basic expectations of quality. Paragraph 2(a), on fitness of goods for "the purposes for which goods of the same *description* would *ordinarily* be used," is similar to UCC 2–314(2)(c). Paragraph 2(b), on fitness for a particular purpose, is similar to UCC 2–315. Paragraph (2)(c), on conformity with a sample or model, is similar to UCC 2–313(1)(c). Paragraph (2)(d), on packaging, is similar to UCC 2–314(2)(e). Paragraph (3), on the effect of the buyer's knowledge of a lack of conformity, is comparable to UCC 2–316(3)(b).

Article 36. Damage to Goods: Effect on Conformity

Goods often arrive in poor condition because of damage that occurred after the risk of loss passed to the buyer. Paragraph (1) of Article 36 makes it clear that the seller is not responsible for defects that result from transit casualties which the buyer has assumed under the contract or under the Convention's rules on risk of loss (Arts. 66–70, *infra*). Paragraph (2) deals with the effect of contractual guarantees that goods will retain a specified quality for a prescribed period of time.

Article 37. Right to Cure Up to the Date for Delivery

Under Article 37 the seller, up to the agreed date for delivery, may remedy defects in the goods and thereby prevent destruction of the contract by "avoidance"—the remedy that in U.S. law is termed "rejection" (UCC 2–601) or "revocation of acceptance" (UCC 2–608). The "cure" provisions of Article 37 closely resemble those of UCC 2–508(1). *Cf.* Art. 48, *infra*, and UCC 2–508(2).

Article 38. Time for Examining the Goods

Article 38 provides rules on how soon the buyer "must examine" the goods. These rules are given legal effect by Article 39(1), which cuts off the buyer's rights if he fails to notify the seller of a nonconformity within a reasonable time after he "ought to have discovered" it. The rules on inspection and notice in Articles 38 and 39(1) are similar to the notice requirement in UCC 2–607(3)).

Article 39. Notice of Lack of Conformity

Article 40. Seller's Knowledge of Non-Conformity

Article 41. Third-Party Ownership Claims to Goods

Article 42. Third-Party Claims Based on Patent or Other Intellectual Property

Article 43. Notice of Claim

One of the limits on the scope of the Convention is set by Article 4: "this Convention . . . is not concerned with . . . (b) the effect which the contract may have on the property in the goods sold." Thus, if a third person claims the goods because of a defect in the seller's title, the question whether the buyer is protected, as a good faith purchaser, against that third-party claim is not governed by the Convention but is left to applicable domestic law.

Article 41 addresses this question: When the seller supplies goods that are subject to a third-party claim, what are the rights of the buyer *against the seller?* Third-party claims "based on industrial property or other intellectual property" (e.g., a patent or copyright) are dealt with in Article 42.

The protection afforded the buyer under Article 41 is similar to the implied warranty of title provided by the Uniform Commercial Code (UCC 2–312(1)). The Code gives the buyer rights against the seller when a third person establishes a claim "by way of infringement or the like" (UCC 2–312(3)), but does not deal with the problems that arise when the buyer encounters an infringement claim in a country where the seller could not have anticipated that the goods would be used or resold. These problems are addressed in Article 42.

The notice provisions of Article 43 do not call for discussion here. *Cf.* Articles 39, 40 and 44, *supra.* (Article 43 does not set a fixed cut-off period for notice comparable to the two-year period in Article 39(2)).

Article 44. Excuse for Failure to Notify

As was mentioned under Article 38, the notice requirement of Article 39(1) is similar to that of UCC 2–607(3). However, Article 39(2) sets an outer limit for notice of two years unless the parties agree otherwise; the UCC states no fixed outer limit for notification. *Cf.* UCC 2–725 (limitation period for actions of four years after delivery). On the other hand, the Uniform Commercial Code extends to claims, including those for personal injury arising out of consumer purchases, where substantial delays in notification may be justified. As we have already seen, the Convention excludes substantially all consumer transactions (Art. 2(a)) and excludes all claims for death or personal injury (Art. 5). Article 44 of the

Convention relaxes the notice requirement of Articles 39(1) and 43(1) to the extent of allowing the buyer to reduce the price (Art. 50) "or claim damages, except for loss of profit" when the buyer "has a reasonable excuse for his failure to give the required notice." This provision, however, does not remove the two-year outer limit for notification set by Article 39(2) or authorize a buyer, who has failed to give notice within a reasonable time, to exercise other remedies such as avoidance of the contract (Art. 49, *cf.* Art. 46).

SECTION III. REMEDIES FOR BREACH OF CONTRACT BY THE SELLER

(Articles 45–52)

Introduction to Section III

A. A Bird's-Eye View of the Section

The first two sections of Chapter II define the seller's duties; Section III defines the buyer's remedies when the seller is in breach.

Section III opens (Art. 45) with a general overview of the remedial system and indicates the relationship of different remedies to each other. *Cf.* UCC 2–711, 2–720. Article 46 states the buyer's right to compel performance by the seller. See Art. 28, *supra,* and UCC 2–716.

Three articles (Arts. 47–49) address the buyer's right to "avoid" the contract, a concept that includes the rejection of goods. *Cf.* UCC 2–601, 2–608. Article 47 empowers the buyer to fix an additional final period for the seller's delivery of the goods—a step that clarifies the buyer's right to avoid the contract for delay in delivery. Article 48 empowers the seller to "cure" defects in performance and thus forestall avoidance of the contract. *Cf.* UCC 2–508. Article 49 states the grounds on which the buyer may avoid the contract. *Cf.* UCC 2–608.

The section closes with three articles dealing with special situations—the buyer's right to reduce the price (Art. 50), the applicability of remedies to only part of the goods (Art. 51; *cf.* UCC 2–601(c), 2–608(1)) and deliveries that are too early or excessive in quantity (Art. 52; *cf.* UCC 2–601(c)). Although the remedy in Article 50 (reduction of price) has its origin in civil law concepts, its formula has been amended so as to approximate the common law right to deduct damages from the price (*Cf.* UCC 2–717).

B. Relationship to Other Parts of the Convention

Section III of the present chapter provides remedies that apply only to breach by the seller; Section III of Chapter III provides comparable remedies for breach by the buyer. These two sections are supplemented by remedial provisions in Chapter V that apply to both parties—*e.g.,* anticipatory breach (Sec. I), the measurement of damages, and interest (Secs. II and III), "exemption" from damages (Sec. IV) and the effects of avoidance of the contract (Sec. V).

C. General Comment

It is not feasible for this legal analysis to analyze in detail the remedial provisions of Articles 45–52. It must suffice to note that, with the encouragement of the United States delegation, UNCITRAL reviewed the 1964 Hague Convention (ULIS), unified and simplified its complex provisions, and thereby met the serious objections of the United States delegation to the 1964 Hague Conference.

CHAPTER III: OBLIGATIONS OF THE BUYER

(Articles 53–65)

Introduction to Chapter III

The structure of Chapter III is similar to that of the preceding chapter on Obligations of the Seller. Two sections state the buyer's duties: to pay the price (Sec. I, Arts. 53–59; *cf.* UCC 2–310(a), 2–507(1)) and to take delivery (Sec. II, Art. 60). The final section defines the remedies that are available to the seller when the buyer fails to perform these duties (Sec. III, Arts. 61–65; *cf.* UCC 2–703). These remedial provisions (like those in Chapter II) are supplemented by general rules on remedies in Chapter V (Arts. 71–88).

Many of the provisions of this chapter on the obligations of the buyer are mirror-images of provisions in the preceding chapter on the obligations of the seller.

CHAPTER IV: PASSING OF RISK

(Articles 66–70)

Introduction to Chapter IV

Casualty to the goods (*e.g.* by theft or fire) may occur in various settings— while the seller holds the goods before delivering them to a carrier or to the buyer, while the goods are in transit, while the buyer is examining the goods, or while the buyer holds the goods after rejecting them. Usually the loss will be covered by insurance. Allocating the risk of loss between seller and buyer should reflect considerations such as these: Which party is in a better position to evaluate the loss and press a claim against the insurer and to salvage or dispose of damaged goods? Who can insure the goods at the least cost? Who is more likely to carry insurance under standard commercial practice? What rules on risk will minimize litigation over negligence in the care and custody of the goods?

The United States delegates to the 1964 Hague Conference on Sales reported their disappointment that risk of loss was governed by concepts that were so abstract that results were unpredictable and unresponsive to commercial needs. In UNCITRAL, on the initiative of the United States and other delegations, these objections were met by a thorough overhaul of these rules. As a result, the 1980 Convention speaks of physical acts of transfers of possession—the "handing over" of the goods to a carrier or to the buyer.

Article 67 deals with the important issue of risk of loss in transit. When the contract (including the parties' established practices—Art. 9) does not solve this problem, the Convention, like the Uniform Commercial Code, provides the general rule that risk passes to the buyer when the goods are handed over to the carrier. Article 67 also echoes the Code in providing that the seller's retention of "documents controlling the disposition of the goods does not affect the passage of the risk." (See UCC 2–509(1)(a)).

Article 68 deals with contracts for the sale of goods that are already in transit when the contract is made, and provides that risk passes at the making of the contract unless the parties otherwise agree or the circumstances indicate an earlier time. The Uniform Commercial Code does not address this problem.

Article 69 deals, among other matters, with non-transit situations, and makes risk pass to the buyer "when he takes over the goods"—an approach that is similar to UCC 2–509(3). Finally, Article 69(1) and 70 deal with the effect of breach of contract on risk; in both approach and result these articles are similar to the Uniform Commercial Code (UCC 2–510).

CHAPTER V. PROVISIONS COMMON TO THE OBLIGATIONS OF THE SELLER AND OF THE BUYER

(Articles 71–88)

This concluding chapter addresses special problems with respect to remedies for breach of contract. Section I, Anticipatory Breach and Installment Contracts (Arts. 71–73), is concerned primarily with protection against impending failure of counter-performance; a party who faces this problem may, in some circumstances, suspend performance (Art. 71; *cf.* UCC 2–609, 2–705) or avoid the contract (Art. 72; *cf.* UCC 2–610). Article 73 deals with similar problems that arise in contracts for the delivery of goods by installments (*Cf.* UCC 2–612). Section II (Arts. 74–77) provides rules for measuring damages. (*Cf.* UCC 2–706—2–710, 2–712 to 2–715, 2–723). Section III consists of a brief provision (Art. 78) allowing the recovery of interest on sums in arrears. Section IV, exemptions (Arts. 78–80), confronts the difficult question of excuse from liability when performance is prevented by an impediment (*e.g., force majeure*). (*Cf.* UCC 2–613, 2–615). Section V, Effects of Avoidance (Arts. 81–84), includes provisions on the restitution of benefits received under a contract that has been avoided (*Cf.* UCC 2–711 (1) & (3)). Section VI, Preservation of the Goods (Arts. 85–88), is designed to prevent the waste or deterioration of goods that have been rejected. *Cf.* UCC 2–602(2)(b), 2–603, 2–604.

PART IV. FINAL PROVISIONS

(Articles 89–101)

A. Introduction

Many of these provisions are ministerial. Articles 89 and 91 are administrative provisions commonly included in United Nations conventions. Article 90 deals with the relationship between the 1980 Convention and any other convention that "contains provisions concerning the matters governed by" the 1980 Convention. The most significant provisions in this part deal with permitted reservations and the Convention's entry into force.

(1) "Declarations" (Reservations)

Articles 92–96 specify those "declarations" (reservations) that may be made by Contracting States to modify their obligations under the Convention.

Article 92 permits a Contracting State to declare that it will not be bound by Part II (Formation of the Contract) or by Part III (Obligations of the Parties under a Contract of Sale). At the 1964 Hague Conference, contrary to the position urged by the United States, separate conventions were adopted on formation of the sales contract and on obligations under the contract. In UNCITRAL, the United States position was accepted. Because of the relationship between Parts II and III, it seems advisable for the United States to ratify the entire Convention without a declaration under Article 92.

Article 93 is designed to permit a declaration (reservation) by a Contracting State with a constitutional system different from the United States (e.g. Canada) that embraces territorial units in which "different systems of law are applicable in relation to the matters dealt with" in the Convention. As already indicated, the Convention applies only to international sales. In view of the Constitutional power of the United States federal government over foreign commerce (Constitution Art. I § 8) and the treaty power (Constitution Art. II § 2; Art. VI), a declaration by the United States pursuant to Article 93 would be unnecessary and inappropriate. In the absence of a United States declaration, the Convention will extend to all territories under the jurisdiction of the United States.

Article 94 seeks to meet the needs of State joined in economic communities (e.g. Benelux) by providing for reservations by two or more Contracting States "which have the same or closely related legal rules on matters governed by" the Convention. If two or more States make declarations under Article 94, the Convention will not apply to transactions among parties in these States but will, of course, apply to transactions that run between parties in these States and parties in other States. See Article I, *supra*. There is no need for the United States to make use of such a reservation.

Article 95 permits a Contracting State to declare that it will not be bound by Article 1(1)(b) which would make the Convention also apply "when the rules of private international law lead to the application of the law of a Contracting State." States that make this declaration would apply the Convention only when the seller and buyer have their places of business in different *Contracting* States (Art. 1(1)(a)). As noted under Article 1, *supra,* it is recommended that the United States ratify subject to this reservation; the reasons are set forth in Appendix 9 to this analysis.

Article 96 permits a declaration by a State that wishes to protect its domestic legislation that "requires contracts of sale to be concluded in or evidenced by writing", *i.e.,* a "statute of frauds." For the reasons given in the discussion of Articles 11 and 12 of the Convention, it is considered inadvisable for the United States to make use of the reservation permitted by this Article.

(2) Entry Into Force

Article 99(1) provides that the Convention enters into force on the first day of the month following the expiration of twelve months after the tenth State has consented to be bound by the Convention. Article 99(2) governs the time when the Convention enters into force with respect to States whose consent to be bound follows that of the ten initial States.

ADDENDUM

PROPOSED UNITED STATES DECLARATION UNDER ARTICLE 95 EXCLUDING APPLICABILITY OF THE CONVENTION BASED ON ARTICLE 1(1)(B)

Under Article 1 the Convention will apply only if two basic requirements are met: (1) The sale must be international—i.e., the seller and the buyer must have their "places of business in different states," and (2) the sale must have a prescribed relationship with one or more States that have adhered to the Convention. This statement is concerned with the second requirement—the relationship between the Convention and one or more Contracting States.

The Convention, in subparagraphs (1)(a) and (1)(b) of Article 1, states two such relationships, either of which will suffice.

(a) *First,* under subparagraph (1)(a) the Convention applies when the places of business of the seller and the buyer are in different Contracting States.

(b) *Second,* under subparagraph (1)(b) the Convention would also apply:

(b) when the rules of private international law lead to the application of the law of a Contracting State.

At the 1980 Diplomatic Conference, delegates of the United States and several other countries proposed the deletion of the second of these grounds for applicability—subparagraphs (1)(b) of Article 1. This proposal was defeated; as a compromise, the Convention's Final Provisions (Part IV) provide in Article 95 that a Contracting State may, by reservation, declare "that it will not be bound by subparagraph (1)(b) or Article 1."

The United States, in signing the Convention, state that ratification subject to the Article 95 reservation was contemplated. This position, recommended by the American Bar Association, will promote maximum clarity in the rules governing the applicability of the Convention. The rules of private international law, on which applicability under subparagraph (1)(b) depends, are subject to uncertainty and international disharmony. On the other hand, applicability based on subparagraph (12)(a) is determined by a clear-cut test: whether the seller and buyer have their places of business in different Contracting States.

A further reason for excluding applicability based on subparagraph (1)(b) is that this provision would displace our own domestic law more frequently than foreign law. By its terms, subparagraph (1)(b) would be relevant only in sales between parties in the United States (a Contracting State) and a *non*-Contracting State. (Transactions that run between the United States and another Contracting State are subject to the Convention by virtue of subparagraph (1)(a). Under subparagraph (1)(b), when private international law points to the law of a foreign *non*-Contracting State the Convention will not displace that foreign law, since subparagraph (1)(b) makes the Convention applicable only when "the rules of private international law lead to the application of the law of a *Contracting* State. Consequently, when those rules point to United States law, subparagraph (1)(b) would normally operate to displace United States law (the Uniform Commercial Code) and would not displace the law of the foreign *non*-Contracting States.

If the United States law were seriously unsuited to international transactions, there might be an advantage in displacing our law in favor of the uniform international rules provided by the Convention. However, the sales law provided by the Uniform Commercial Code is relatively modern and includes provisions that address the special problems that arise in international trade.

For these reasons it seems advisable for the United States to exclude applicability of the Convention under sub-paragraph (1)(b) by the declaration (reservation) permitted by Article 95. Fortunately, this position will not interfere with broad application of the Convention to international sales. Widespread adoption of the Convention can be anticipated; hence it is expected that eventually a substantial portion of United States international trade will involve other Contracting States and will receive the benefits of the Convention by virtue of subparagraph (1)(a) of Article 1. Moreover, parties who wish to apply the Convention to international sales contracts not covered by Article 9(1)(a) may provide by their contract that the Convention will apply.

[1]The instrument of accession by the Government of Argentina contains the following declaration:

(Translation) (Original: Spanish)

In accordance with Articles 96 and 12 of the United Nations Convention on Contracts for the International Sale of Goods, any provisions of article 11, Article 29 or Part II of the Convention that allows a contract of sale or its modification or termination by agreement or any offer, acceptance or other indication of intention to be made in any form other than in writing does not apply where any party has his place of business in the Argentine Republic.

[2]The instrument of accession by the Government of Australia contains the following declaration:

"The Convention shall apply to all Australian States and mainland territories and to all external territories except the territories of Christmas Island, the Cocos (Keeling) Islands and the Ashmore and Cartier Islands."

[3]The instrument of accession by the Government of Belarus contains the following declaration:

(Translation) (Original: Russian)

"Belarus, in accordance with articles 12 and 96 of the Convention declares that any provision of article 11, article 29 or Part II of this Convention that allows a contract of sale or its modification or termination by agreement or any offer, acceptance or other indication of intention to be made in any form other than in writing does not apply where any party has his place of business in Belarus."

[4]The instrument of accession by the Government of Canada contains the following declarations:

"The Government of Canada declares, in accordance with Article 93 of the Convention, that the Convention will extend to Alberta, British Columbia, Manitoba, New Brunswick, Newfoundland, Nova Scotia, Ontario, Prince Edward Island and the Northwest Territories;

The Government of Canada also declares, in accordance with Article 95 of the Convention, that, with respect to British Columbia, it will not be bound by Article 1.1 b) of the Convention."

[5]The instrument of ratification by the Government of Chile contains the following declaration:

(Translation) (Original: Spanish)

"The State of Chile declares, in accordance with articles 12 and 96 of the Convention, that any provision of article 11, article 29 or Part II of the Convention that allows a contract of sale or its modification or termination by mutual agreement or any offer, acceptance or other indication of intention to be made in any other form than in writing, does not apply where any party has its place of business in Chile."

[6]The instrument of approval by the Government of China contains the following declaration:

(Courtesy Translation) (Original: Chinese)

The People's Republic of China does not consider itself to be bound by subparagraph (b) of paragraph 1 of Article 1 and Article 11 as well as the provisions in the Convention relating to the content of Article 11.

[7]The instrument of ratification by the Government of Czechoslovakia contains the following declaration:
(Courtesy Translation) (Original: Czechoslovak)

"Pursuant to Article 95, the Czechoslovak Socialist Republic declares that it shall not consider itself bound by the provision of Article 1, paragraph 1, item b), of the Convention."

[8]The instrument of ratification by the Government of Denmark was accompanied by the following declaration:
(Original: English)

"Upon ratifying the Convention, the Kingdom of Denmark declares:

"1) under paragraph 1 of Article 92 that Denmark will not be bound by Part II of the Convention,

"2) under paragraph 1 of Article 93 that the Convention shall not apply to the Faroe Islands and Greenland,

"3) under paragraph 1 cf. paragraph 3 of Article 94 that the Convention shall not apply to contracts of sale where one of the parties has his place of business in Denmark, Finland, Norway or Sweden and the other party has his place of business in another of the said states,

"4) under paragraph 2 of Article 94 that the Convention is not to apply to contracts of sale where one of the parties has his place of business in Denmark, Finland, Norway or Sweden and the other party has his place of business in Iceland."

[9]In accordance with article 99(2), the Convention will enter into force for Ecuador on 1 February 1993.

[10]The instrument of ratification by the Government of Finland contains the following declarations:

(Original: English)

"1. With reference to Article 92, Finland will not be bound by Part II of this Convention (Formation of the Contract).

2. With reference to Article 94, in respect of Sweden in accordance with paragraph (1) and otherwise in accordance with paragraph (2) the Convention will not apply to contracts of sale where the parties have their places of business in Finland, Sweden, Denmark, Iceland or Norway."

[11]On October 3, 1990 the German Democratic Republic acceded to the Federal Republic of Germany.

The instrument of ratification by the Government of the Federal Republic of Germany contains the following declaration:

(Courtesy Translation) (Original: German)

"The Government of the Federal Republic of Germany holds the view that Parties to the Convention that have made a declaration under article 95 of the Convention are not considered Contracting States within the meaning of subparagraph (1)(b) of article 1 of the Convention. Accordingly, there is no obligation to apply—and the Federal Republic of Germany assumes no obligation to apply—this provision when the rules of private international law lead to the application of the law of a Party that has made a declaration to the effect that it will not be bound by subparagraph (1)(b) of article 1 of the Convention. Subject to this observation the Government of the Federal Republic of Germany makes no declaration under article 95 of the Convention."

In a note accompanying the instrument of ratification the Government of the Federal Republic of Germany stated that the said Convention shall also apply to Berlin (West) with effect from the date on which it enters into force for the Federal Republic of Germany.

The Federal Republic of Germany denounced, on 1 January 1990, the Conventions relating to the formation of contracts for the international sale of goods and the international sale of such goods, both done at The Hague on 1 July 1964. These denunciations shall take effect on 31 December 1990, and the present Convention will therefore enter into force for the Federal Republic of Germany on 1 January 1991, in accordance with paragraphs 2 and 6 of article 99.

[12]In accordance with article 99(2), the Convention will enter into force for Guinea on 1 February 1992.

[13]In a note accompanying its instrument of ratification, the Government of Hungary made the following declarations:

"It [Hungary] considers the General Conditions of Delivery of Goods between Organizations of the Member Countries of the Council for Mutual Economic Assistance/GCD

CMEA, 1968/1975, version of 1979/ to be subject to the provisions of article 90 of the Convention;

[14]It states, in accordance with articles 12 and 96 of the Convention, that any provision of article 11, article 29, or part II of the Convention that allows a contract of sale or its modification or termination by agreement of any offer, acceptance or other indication of intention to be made in any form other than in writing, does not apply where any party has his place of business in the Hungarian People's Republic."

[14]The instrument of ratification by the Government of Norway contains the following declarations:

(Original: English)

"1. In accordance with Article 92, paragraph (1), the Government of the Kingdom of Norway declares that Norway will not be bound by Part II of this Convention (Formation of the Contract).

"2. With reference to Article 94, in respect of Finland and Sweden in accordance with paragraph (1) and otherwise in accordance with paragraph (2), the Government of the Kingdom of Norway declares that the Convention will not apply to contracts of sale where the parties have their places of business in Norway, Denmark, Finland, Iceland or Sweden."

[15]The instrument of accession by the Government of the [Russian Federation] contains the following declaration:

(Translation) (Original: Russian)

"In accordance with articles 12 and 96 of the Convention, the [Russian Federation] declares that any provision of article 11, article 29 or Part II of the Convention that allows a contract of sale or its modification or termination by agreement or any offer, acceptance or other indication of intention to be made in any form other than in writing does not apply where any party has his place of business in the [Russian Federation]."

[16]The instrument of ratification by the Government of Sweden contains the following declarations:

(Original: English)

"1. With reference to Article 92, Sweden will not be bound by Part II of this Convention (Formation of the Contract).

"2. With reference to Article 94, in respect of Finland in accordance with paragraph (1) and otherwise in accordance with paragraph (2) the Convention will not apply to contracts of sale where the parties have their places of business in Sweden, Finland, Denmark, Iceland or Norway."

[17]In accordance with article 99(2), the Convention will enter into force for Uganda on 1 March 1993.

[18]The instrument of accession by the Government of [Ukraine] contains the following declaration:

(Translation) (Original: Russian)

"In accordance with articles 12 and 96 of the Convention, [Ukraine] declares that any provision of article 11, article 29 or Part II of the Convention that allows a contract of sale or its modification or termination by agreement or any offer, acceptance or other indication of intention to be made in any form other than in writing does not apply where any party has his place of business in [Ukraine]."

[19]The instrument of ratification by the Government of the United States contains the following declaration:

"Pursuant to article 95 the United States will not be bound by subparagraph (1)(b) of Article 1."

Cumulative Index

(Note: Page references to the Supplement are preceded by "S" and are in boldface)